Introducing Christian Ministry Leadership

Introducing Christian Ministry Leadership

Context, Calling, Character, and Practice

William D. M. Carrell

WIPF & STOCK · Eugene, Oregon

INTRODUCING CHRISTIAN MINISTRY LEADERSHIP
Context, Calling, Character, and Practice

Copyright © 2022 William D. M. Carrell. All rights reserved. Except for brief quotations in critical publications or reviews, no part of this book may be reproduced in any manner without prior written permission from the publisher. Write: Permissions, Wipf and Stock Publishers, 199 W. 8th Ave., Suite 3, Eugene, OR 97401.

Wipf & Stock
An Imprint of Wipf and Stock Publishers
199 W. 8th Ave., Suite 3
Eugene, OR 97401

www.wipfandstock.com

PAPERBACK ISBN: 978-1-6667-3285-6
HARDCOVER ISBN: 978-1-6667-2700-5
EBOOK ISBN: 978-1-6667-2701-2

09/19/22

Unless otherwise designated, all Scripture quotations are from the NRSV, New Revised Standard Version Bible, copyright © 1989 National Council of the Churches of Christ in the United States of America. Used by permission. All rights reserved worldwide.

Scripture quotations marked KJV are from the King James or Authorized Version of the Bible.

Emphases have been added to some Scripture quotations.

Contents

List of Figures & Tables | viii
Acknowledgements | xi
Introduction | xiii

Part One: The Context of Ministry Leadership | 1

Chapter 1: The Biblical Story | 3
    God's Relationship with the Creation 5
    The New Covenant and the Kingdom of God 6
    Reconciliation 8
    Shalom 10

Chapter 2: The Church | 12
    Models of Church Governance 12
    A Congregational View of the Church 14
    The Mission of God 20
    The Community of Salvation 23

Part Two: The Calling of Ministry Leadership | 29

Chapter 3: The Meaning of Calling | 31
    Biblical Foundations 31
    Calling in Christian History 34
    Classifications of Calling 39

CONTENTS

Chapter 4: General and Individual Calling | 42
    Responding to the General Call   42
    Discerning the Individual Call   47
    The Call to Ministry Leadership   61
    Ordination to Ministry Leadership   61

Part Three: The Character of Ministry Leaders | 65

Chapter 5: The Content of Character | 67
    The Easy Yoke   67
    Formation of Moral Norms   68
    Character Traits of Ministry Leaders   70

Chapter 6: The Integrity of Conduct | 83
    Making Space for God   83
    Actions of Integrity   87
    Self-Management   88
    Becoming a Shepherd Leader   92

Part Four: The Practice of Ministry Leadership —Proclamation, Care, and Guidance | 99

Chapter 7: Proclamation as Witness | 103
    Communicating the Gospel   103
    Relationship   105
    Testimony   106
    Gospel   109
    The Evangelistic Conversation   114

Chapter 8: Proclamation as Preaching | 117
    The Authoritative Source   118
    Hermeneutics   120
    Biblical Exegesis   121
    Basic Sermon Types   127

CONTENTS

Chapter 9: Care as Counsel | 131
    Ministry Leaders as Counselors   132
    Brief Pastoral Counseling   134
    Active Listening   135

Chapter 10: Care as Comfort | 143
    Thinking Theologically about Suffering   144
    Comforting the Sick   149
    Comforting the Grieving   154
    The Moment of Death and the Funeral   156
    After the Funeral   161

Chapter 11: Guidance of Worship | 163
    Elements of Worship   164
    Balancing of Worship Approaches   168
    Following the Christian Year   170
    Using the Lectionary   172
    Sacraments or Ordinances   173

Chapter 12: Guidance of Work | 176
    Setting Forth the Vision   176
    Instructing in the Faith   180
    Sending Out to Serve   185

Bibliography | 191

Figures and Tables

Figures

1.1 The Biblical Story   4
4.1 Layers of Personality   52
4.2 The "Big Five" Personality Traits   53
5.1 Formation of Moral Norms   70
6.1 Example of a Twenty-One-Period Schedule   90
7.1 The Practices of Ministry Leaders: Proclaim, Care, Guide   101
7.2 Priorities of Witness Based on Thompson   106
8.1 The Hermeneutical Arch   129
9.1 Attending Posture   136
11.1 Worship Emphases: Action, Thought, and Emotion   169
12.1 Bloom's Taxonomy (Revised)   183

Tables

2.1 Three Models of Church Governance or Polity   13
2.2 The Process of Salvation   23
3.1 Comparison of Historical Views of Calling   39
4.1 Spiritual Gifts   58
5.1 Character Traits of Ministry Leaders   72
5.2 Biblical Examples of Women in Ministry Leadership   75

FIGURES AND TABLES

7.1 Four Themes of the Gospel with Biblical References   111
9.1 Words for Clarifying Various Emotions   139
11.1 The Elements of Worship   166
11.2 The Christian Year   171
11.3 Example of the Revised Common Lectionary   173

Acknowledgements

THE WRITING OF THIS book would not have been possible without the support of the administration of the University of Mary Hardin-Baylor, my teaching home for most of the past two decades. The university provided two summer research grants, which furnished me the time and resources to complete the book. I am particularly grateful to our president, Dr. Randy O'Rear, and to our provost, Dr. John Vassar, for their support of our faculty and for their commitment to our professional development. I am also indebted to my dean and friend, Dr. Tim Crawford, who encouraged this project from the start. The students in my Introduction to Christian Ministry Leadership courses have been very helpful in shaping the final form of the book by their responses to early drafts of the work. I am especially appreciative of Alan Arthur, my student teaching assistant, who read early chapters and made important suggestions for improvement. My current pastor and former student, Rev. Maddie Rarick, also helped me make significant improvements by her careful reading, questions, and observations. Esther Crawford, a fellow church member and UMHB graduate, greatly enhanced the various figures and diagrams in the book. The members of the churches in which I have served, former students at Bluefield College and at UMHB, and colleagues in the Association of Ministry Guidance Professionals (AMGP)—all have contributed in countless ways to my understanding of ministry leadership. Finally, the love and support of my wife, Martha, have sustained me throughout the writing of the book, as they have throughout the years of our life and ministry together.

Introduction

FORTY YEARS AGO, AS a newly-minted seminary graduate, I endeavored to start a new church. I soon discovered, however, that I had no clear idea of what I was doing or why I was doing it. I assumed my education in Bible, church history, theology, and Christian ethics had given me what I needed to establish and serve as pastor of this new church, but it became painfully clear that I had much to learn. Among the many things that I understood poorly in those early days was how my work fit within the larger context of what God is doing in the world. I was focused on getting a church started as if I was starting a new business, and I thought it was all up to me to make it happen. I thought of my work as something I was doing *for* God, not *with* God and *by* the power of the Spirit. I also did not understand my own calling to ministry very well. In those days, it was common to stress the importance of calling but uncommon to hear explanations of how to understand and to discern calling. The personal character required for ministry also eluded me. Not only was I not sure of what I was supposed to do, I was also not sure of whom I was supposed to *be*. Finally, I thought I understood how to perform the basic practices of ministry leadership, but I soon realized that I had few skills or the wisdom to know how to use them well. My struggle to understand and develop the skills for ministry leadership sowed the seeds from which this book has emerged. Indeed, this book reflects experiential learning from mistakes more than from successes. Over the years, I have found that beginning ministry leaders cannot avoid making mistakes, but they can make better sense of those mistakes and make quicker progress in overcoming them by reflecting on their experience in light of the context, calling, character, and practice of ministry leadership as described in a book like this.

INTRODUCTION

This book is designed for students who are exploring a call to ministry leadership. It reflects my own practical theology. Although the book is structured in a logical sequence beginning with the divine revelation of the biblical story and concluding with specific roles and methods of ministry leadership, the book was not generated in this sequence. I did not come to my understanding by learning theoretical principles and then simply putting them into practice. The book is an integration of my own practical experience as a ministry leader and my theological reflection on that experience. Today we have become aware that theology and practice go hand in hand. In the words of Dan Browning, "All our practices, even our religious practices, have theories behind and within them."[1] So theology does not precede practice but is *embedded* in practice. Anderson describes how this new awareness has given rise to an interactive approach to practical theology: "Theory is no longer regarded as a set of mental constructs that can exist independently of their embodiment in the physical, psychological and social structures of life. Theory and practice inform and influence each other in such a way that all practice includes theory, and theory can only be discerned through practice."[2]

Practice, therefore, is essential to learning. In learning to play the piano or to play golf, one has to start by playing. At first, there are wrong notes and shanked drives, but the more one makes mistakes and corrects them through reflection (e.g., "What am I doing wrong? How can I improve?"), the better one gets at playing. Learning the practice of ministry leadership is no different. Ministry leadership is learned only through the combination of hands-on experience (practice) and theological reflection and instruction (theory), followed by application of new insights in hands-on ministry leadership (practice). This textbook is designed for the middle process of theological reflection and instruction, but the assumption is that students cannot learn ministry leadership just by reading the book. There is no substitute for learning by doing. Three pedagogical assumptions, therefore, form the approach of this textbook.

The first assumption is that students exploring a call to ministry leadership need to be engaged in some kind of hands-on ministry throughout the learning process. Most students already are or have been active in congregational life. They have been in worship, heard many sermons, participated in Bible studies, traveled on mission trips, shared

1. Browning, *Fundamental Practical Theology*, 6.
2. Anderson, *Shape of Practical Theology*, 21.

their faith, worked in food pantries, and assisted their ministry leaders in various ways. So they already have practical experience in ministry, but they must continue to involve themselves in congregational life and be active in ministry. Learning ministry leadership is a spiral, not a linear process. Students learn best when they are engaged in ministry practice at the same time they are conceptualizing and reflecting on that practice. In my own introductory course in Christian ministry, I require a minimum of two hours a week of hands-on ministry either in a local church or in a community outreach ministry. Teaching the practice of ministry leadership to students who are not engaged in ministry is like teaching a dance class in which students never dance.

The second pedagogical assumption is that beginning students in ministry leadership need a conceptual framework of vocabulary, backgrounds, and traditions in order to make sense of their practical experience and to prepare them for deeper theological reflection in advanced and specialized courses in ministry leadership. An important aspect in regard to vocabulary are the words used to describe the subject-matter of this book. A book like this might be called *Introduction to Ministry*, or *The Basics of Pastoral Ministry*, etc., but I have grown uncomfortable with the use of the words minister and ministry by themselves to describe ministry leaders. There is no reference in the New Testament to a particular clergy class who do ministry *for* the church. All Christians are called to do the work of ministry.

The Scripture makes it clear that the work of ministry is to be performed by all Christians with the help of ministry leaders: "The gifts he gave were that some would be apostles, some prophets, some evangelists, some pastors and teachers, *to equip the saints for the work of ministry*" (Eph 4:11–13, emphasis added). The specific roles listed in Ephesians (apostles, prophets, evangelists, pastors, and teachers) describe some of the ways that ministry leaders may be gifted; in this book, however, I have chosen to use more generic designations to indicate what all those who lead and equip others in ministry need to know. My choice of terminology also indicates that the call to ministry leadership is not a *higher* calling than that of all Christians. Ministry leadership is simply one kind of role among all the other kinds of ministry roles. In the New Testament, the primary Greek word for ministry is *diakonia* ("service") and the word for minister is *diakonos* ("servant"). Ministry is simply serving God and others. Throughout the book, therefore, I use the designations *ministry leader* or *ministry leadership* rather than *minister* or *ministry* alone to designate those who equip and lead others in Christian ministry.

One other reason for the use of the more generic vocabulary is to try to avoid traditional terms that are often read through a patriarchal lens. The Bible says that the Spirit of God has been poured out on all Christians, both men and women (Acts 2:17–18). As Acts 2 clearly states, both men and women "shall prophesy," and Paul clearly teaches that the gospel of Jesus Christ brings equality: "There is neither Jew nor Greek, there is neither slave nor free, there is neither male nor female: for you are all one in Christ Jesus" (Gal 3:28). In chapter 5, I address more specifically women serving in all roles of ministry leadership, but it is important for the reader to know at the outset that, in the words of Peter in Acts 10, "truly I perceive that God shows no partiality."

The third pedagogical assumption is that the core practice of students and instructors in Christian ministry leadership is *Christopraxis*. As Anderson insists, the presence of Christ through the Holy Spirit is at the core of the practical experience of Christians. Christ, through the Holy Spirit, participates with us in the practice of ministry:

> Christopraxis, I have argued, is the normative and authoritative grounding of all reflection in the divine act of God consummated in Jesus Christ and continued through the power and presence of the Holy Spirit in the body of Christ. Practical theology is an ongoing pursuit of competence through critical theological reflection. This competence does not arise merely through repetition and practice of methods but is gained through participation in the work of God in such a way that accountability for the judgments made in ministry situations are congruent with Christ's own purpose as he stands within the situation and acts through and with us.[3]

The emphasis on Christopraxis removes the individualism and isolation that ministry leaders may feel in their work. Everything does not depend solely on their efforts and expertise. The work of leadership in ministry is first and foremost the work of Christ, and we who lead must lead according to the will of Christ the King by the power of the Holy Spirit.

These three pedagogical assumptions—the ongoing engagement in the practice of ministry, the need for a conceptual framework, and the presence of Christ with us in the work—shape the outlook and format of the book. The first three parts of the book each contain two chapters,

---

3. Anderson, *Shape of Practical Theology*, 52–53.

INTRODUCTION

and the final part contains six chapters. The total of twelve chapters corresponds to the weeks of the course I currently teach in Introduction to Christian Ministry Leadership. The first part of the book leads off with the idea that for ministry leaders to know who they are and what they are supposed to do, they need to understand the context of ministry leadership. Chapter 1 describes the biblical story as the larger context within which ministry is understood. By having in mind this larger context, ministry leaders are humbled, motivated, and guided. The larger context helps ministry leaders to understand that they are servants who work alongside countless other servants of God to bring about God's purposes. What matters most is not the personal success of ministry leaders but the rule of Christ the King and the coming of his kingdom. Chapter 2 narrows the focus to the immediate context of ministry leadership, the church. Through the church, God is on mission in the world to seek and to save the lost and to reconcile and to restore the relationship of trust and love between God and the entire creation. So the church is a means to that end, not an end in itself. Ministry leaders have the great privilege of being agents in God's work of reconciliation.

The second part of the book examines the call to ministry leadership. Chapter 3 is a study of the biblical and historical background of calling with particular attention given to the ways the Protestant reformers interpreted calling in reaction to earlier views. This chapter is followed in chapter 4 by my own interpretation and approach toward calling in a general sense and calling in an individual sense. My conclusion is that all Christians are called to ministry, and the call to ministry leadership is one kind of calling among others. Ministry leadership, however, places special demands on a person that other ministry roles may not require or emphasize as strongly. Discerning a call to ministry leadership takes time and intentional self-examination, and it takes the confirmation and call of a community of Christians that has observed the gifting for ministry leadership that the individual also has perceived from within.

The third part of the book examines the moral aspects of ministry leadership in the light of Christian character ethics. Chapter 5 describes the nature of character formation and the moral qualifications for ministry leaders. The Bible has little to say about the skills or training of ministry leaders, but it has much to say about the ethical character of ministry leaders. Skills are important, but those who lead others in the work of God, first and foremost, must be people of exemplary moral traits. Chapter 6 addresses the need for ministry leaders to cultivate integrity and develop the habits that maintain ethical conduct. The integrity of ministry leaders bears directly, for good or for ill, on the effectiveness of ministry. The last part of the book turns to an examination of three primary areas of ministry leadership: proclamation, care, and guidance. Following the roles of Jesus's own ministry as Prophet, Priest, and King, the final six chapters of the book give basic instruction for witness, preaching, counsel, comfort, worship, and work. Each of these chapters is intended to be introductory but also immediately useful for students who are already in or soon to be in the midst of ministry leadership.

Those who write to instruct others in Christian ministry do so from within a particular ecclesiastical tradition, and it is no different with me. I write from the perspective of a life of serving within the Baptist tradition, so I understand the church to be confessional and congregational in nature. It is inevitable that this book will contain descriptions that reflect my Baptist heritage; however, the book is not intended for Baptists per se. My hope is that students of any Christian tradition will find this text helpful for understanding the call to ministry leadership.

Part One

The Context of Ministry Leadership

How are we to understand the nature, roles, and functions of Christian ministers? As we shall see, leadership in ministry is a multifaceted calling, and it is easy to get overwhelmed with diverse responsibilities and expectations. So, it is vital in introducing anyone to this great calling to provide a way to sort through the various demands and be able to distinguish major from minor concerns. Context enables ministry leaders to distinguish the important from the unimportant in their responsibilities. Context refers to the matrix of interrelated elements that help to define something. The English word context comes from the Latin *contexere*, meaning "to weave." To create a functional piece of cloth, a "textile," a single thread must be interlaced with many other threads. To create a purposeful ministry, the biblical story must be interlaced and interwoven in one's mind and heart.

James Childs explains why context or a "larger framework of meaning" is vital to any kind of work. He argues that people often try to find their purpose or sense of self-worth through work itself, but purpose and self-worth are what people *bring to*, not *derive from* their work. "Despite the importance with which we endow our occupations in determining self-worth, it is the larger framework of meaning and value to which people hold, their 'faith,' that gives meaning to work and the institutions of work, not the reverse."[1] Too often people try to get meaning out of work itself, but work without a context is work without meaning. The story of the three rock masons makes this point clear: "Three workers were breaking rock into pieces. Asked what they were doing, the first answered, 'Making little rocks out of big ones.' The second replied, 'Making

---

1. Childs, *Ethics in Business*, 17.

a living.' And the third said, 'Building a cathedral.'"[2] Each worker was doing the same work, but each one saw their work differently. Context made the difference. Work of any kind involves small, mundane tasks. Without a larger context, however, we see only small, momentary actions. With the increase of context, we perceive the greater purpose into which those actions fit. It is this bigger picture or the larger context of meaning that forms vision and motivates work.

Context, therefore, enables ministry leaders to understand their work. Ministry leaders must reflect deeply on the words of the biblical text and their own personal experience with God. Healthy ministry leaders understand that they do not derive meaning from their work itself but from their faith and understanding of how their work fits into the larger framework of God's work. Ministry leaders who try to get meaning only from the work itself—preaching sermons, crafting worship, visiting the sick, holding meetings, teaching lessons, counseling the despondent, growing a church, promoting to important positions, etc.—may find life in ministry leadership shallow and unrewarding. Often such leaders become either workaholics or work avoiders who are prone to burnout. So, the context through which ministry leaders view their work is absolutely important for healthy, effective, and fulfilling life in ministry leadership. The path to fulfillment and effectiveness in ministry leadership starts with knowing what God is doing in the world. The broad story of God's work forms the context that enables ministry leaders to make sense of their own experience and work. In the words of Smith and Pattison, "the vital question is: what is the primary story around which we shape our lives?"[3]

---

2. Meilaender, *Working*, 1.
3. C. Smith and Pattison, *Slow Church*, 64.

1

The Biblical Story

The biblical story is the larger context of meaning for understanding the purpose and the practices of ministry leadership. Before ministry leaders rise to explain the Bible to others, they must immerse themselves in the story that frames and forms their own purpose and role in ministry. It is not uncommon for ministry leaders to view the Bible as a tool of their trade, as a resource for preaching, teaching, or counseling. Such a view of the Bible, however, represents a profound misunderstanding of the place and role of the Bible in Christian ministry leadership. The biblical story is not a means to some end (e.g., advice for living, a way to happiness, or even a way to salvation); instead, the biblical story is the end of all of our means. This story must *form* us before we can *inform* others. The biblical story is the larger context that explains why we are here and what we are supposed to do. Therefore, Christian ministry leaders must learn and relearn this story to be able to understand and perform their roles in that story.

Overview of the Story

The Bible consists of many diverse writings composed by many different authors at different times and places and with different points of view. These writings, when viewed as a whole, however, tell a unified story. The overarching story that rises from the Bible's many narratives, poems, proverbs, parables, prophesies, and prayers is the story of the God who creates, loves, suffers with, and saves the world. The biblical story opens with God's creation of the world and concludes with the restoration of the creation in the kingdom of God (see fig. 1.1).

Figure 1.1 The Biblical Story

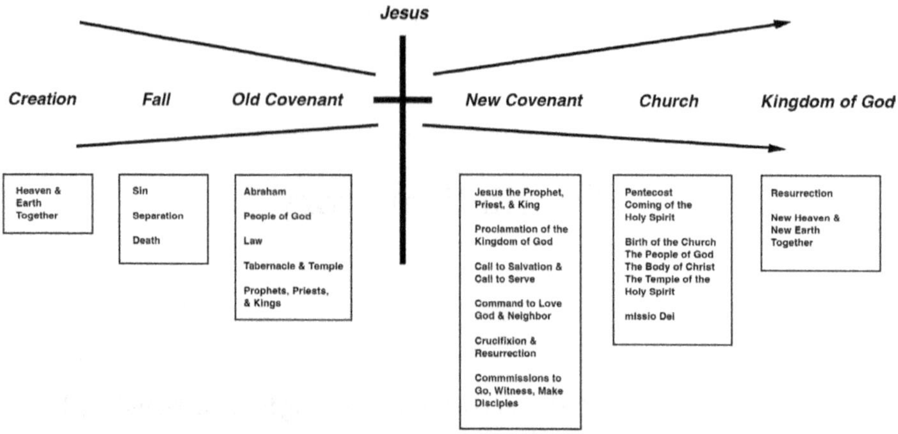

```
                              Jesus
      ──────────────────────┐     ┌──────────────────────────→
                             \   /
  Creation    Fall    Old Covenant ─┼─ New Covenant    Church    Kingdom of God
                             /   \
      ─────────────────────┘      └──────────────────────────→
```

Creation	Fall	Old Covenant	New Covenant	Church	Kingdom of God
Heaven & Earth Together	Sin / Separation / Death	Abraham / People of God / Law / Tabernacle & Temple / Prophets, Priests, & Kings	Jesus the Prophet, Priest, & King / Proclamation of the Kingdom of God / Call to Salvation & Call to Serve / Command to Love God & Neighbor / Crucifixion & Resurrection / Commissions to Go, Witness, Make Disciples	Pentecost / Coming of the Holy Spirit / Birth of the Church / The People of God / The Body of Christ / The Temple of the Holy Spirit / missio Dei	Resurrection / New Heaven & New Earth Together

Between the creation and the kingdom is God's long-suffering work to restore the relationship that was broken by human sin. The fall into sin fractured the close fellowship between humans and God. The result was human suffering and death. God did not abandon the creation, however. He continued to sustain all peoples of the earth while narrowing his restorative work to a single human family. Through his covenant with Abraham and his descendants, God raised up a people who would know him and obey his commands. He graciously preserved this family through countless threats and their own unfaithfulness to the covenant.[1] God raised up leaders and deliverers like Joseph, Moses, Joshua, and, later, judges, prophets, priests, and kings. He provided laws to keep the people faithful to him and to create a just society. He provided a place and procedures for worship to help the people know him, deal with their sins, and remain in relation with him. The descendants of Abraham, Isaac, and Jacob had moments of greatness, but inevitably the nation failed to be faithful to the covenant. The Northern and Southern Kingdoms were destroyed, Jerusalem was destroyed, the temple that had stood for four hundred years was destroyed, and the people were exiled from the land that God had given them over a thousand years earlier. The nation was finished, but God was not finished with the people. He promised to renew the covenant, to bring the people back from exile, and to

---

1. By my use of masculine pronouns to refer to God, I do not intend to suggest that God is male as opposed to female. The use of the masculine pronoun is congruous with the biblical text and avoids monotonous repetition of the proper noun or awkward alternation between "he" and "she."

restore the kingdom. What the people of Israel did not yet understand was that the restored kingdom would incorporate believers from all nations, not merely their own. The unfolding story reached its zenith with the coming of Jesus Christ. In Jesus, the full nature of God as love and his purpose of reconciling and restoring his entire creation became clear.

God's Relationship with the Creation

The biblical story opens in Gen 1 with God's methodical creation of the world. Two things we learn about God in this chapter are that he is all powerful and that he is all good. God creates simply by words, "Let there be . . . ," and all that comes to exist through his words is deemed *good*. The goodness of the creation reflects God's own moral or ethical nature. What is good and right for the creation are of highest concern to God, because the essence of God's character is love. God cares deeply for his creation, and the world he establishes reflects his own moral nature. At the center of that creation are self-conscious, morally responsible creatures—human beings. God's gift of moral responsibility creates the possibility for a mutual relationship. To act responsibly, one has to be able to comprehend alternatives and to choose what is right over what is wrong. It is only with these moral capabilities that one is able to love. The Bible says that God is love (1 John 4:8, 16), so his purpose in creating the world was to extend his own loving nature by creating morally responsible beings with the potential to receive his love and to give love to others.

All real love requires both distance and nearness. Along with power and love, we find two additional aspects of God's nature. Genesis 1 and 2 testify to God's *transcendence* and *immanence*. In Gen 1, God is shrouded in absolute mystery. God is above and beyond the creation. He *transcends* the world. In Gen 2, God freely enters the creation and relates personally with his creatures. God is close; he is *immanent*. Thus, the Bible presents the paradoxical truth that God is both far and near. Because God has the power to be both distant and near, a real relationship of love is possible. Four qualities, therefore, combine to form the unique Judeo-Christian understanding of God. God's power, love, transcendence, and immanence mean that God has lovingly chosen to remain *interconnected* with his creation, and this interconnectedness is at the heart of Christian theology and ministry. N. T. Wright stresses that interconnectedness is foundational to the Christian view of God and the belief that God loves the world:

> But for the ancient Israelite and the early Christian, the creation of the world was the free outpouring of God's love. The one true God made a world that was other than himself, because that is what love delights to do. And, having made such a world, he has remained in a close, dynamic, and intimate relationship with it, without in any way being contained within it or having it contained within himself.[2]

Wright's concern is to distinguish the unique monotheism of Judaism and Christianity from either pantheism or deism. In pantheism, there is no distinction between god and the world; they are the same thing. There is no *other* with whom to relate. In deism, after an initial "first cause," god and the world never interact. There is no *relation* with the other. Neither pantheism nor deism are adequate to describe the biblical witness that God is love. Only where God is both *other* and *in relation* with the creation can God love and humans respond in kind. Only in the ethical monotheism (belief in a single, moral God) of Jews and Christians is God simultaneously *holy* and loving.

Such holy love is not without pain, however. In choosing to stay in relationship with sinful humanity, God also chooses to suffer the pain of rejection. In the Judeo-Christian view, God suffers with the creation. The cross of Jesus Christ was not a mistake but the ultimate demonstration of the very nature of God. To love is to suffer, and it is in the mystery of God's suffering love that we find the core context of Christian ministry leadership.

The New Covenant and the Kingdom of God

The evening prior to his crucifixion, Jesus offered bread and wine to his disciples as symbols of the new covenant he was bringing through his death and resurrection. Six centuries earlier, Jeremiah described this new covenant as one that would be written on the heart, not on stone tablets, an internal and universal covenant fulfilling and completing the purposes of the original covenant God formed exclusively with the nation of Israel (Jer 31:31–34). This new covenant made possible a relationship with God now based on faith in Jesus as the incarnation of God and his *hesed*.

The Hebrew word *hesed* is the term for God's covenant love throughout the Old Testament. It is often translated as "mercy," "kindness," or "lovingkindness" in the King James Version and "steadfast love" in the

---

2. N. Wright, *Simply Christian*, 65–66.

New Revised Standard Version. *Hesed* is a relational word that expresses the depth of God's grace and love for Israel. The word conveys a familial relationship of deep feeling and enduring commitment. The new covenant and the *hesed* of God are important elements for understanding Jesus's announcement of the arrival of the kingdom of God. In essence, Jesus was announcing the reestablishment of God's rule and reign over the creation. The odd thing about this reign was that it was not the forceful exercise of God's power, as one might expect when a king acquires a kingdom. Jesus's work of restoring the kingdom was through the renunciation of his divine power. Relationships cannot be restored by force. Relationships are restored by the *giving and receiving* of forgiveness. Just as humans willfully separated themselves from their Creator, they are restored only by willful acts of repenting of sin and receiving of forgiveness. God's work of reconciliation, therefore, is work that bears upon the human will, not through coercion but through the power of persuasive love.

Only in the context of willful human alienation does God's work of reconciliation through the life and death of Jesus make sense. God is not merely rescuing individuals from future punishment after death but restoring the entire creation from the hell of this current existence. The biblical story is that the world fell under a curse, or as Paul describes it, the world was "subjected to futility":

> I consider that the sufferings of this present time are not worth comparing with the glory about to be revealed to us. For the creation waits with eager longing for the revealing of the children of God; for the creation was subjected to futility, not of its own will but by the will of the one who subjected it, in hope that the creation itself will be set free from its bondage to decay and will obtain the freedom of the glory of the children of God. (Rom 8:18–21)

Futility implies a frustration and failure to achieve a purpose or a goal. God subjected the creation to a wilderness of wandering where humans experienced the dire consequences of their own choices to stray away from God. Something important happens, however, in the turn away from God. The recognition of the futility of life apart from God is a necessary step in God's great purpose and work.

God is not controlling puppets but fostering mature moral agency in his creation. He can do so only by taking the risk of imprinting his own morally free, responsible image upon humanity. Wright describes the underlying theme or pattern of the biblical story as "the story of going away and coming back home again."[3] This pattern is repeated over and over in the biblical text in the journeys of Abraham and the patriarchs and matriarchs, in the enslavement and exodus of the people of Israel from Egypt, in the exile and return of the Jews from Babylon, in the incarnation and ascension of Jesus, and finally in the restoration of Eden in the new heaven and new earth. When humans distance themselves from God, they find themselves in a wilderness surrounded by mortal threats, suffering hunger and thirst, and struggling to survive. In the incarnation, Jesus fully identified himself with alienated humanity by emptying himself (Phil 2:6) of divine power and placing himself in exile in a world of sin and death. Jesus embodied the pattern of leaving home and coming back again in his life, death, and resurrection, and he foreshadowed the full restoration and resurrection of the creation. Jesus's parable of the father and his two sons brings this theme into perspective (Luke 15:11–32).

The loving father did not force his sons to do his will but gave them their freedom. Yet, he never stopped waiting and loving. The sons both rejected the father, whether by straying away to a far country or by staying home in hateful resentment. Both sons had to "come to themselves" and realize that the father was good and always had their best interest at heart. Here, then, is the great context of ministry leadership—the ministry of the good and loving God who actively pursues but also waits for the creation to return home. Ministry leaders who keep this larger framework of meaning constantly in mind know why they do what they do, and it is in knowing why that leaders find the continuing motivation and joy in ministry. That motivation and joy are products of God's primary work, the work of reconciliation.

Reconciliation

The grand sweep of the biblical story from creation to culmination is the story of God's ministry of reconciliation. In the christological hymn in Colossians, God's presence and work are described in terms of reconciliation: "For in him [Christ] all the fullness of God was pleased to dwell, and through him God was pleased to reconcile to himself all things, whether on earth or in heaven, by making peace through the blood of his cross" (Col 1:19–20). God's reconciling work in Christ is the larger framework from which to understand and to carry out the countless smaller acts of

3. N. Wright, *Simply Christian*, 75.

Christian ministry. Every aspect of Christian ministry, proclamation, care, and guidance makes sense only within the larger context of God's work to reconcile to himself "all things" in the kingdom of God.

In 2 Corinthians, Paul describes the connection between God's work of reconciliation and Christian's work as "ambassadors" of the gospel message of reconciliation:

> All this is from God, who reconciled us to himself through Christ, and has given us the ministry of reconciliation; that is, in Christ God was reconciling the world to himself, not counting their trespasses against them, and entrusting the message of reconciliation to us. So we are ambassadors for Christ, since God is making his appeal through us; we entreat you on behalf of Christ, be reconciled to God. For our sake he made him to be sin who knew no sin, so that in him we might become the righteousness of God. (2 Cor 5:18–21)

Paul uses the Greek word for reconciliation, *katallagē*, in various noun and verb forms no less than five times in three verses. The word conveyed the idea of the change in a relationship from estrangement to reunion. Paul makes this clear when he describes humans as "enemies" of God:

> But God proves his love for us in that while we were still sinners Christ died for us. Much more surely then, now we have been justified by his blood, we will be saved through him from the wrath of God. For if while we were enemies, we were reconciled to God through the death of his Son, much more surely, having been reconciled, we will be saved by his life. But much more than that, we even boast in God through our Lord Jesus Christ, through whom we have now received reconciliation. (Rom 5:8–11)

The alienation of the creation was so severe that it took nothing less than the crucifixion of Jesus to bring about the reconciliation.

How Jesus's death brings about reconciliation is one of the great theological mysteries. There have been many atonement theories throughout Christian history. The word atone means to make amends or to make up for some hurt or injury to another. An atonement theory is an explanation of how the death of Jesus atones or saves us from our sins. There are theories that see the death of Jesus as a victory over the spiritual powers of evil or as the payment of a ransom to free us from Satan and enslavement to sin. Other theories view Jesus's death as a satisfaction of God's requirement for justice or as a substitutionary punishment of Jesus in place of the punishment deserved by humanity. Still other theories explain the death of Jesus purely as an act of love that influences or moves hearts and minds to repentance and love for God. All these views, and many others, endeavor to explain how Jesus's death was necessary for God to forgive the sins of the world.

Whichever theory of atonement one adopts, the Bible makes it clear that reconciliation was the act of God *in* Christ, and this act was supremely an act of forgiveness. "That is, in Christ God was reconciling the world to himself, not counting their trespasses against them" (2 Cor 5:19). When one person hurts another, the relationship between them is damaged or broken. No amount of money or punishment can restore the relationship unless there is a change of heart. The demand for justice, the need for payback, has to give way to forgiveness. In Jesus's dying and rising, we see divine forgiveness on a cosmic scale. The love of God overcame human sin not by force but by forgiveness. Jesus died as the supreme act of God's mercy. God bore human sin, so that a new relationship could be established. In Jesus's death and resurrection, therefore, ministry leaders discover the coherent context of all Christian service—love, forgiveness, mercy, and reconciliation. Here we find the kingdom of God, the realm where grace rules. When Christian ministry leaders do kingdom work, they extend that kingdom of forgiveness. They become ambassadors of reconciliation, extending God's message of reconciliation in countless small ways, building a cathedral of mercy, a reconciled and reunited heaven and earth where we again walk and talk with our Creator and worship our King. Within the context of the kingdom of forgiveness, ministry leaders also find their own peace in the conduct of life and ministry.

Shalom

How Christian ministry leaders think about God and what he is doing determines their vision, motivation, priorities, choices, decisions, and ultimately their own *shalom*—their well-being. Shalom is a Hebrew word usually defined as "peace." In the context of the Bible, however, the meaning of shalom is much richer than the English word peace might suggest. English words for shalom include harmony, wholeness, completeness, prosperity, welfare, and tranquility. Proverbs 3:17 indicates that shalom is directly related to wisdom: "Her [wisdom's] ways are ways of pleasantness, and all her paths are peace." Psalm 122 encourages the pilgrims as they ascend to the Holy City for worship to "pray for the peace of Jerusalem:

'May they prosper who love you. Peace be within your walls, and security within your towers.' For the sake of my relatives and friends I will say, 'Peace be within you.' For the sake of the house of the LORD our God, I will seek your good'" (Ps 122:6-9). Praying for the shalom of Jerusalem is the same as seeking the *good* of the city.

Those who experience shalom in the conduct of ministry leadership are those who have found the good, the well-being, that comes from knowing the grace and peace of God and knowing something of how their work fits within God's work. These ministry leaders define their success relative to their relationship with a gracious and loving God who is working to restore the creation and reconcile humanity in the kingdom of God. His work of restoration and reconciliation are at the heart of the biblical story that births and forms the community of Christ, and that story enables ministers to understand the purpose and nature of the church.

2

The Church

THE BIBLICAL STORY FORMS the larger context of meaning for understanding Christian ministry leadership. Within this story, the church emerges as the immediate context of God's work of reconciliation and restoration of the world. The roles of ministry leaders are functions of the church and are understood only within the setting of the church. So it is imperative that those who pursue the call to ministry leadership have a clear view of the nature of the church. That said, it is painfully obvious that Christians have understood the nature of the church in many different ways in the long history of Christianity. No matter the Christian tradition in which one serves, however, it is essential to understand the various views of the nature and governance of the church for clarity about the purpose and functions of Christian ministry leadership.

Models of Church Governance

A wide variety of organizational models and administrative processes have developed throughout Christian history. Models of church governance or church polity may be categorized by the following adjectives: *episcopal, presbyterian,* or *congregational* (see table 2.1). These words are also used to describe particular Christian denominations, but that is not the intention here. For example, as a general model of church governance, episcopal describes a *way* of organizing and administering a church, not the Episcopal Church in particular. The governance of some churches may be clearly defined by one of these three kinds of polity. Other churches may combine or modify the three models in some way.

Table 2.1 Three Models of Church Governance or Polity

Episcopal Polity	Presbyterian Polity	Congregational Polity
Monarchical	Representative	Democratic
Authority is centered in a single bishop (*episcopos*) or in a hierarchy of bishops	Authority is centered in designated elders (*presbuteros*) from local churches	Authority is centered in the members of each local church
Examples: Roman Catholic Church, Eastern Orthodox Church, Episcopal churches, Methodist churches	Examples: Presbyterian churches, Churches of Christ, Bible churches	Examples: Baptist churches, some nondenominational churches

Episcopal polity takes its name from the Greek word *episkopos*, meaning "bishop" or "overseer." Authority is vested in a single individual (monarchical). A bishop presides over a unified organization comprised of multiple local congregations. Depending on the particular denominational expression, there may be only a single level of monarchical bishop (e.g., Methodist Church) or a hierarchy of monarchical bishops (e.g., the Roman Catholic Church). Presbyterian polity takes its name from the Greek word *presbuteros*, meaning "elder." Presbyterian polity centers authority in designated church elders who form a board or a "session" that governs a congregation. Elders from local congregations may also represent their churches in meetings of denominational governing bodies (e.g., synods or general assemblies) on regional or national levels. This representative form of polity is common in Reformed (or Calvinistic) churches and increasingly in many Baptist and nondenominational churches. In congregational polity the members of a local congregation together govern themselves. Each church is independent and autonomous. Through deliberative processes, congregations vote to elect their leaders and delegate limited authority to individuals, committees, or teams for the performance of specific tasks. These churches may choose to associate themselves with other churches to accomplish greater purposes (e.g., supporting missionaries or funding theological education), but they do not surrender their self-governance in doing so. The three types of church polity, therefore, shape differing contexts within which ministry leaders serve. The inclination of this book is toward ministry leaders who serve in congregational traditions, so it is incumbent to take a closer look at a congregational understanding of the nature of the church.

A Congregational View of the Church

The English word church is often thought of as a building or institution. In the New Testament, however, the Greek word for church did not refer to a building but to the people of God. The word *ekklēsia* was derived from the combination of two words, *ek* ("out") and *kaleō* ("call"), meaning "to call out" as in inviting people to meet together. In the Septuagint (the Greek translation of the Hebrew Old Testament) *ekklēsia* was used to translate two Hebrew words, *edah* for the nation of Israel and *qahal* for the gathered assembly of the Israelites.[1] Alongside *ekklēsia*, three important descriptions attest to the relationship of God to the church. Peter describes the church as the people of God (1 Pet 2:9–10), and Paul contributes two other descriptions: the body of Christ (Rom 12:5) and the temple of the Spirit (1 Cor 3:16–17). These three phrases show that the divine Trinity is closely identified with the church. The church is the Father's adopted family, Jesus's body, and the Spirit's dwelling place. The biblical descriptions, therefore, clearly demonstrate that the church is, in essence, a people, not a building.

Whether ministers see themselves primarily as operators of institutions or as guides of people determines how they view their own identity and their purpose. The example of Jesus himself helps us here to better understand the nature of the church. Jesus indicated that the church would be the place of his continuing presence on earth after his resurrection and ascension. In Matthew's Gospel, Jesus said he would be present in even the smallest of gatherings: "For where two or three are gathered in my name, I am there among them" (Matt 18:20). The church in essence was to be a spiritual, interpersonal relationship of Jesus and his people. The earliest Christians came to understand that the presence of God was no longer to be identified with the temple in Jerusalem but with believers in Jesus in whom the Spirit of God was now present. In Stephen's last sermon before he was stoned to death in the book of Acts, he made it clear that God "does not dwell in houses made with human hands" (Acts 7:48). Stephen's point was that God dwells in the person of Jesus, and, through the Holy Spirit, he also indwells all who believe in Jesus. In the dramatic story of the conversion of Saul (Paul) on the Damascus road, Saul saw a

---

1. Kicklighter, "Origin of the Church," 30–32.

bright light and heard a voice saying, "Saul, Saul why are you persecuting me?" When Saul asked who was speaking, the voice replied, "I am Jesus, whom you are persecuting" (Acts 9:4–5). Jesus did not say Saul was persecuting "my people" or "my disciples"; he said "*me*"!

The solidarity of Jesus with his followers indicates that the church was his chosen place to abide in Spirit and truth. John's Gospel, in particular, emphasizes the continuing presence of Jesus with his followers in the Holy Spirit:

> And I will ask the Father, and he will give you another Advocate, to be with you forever. This is the Spirit of truth, whom the world cannot receive, because it neither sees him nor knows him. You know him, because he abides with you, and he will be in you.... But the Advocate, the Holy Spirit, whom the Father will send in my name, will teach you everything, and remind you of all that I have said to you. Peace I leave with you; my peace I give to you. I do not give to you as the world gives. Do not let your hearts be troubled, and do not let them be afraid. (John 14:16–17, 26–27)

The Spirit's great continuing work was the bestowal of peace on the gathered community of Jesus. He bestowed peace in the full sense of shalom, the well-being produced by faith in the abiding presence of God.

Jesus explained further that the Holy Spirit would be with his disciples and help them to know what was morally right and to be able to discern truth. Most importantly, the Spirit would keep the disciples grounded in the person and the glory of Jesus:

> Nevertheless I tell you the truth: it is to your advantage that I go away, for if I do not go away, the Advocate will not come to you; but if I go, I will send him to you. And when he comes, he will prove the world wrong about sin and righteousness and judgment: about sin, because they do not believe in me; about righteousness, because I am going to the Father and you will see me no longer; about judgment, because the ruler of this world has been condemned. I still have many things to say to you, but you cannot bear them now. When the Spirit of truth comes, he will guide you into all the truth; for he will not speak on his own, but will speak whatever he hears, and he will declare to you the things that are to come. He will glorify me, because he will take what is mine and declare it to you. All that the Father has is mine. For this reason I said that he will take what is mine and declare it to you. (John 16:7–15)

The implication is that when the people of the church gather, they do not beckon a distant deity to hear their voices. Rather, through Jesus and by the Holy Spirit, God is already present bestowing grace and peace, enabling worship and work. This divine presence, therefore, forms the immediate context of Christian ministry. Ministry leaders are never alone in their work, and, the more clearly they understand that Jesus is already present, the less pressure they place on themselves to make something happen. In the context of the continual presence of Jesus, we can better understand the power of ministry leaders to "bind" and "loose."

Jesus's use of *ekklēsia* is recorded in only one Gospel and in only two brief texts in which he portrays the church as an essential outcome of his work of reconciliation and as the locus of kingdom authority for "binding and loosing":

> Simon Peter answered, "You are the Messiah, the Son of the living God." And Jesus answered him, "Blessed are you, Simon son of Jonah! For flesh and blood has not revealed this to you but my Father in heaven. And I tell you, you are Peter, and on this rock I will build my church, and the gates of Hades will not prevail against it. I will give you the keys of the kingdom of heaven, and whatever you bind on earth will be bound in heaven, and whatever you loose on earth will be loosed in heaven. (Matt 16:16–19)

> If the member refuses to listen to them, tell it to the church; and if the offender refuses to listen even to the church, let such a one be to you as a Gentile and a tax collector. Truly I tell you, whatever you bind on earth will be bound in heaven, and whatever you loose on earth will be loosed in heaven. (Matt 18:17–18)

In John's Gospel, Jesus says something similar when he commissions his disciples after the resurrection, "When he had said this, he breathed on them and said to them, 'Receive the Holy Spirit. If you forgive the sins of any, they are forgiven them; if you retain the sins of any, they are retained'" (John 20:22–23). The ways these texts have been interpreted has produced major divisions in Christianity.

The most basic division is between churches that view apostolic authority as *person-centered* and those that view apostolic authority as *confession-centered*. The first group holds that Jesus empowered the disciples themselves to determine doctrine and to include or exclude people from salvation and the church. The second group holds that Jesus referred to the power of the *confession* or *testimony* of Peter, not to the person of

Peter himself. In the first view, expressed primarily in the Roman Catholic and Orthodox traditions, the apostles and their successors were given the authority to "forbid and permit."[2] The background of this idea is found in Jewish rabbinical traditions relating to interpretation of the law. The rabbis interpreted what was forbidden and what was permitted regarding the proper keeping of the law. The influence of rabbinical traditions is evident in churches that view the apostles and their successors as having the authority to interpret the faith, to forgive sin, and to determine who may be included or excluded from the church.

In the second view, typical of Baptist and other congregational traditions, the confession itself and the body of Christ formed by that confession have the authority to bind and loose. When the church communicates the gospel of Jesus, it offers the message that binds or liberates according to the response of each person. The church as a corporate body of believers has the authority to interpret the faith, but the binding and loosing are not lodged in a bishop or hierarchy of bishops, such as the magisterium of the Roman Catholic Church. The locus of authority in congregational traditions is the Bible and the Holy Spirit who dwells within each believer. Believers read the Scripture individually and corporately and live out the biblical narrative in a community of faith. The only *control* on interpretation is the biblical story itself and the inner testimony of the Holy Spirit as past and present communities of faith have understood them. So the hearing, interpreting, and imparting of the gospel message are the privilege and responsibility of all believers. Professionally trained, occupational ministry leaders serve an important function in equipping and enabling churches to carry out the commission and commands of Christ. Yet, the congregational view undermines hard and fast distinctions between clergy and laity, in which only ordained clergy have interpretive authority and can perform certain rituals for the laity.

The congregational view also bears upon how Christians understand the idea of sacrament. On the one hand, in churches that adhere to some form of apostolic succession and sacerdotal (priestly) authority, the power to bestow sacraments goes hand in hand with this authority. Sacrament is a difficult word to define, because it is an inherently mysterious and spiritual idea. The definition culled from St. Augustine, a visible sign of an invisible grace, has long held sway.[3] A sacrament is a ritual administered by

---

2. Kohler, "Binding and Loosing," 215.
3. Augustine, *Doctrinal Treatises*, 312.

ordained clergy that mysteriously imparts the grace of God. Sacraments are inherently efficacious based upon the authority of the church and the clergy who administer them. In the Roman Catholic and Orthodox traditions there are multiple sacraments performed at significant moments or situations in life: birth (baptism), adolescence (confirmation), post-baptismal sins (communion), marriage, anointing of the sick, confession of sin, and ordination. The clergy, empowered by their own sacrament of "holy orders" (the rite of ordination), have the authority, as representatives of Christ, to distribute the sacraments.

On the other hand, in congregational traditions, clerical authority and sacrament are replaced by the priesthood of all believers and personal grace and faith. Each individual person hears and confesses faith in the truth of the gospel message. Through conscious and willful repentance of sin, belief in Jesus as the risen Lord, and receipt of the gracious forgiveness of God, each person enters a new personal relationship with God and with the people of Christ's church. The person now is one of the people of God, a member of the body of Christ, and part of the temple of the Spirit. Instead of sacraments, therefore, confessional traditions observe two memorial ordinances, baptism and the Lord's Supper. Christ himself commanded these two symbolic rituals, so congregational churches view them as acts of personal obedience but not conduits for sacramental grace. Grace cannot be bestowed like a commodity by a priest. God bestows grace directly and personally when someone places his or her trust in Christ and his forgiveness. So the ordinances are symbolic demonstrations and reminders of that faith. Although these congregations do not believe in self-efficacious sacraments or sacerdotal clergy, they may still have room for a reinterpretation of the idea of sacrament.

In essence, the idea of sacrament conveys the power and freedom of God to be present in and through anything in his creation. In the Roman Catholic Mass, the moment of receiving the Eucharist (the Lord's Supper) is the consumption of the actual body and blood of Jesus. This Roman Catholic belief in the *transubstantiation* of the bread and wine into the actual body and blood of Jesus conveys the profound meaning that Jesus is physically present in that moment with his people. In congregational traditions there is little to compare with such a tangible ritual of Christ's presence, so ministry leaders in these traditions may feel compelled to produce spiritual experiences by contrived means (e.g., manipulative sermons and altar calls, heart-pounding music, overreliance on technology and ambiance, etc.). These contrivances may draw a crowd and stir emotions, but they can soon become routine and hollow. Few things lead to depression and burnout among ministry leaders quicker than the sense that they are just putting on a show each week in the attempt to "gin up" the spirit. In the words of an old Baptist wag, "sometimes it seems that we are building windmills in a land where the wind never blows."

By retaining a core insight of the sacramental traditions, however, congregational traditions may find something they have lost. At the heart of the idea of sacrament is the belief that God is *already* present with God's people. When Jesus told his followers that wherever two or three were gathered, he would be there in their midst, he laid the groundwork for a healthy sacramental theology. Dietrich Bonhoeffer captures this when he says, "Christianity means community through Jesus Christ and in Jesus Christ. No Christian community is more or less than this. Whether it be a brief, single encounter or the daily fellowship of years, Christian community is only this. We belong to one another only through and in Jesus Christ."[4] Christ is truly present in his church—in the midst of his people, so that his presence is not limited to special rituals or physical elements like bread, wine, water, or oil. Christ's presence is spiritual and personal. The difference of interpretation here has profound implications for how Christian ministers understand their purpose in serving the church. The role of ministers in leading the church is not to provide spiritual experiences or stir emotions but to help their people to recognize and believe the God who is already graciously present. In Jesus and by the Holy Spirit, God indwells the church. The "visible sign" of the "invisible grace" is the actual gathering of two or more of Christ's followers in worship. The gathering of the people of the church is more than the sum of the individual members. Christ is sacramentally present in the gathering. We experience Christ in the presence of one another; we are strengthened by Christ in the presence of one another; we are challenged by Christ in the presence of one another; we are blessed by Christ in the presence of one another. Again, in the words of Bonhoeffer, "The physical presence of other Christians is a source of incomparable joy and strength to the believer."[5] The sacramental nature of the church as the earthly presence of Christ is not only for the purpose of blessing the gathered members, however. Christ's presence always calls and directs the church to the world.

4. Bonhoeffer, *Life Together*, 21.
5. Bonhoeffer, *Life Together*, 19.

PART ONE: THE CONTEXT OF MINISTRY LEADERSHIP

The Mission of God

When Jesus commissioned his disciples following his resurrection, he described their subsequent work as the mission of spreading of his message to the world:

> Then he opened their minds to understand the scriptures, and he said to them, "Thus it is written, that the Messiah is to suffer and to rise from the dead on the third day, and that repentance and forgiveness of sins is to be proclaimed in his name to all nations, beginning from Jerusalem. You are witnesses of these things. (Luke 24:45–48)

> Go therefore and make disciples of all nations, baptizing them in the name of the Father and of the Son and of the Holy Spirit, and teaching them to obey everything that I have commanded you. And remember, I am with you always, to the end of the age. (Matt 28:19–20)

> But you will receive power when the Holy Spirit has come upon you; and you will be my witnesses in Jerusalem, in all Judea and Samaria, and to the ends of the earth. (Acts 1:8)

Mission is the ultimate purpose of the church. Dale Moody makes this clear: "Mission is basic to the meaning of the church. Indeed, the church is mission, and where there is no mission there is no church. God has called the church from the world to send her back into the world with a message and a mission."[6] The English word mission comes from the Latin *missio*, meaning "to send"; in turn, the Latin word translates the New Testament Greek word *apostellō*, also meaning "to send" or "to send out someone." The church is essentially apostolic or missional, not in the sense of being governed by apostles but in the sense of being sent out to the world by God.

The "missional" church movement of the past few decades has helped to recover the idea that the church is not just a missionary-sending institution but an entire people on mission. The difference is again one of context. When a church views itself in the context of a dominant center of Christian culture, then that church sends missionaries to convert those of other cultures to its own culture. On the other hand, when a church views itself in context of a marginal people in a foreign land, then it bears witness to the Christ who is reconciling all (inside and outside the church) to himself. A truly missional church sees itself as undergoing reconciliation and

---

6. Moody, *Word of Truth*, 427.

transformation by Christ even as it invites others to believe in Christ and participate in that same reconciliation and transformation.

The church truly is a body of wounded healers, the sick reaching out to the sick. As Jesus said, "No one is good but God alone" (Mark 10:18), so there is no place for cultural pride or self-righteous religion. The fundamental humility of such a church reflects the very nature of Jesus himself. Jesus's mindset was that of the emptying of self for the sake of others (Phil 2:5–11). His mission required the denial of himself and the laying down of his life for humanity. In so doing, Jesus reflected the missional nature of God. The Father, Son, and Holy Spirit are essentially missional, and this means that the church also is missional. According to David Bosch, "the classical doctrine on the *missio Dei* as God the Father sending the Son, and God the Father and the Son sending the Spirit, was expanded to include yet another 'movement': Father, Son, and Holy Spirit sending the church into the world."[7]

The sending work of the missional God involves two rhythmic actions: gathering and dispersing. The missional nature of the church emerges from the God that both attracts and disseminates. In both Testaments, God took the initiative to call people to be holy, set apart only for himself. Moses told the people of Israel, "You are a people holy to the LORD your God; the LORD your God has chosen you out of all the peoples on earth to be his people, his treasured possession" (Deut 7:6). Moses's words were echoed in those of Peter speaking of the church as the new people of God: "But you are a chosen race, a royal priesthood, a holy nation, God's own people. . . . Once you were not a people, but now you are God's people; once you had not received mercy, but now you have received mercy" (1 Pet 2:9–10). The first impulse of God's work is attractional, and a basic aspect of the missional nature of the church is to attract people into relationship with God through Jesus and the followers of Jesus.

Paradoxically, the call of God that attracts and gathers is, at the same time, the call that disseminates and disperses the people of God into the world. To be called by God not only is to be *drawn to* but also to be *sent forth*. The sending was already there in the covenant with Abraham. His call to follow was also a call to bless the nations: "Now the LORD said to Abram, 'Go from your country and your kindred and your father's house to the land that I will show you. I will make of you a great nation, and I will bless you, and make your name great, so that you will be a blessing. I will bless

---

7. Bosch, *Transforming Mission*, 399.

those who bless you, and the one who curses you I will curse; and in you all the families of the earth shall be blessed'" (Gen 12:1-3). The attracting and sending forth were also there in Jesus's call to his disciples. He called them to be with him and to be sent out: "Follow me and I will make you fish for people" (Mark 1:17); "and he appointed the twelve, who he also named apostles [sent ones], to be with him, and to be sent out to proclaim the message" (Mark 3:14). To be called is both to abide (dwell) in Christ and also to bear fruit (John 15:5). Attracting and sending forth stem from the fact that Christians are "in the world but not of the world." Jesus himself spoke of this dual reality: "They do not belong to the world, just as I do not belong to the world. . . . As you have sent me into the world, so I have sent them into the world" (John 17:16-18). Christians can be salt and light (Matt 5:13-14) to the world, precisely because they are now citizens of another place. According to Peter, Christians are aliens and strangers, a people of the kingdom of God living in a world in rebellion against God (1 Pet 2:11).

When the church views its context as that of a foreign people living in a strange land, it has the power to speak from the margins of humility, love, and forgiveness to a world centered on pride, indifference, and blame. Christian ministers serving such churches have no illusions about where they serve and the difficulties they face. They know that they themselves and the people with whom they work are still very much engaged with their own personal battles and societal struggles with the sins of pride, indifference and blame. When viewed from the margin rather than from the center of culture, ministry leaders can see the corruptions of the church and the world more clearly and offer a message that brings true reconciliation and shalom. The writer of Hebrews understood how ministers from the margins, strangers, and foreigners in this world are not satisfied with this world but hunger for a better country. These ministers have a vision for the kingdom of God and know that their journey home is not yet complete:

> They confessed that they were strangers and foreigners on the earth, for people who speak in this way make it clear that they are seeking a homeland. If they had been thinking of the land that they had left behind, they would have had opportunity to return. But as it is, they desire a better country, that is, a heavenly one. Therefore, God is not ashamed to be called their God; indeed, he has prepared a city for them. (Heb 11:13-16)

The Community of Salvation

The church attracts people from the world and sends them back into the world, but what happens between the attracting and the sending? What happens while the church is together? There are many activities in congregational life—worship, learning, caring, and even playing together. The primary purpose, however, is salvation. Salvation is not merely a one-time transaction in which people get tickets to heaven. It is the transformation of their character. Salvation entails not only the forgiveness by God but also the reformation of attitudes and actions. Transformation and reformation of character happen primarily in community with fellow believers. Stanley Grenz described the church as the community of salvation.[8] He meant that the church not only proclaims God's *message* of salvation but also that the church is God's *method* of salvation. It is common for Christians to think of salvation as a single moment in their lives, but the Scripture indicates that salvation is actually a process with a beginning, continuing action, and a future goal. Salvation begins with the receiving of God's forgiving grace by faith in Jesus Christ. Faith in Christ justifies the sinner, or makes a person right with God. The forgiven, justified sinner, however, still needs to grow in obedience to Christ. This growth is called sanctification. Sinners have been *declared* holy in justification, but sinners also must *become* holy through sanctification. Finally, the process of salvation comes to completion with glorification, the resurrection from the dead and entrance into the kingdom of God. At every step in the process of salvation the Spirit of God is working, and the believer cooperates with the Spirit's work through faith and obedience.

Table 2.2 The Process of Salvation

Beginning	Continuing Action	Future Goal
"Been Saved"	"Being Saved"	"Will Be Saved"
Justification	Sanctification	Glorification
Forgiveness of Sin	Transformation of Character	Resurrection to New Life

---

8. Grenz, *Theology for the Community*, 627.

Beginning	Continuing Action	Future Goal
Eph 2:8: "For by grace you *have been saved* through faith, this is not your own doing; it is the gift of God."	1 Cor 1:18: "For the message of the cross is foolishness to those who are perishing, but to us who are *being saved* it is the power of God."	Rom 8:10: "For if while we were enemies, we were reconciled to God through the death of his Son, much more surely, having been reconciled, we *will be saved* by his life."
2 Tim 2:9: "[God] *who saved* us and called us with a holy calling, not according to our works but according to his own purpose and grace."	1 Pet 2:1–2: "Rid yourselves of all malice, and all guile, insincerity, envy, and all slander. Like new born infants, long for the pure spiritual milk, so that by it you may grow into salvation."	Phil 3:10–11, 14: "I want to know Christ and the power of his resurrection and the sharing of his sufferings by becoming like him in his death, if somehow I may attain the resurrection from the dead. . . . I press on toward the goal for the prize of the heavenly call of God in Christ Jesus."
Rom 5:1: "Therefore, since we are justified by faith, we have peace with God through our Lord Jesus Christ."	Phil 2:12: "Therefore, my beloved, just as you have always obeyed me, not only in my presence but much more now in my absence, work out your own salvation with fear and trembling."	

Sanctification happens through life in the community of believers. Fallen and alienated people who have forgotten how to love must relearn love through participation in community and the practice of loving acts.

Paul's letters typically have two parts. In the first, part Paul states the basic beliefs of the gospel, and in the second part he encourages believers to live in accord with those beliefs. Paul's indicative statements are followed by imperative statements. Paul contends that believers must work out their salvation (Phil 2:15). He implores the church not to be content with God's gift of grace and forgiveness but to go on to full sanctification by intentional acts of humility, self-denial, and forgiveness that bring about the transformation of character and enable genuine love:

> I appeal to you therefore, brothers and sisters, by the mercies of God, to present your bodies as a living sacrifice, holy and

> acceptable to God, which is your spiritual worship. Do not be conformed to this world but be transformed by the renewing of your minds, so that you may discern what is the will of God—what is good and acceptable and perfect. For by the grace given to me I say to everyone among you not to think of yourself more highly than you ought to think, but to think with sober judgment, each according to the measure of faith that God has assigned. . . . Let love be genuine; hate what is evil, hold fast to what is good; love one another with mutual affection; outdo one another in showing honor. Do not lag in zeal, be ardent in spirit, serve the Lord. Rejoice in hope, be patient in suffering, persevere in prayer. Contribute to the needs of the saints; extend hospitality to strangers. (Rom 12:1–3, 9–13)

Likewise, James, who sometimes is thought to contradict Paul, sounds exactly the same note about the corporate nature of salvation when he insists that the "royal law" of loving one's neighbor must be evident in the church as a result and demonstration of faith,

> You do well if you really fulfill the royal law according to the scripture, You shall love your neighbor as yourself. . . . What good is it, my brothers and sisters, if you say you have faith but do not have works? Can faith save you? If a brother or sister is naked and lacks daily food, and one of you says to them, "Go in peace; keep warm and eat your fill," and yet you do not supply their bodily needs, what is the good of that? So faith by itself, if it has no works, is dead. (Jas 2:8, 14–17)

When comparing Paul and James, it is helpful to be aware of the different ways they use the word "works." When Paul says that we are saved by faith, not by works, he is referring to works as the laws that were particular to Jewish identity, most prominently circumcision. According to Paul, becoming a Jew and doing the Jewish law do not save a person; only Christ through his grace can do that. When James refers to works, however, he means the actions of loving one's neighbor. He is referring to the actions of those who have *already* been saved and are now living the Christian life. For James, the works of loving others should be evident among God's people. Paul would not object to the idea that a true believer is one who practices the law of love as the result of true faith in Jesus.

Not only Paul and James, but the consensus of New Testament writers points to the relational aspect of salvation. Peter sounds the note when he says that young believers need to grow into their salvation by learning how to love: "Rid yourselves, therefore, of all malice, and all guile, insincerity, envy, and all slander. Like newborn infants, long for the pure, spiritual milk, so that by it you may grow into salvation—if indeed you have tasted that the Lord is good" (1 Pet 2:1–3). The writer of Hebrews testifies to the community's role in salvation: "And let us consider how to provoke one another to love and good deeds, not neglecting to meet together, as is the habit of some, but encouraging one another, and all the more as you see the Day approaching" (Heb 10:24–25). The First Letter of John echoes the same note by insisting that the church must be characterized by love for one another: "We love because he first loved us. Those who say, 'I love God,' and hate their brothers or sisters, are liars; for those who do not love a brother or sister whom they have seen, cannot love God whom they have not seen. The commandment we have from him is this: those who love God must love their brothers and sisters also" (1 John 4:19–21).

Indeed, throughout the New Testament, from the moment Jesus called his first disciples to the ingathering of thousands of new believers at Pentecost, following Jesus resulted in corporate living. To follow Christ is to enter a new family, and like all families the members are not of their own choosing. Left to ourselves, we would choose the people we like, or we might not choose anyone at all. In the community of Christ, however, we find ourselves knit together with those God has chosen. These people, not some other people, are the ones with whom we learn how to love:

> But now in Christ Jesus you who once were far off have been brought near by the blood of Christ. For he is our peace; in his flesh he has made both groups into one and has broken down the dividing wall, that is, the hostility between us. He has abolished the law with its commandments and ordinances, that he might create in himself one new humanity in place of the two, thus making peace, and might reconcile both groups to God in one body through the cross, thus putting to death that hostility through it. (Eph 2:13–16)

Effective ministry leaders understand two things. First, they know that God's method of complete salvation is the church, and second, they know that the church is not an easy place to work. The work of reconciliation is hard. The people who are engaged in it are just learning how to truly care for each other. Such love and care do not come naturally. The natural inclinations of sinful humans to pride, envy, and fear make real relationship almost impossible. Only the Holy Spirit working intrapersonally and interpersonally can move us to humility, generosity, and trust.

The church, therefore, is the immediate context of ministry leadership within the larger context of the biblical story. Ministry leaders who maintain the perspective that their work is a small but important part of the greater work of God have a much greater potential to keep themselves mentally and spiritually balanced. They will not see their work as just breaking rocks or making a living but as building a cathedral—contributing to the kingdom that God is building through the work of countless ministers and ministry leaders.

Part Two

The Call to Ministry Leadership

As we turn to consider the calling of ministry leadership, we shift our focus from the macro to the micro. We shift from the great, comprehensive work of God to our own personal place and role in that grand scheme. Even as we narrow our focus, however, we must not forget that our own calling makes sense only within the larger story of God's purpose and work for the entire creation. Within that larger story, we find that God calls humans to participate in his work, and we find that it is only within that calling that we gain our true identity and purpose in life. In the Bible, we find calling spoken of in two complementary ways: the call to salvation and the call to service. The salvation call is God's gracious invitation to all people to repent of sin, believe in Jesus Christ, and enter the kingdom of God. The service call is God's invitation to follow Jesus in self-sacrificial ministry for others.

Throughout the course of Christian history, the basic biblical depictions of calling have gone through significant development and variation in response to social, political, and theological changes. The lasting influence of these disparate views creates significant confusion about the meaning of calling today. In order to gain some clarity, therefore, we must review the biblical and historical background.

3

The Meaning of Calling

Biblical Foundations

CALLING IS DEEPLY EMBEDDED in the biblical narrative. From Genesis to Revelation, God's voice reaches out to humanity. The initial call of God occurs in Gen 3 after the harmonious relationship with humans was shattered by their sin. Humans, ashamed and afraid, hid themselves from God, so he now had to search for them. As he searched, he called out to them: "But the LORD God called to the man, and said to him, 'Where are you?' He said, 'I heard the sound of you in the garden, and I was afraid, because I was naked; and I hid myself'" (Gen 3:9–10). The context of God's calling both for the first humans and for us today is the separation created by our sin. God's voice reaches across the divide, but his voice is often not heard. The result of hiding from God is that God becomes hidden to us; "for you have hidden your face from us, and have delivered us into the hand of our iniquity" (Isa 64:7). Paul explains the terrible consequences of hiding from God: "For though they knew God, they did not honor him as God or give thanks to him, but they became futile in their thinking, and their senseless minds were darkened" (Rom 1:20–23). Sin against God contained its own punishment, estrangement from the Creator.

Yet, God stayed in the relationship, and his voice still penetrated the darkness. Though God was now hidden, he could still be heard, if at times only as an echo. N. T. Wright uses the metaphor of echoes to describe our vague and fragmentary awareness of God's voice stirring fallen humanity to seek justice, to thirst for spirituality, to desire lasting relationship, and to be moved by beauty. These mystical influences and urgings point to a time and place in which these higher values and deeper experiences were clear and whole.[1] These echoes of God's voice now call humanity to reach for "something more" than the material world. Ultimately, they reveal that life has profound meaning and purpose.

The remainder of the Old Testament records the stories of how select individuals heard and believed God's call and received his promises. Noah heard and believed God's call to preserve the creation through a storm of destruction, and he received the promise of hope. Abraham and Sarah heard and believed God's call to birth a people of God, and they received the promises of children, land, and blessing. Moses heard and believed God's call to deliver his people, and he received the promise of the formation of a holy nation. David heard and believed God's call to rule over Israel, and he received the promise of a lineage of kings. Elijah heard and believed God's call to preach truth to power, and he received the promise of victory over false gods. Isaiah heard and believed God's call to preach truth to a people who would not listen, and he received the promise of the future restoration of his people. Jeremiah heard and believed God's call to proclaim the death of the nation, and he received the promise of the transformation of his people with the coming of the new covenant.

These examples of God's call to particular people within Israel foreshadowed the universal call to all people and nations in the New Testament. In Jeremiah's prophecy of the new covenant, he described a situation in which all would know God and hear God's voice:

> But this is the covenant that I will make with the house of Israel after those days, says the LORD: I will put my law within them, and I will write it on their hearts; and I will be their God, and they shall be my people. No longer shall they teach one another, or say to each other, "Know the LORD," for they shall all know me, from the least of them to the greatest, says the LORD; for I will forgive their iniquity, and remember their sin no more. (Jer 31:33–34)

In this new covenant, all who hear and believe God's call receive the promise of salvation and the privilege of serving alongside Christ in the work of ministry.

In the New Testament, the Greek noun for call or calling is *klesis*, and the verb (to call) is *kaleō*. The predominant use of the word in the New Testament is the invitation to salvation:

---

1. N. Wright, *Simply Christian*, 3–51.

> I [Jesus] have come to call not the righteous but sinners to repentance. (Luke 5:32; cf. Mark 2:17, Matt 9:13)
>
> To the church of God that is in Corinth, to those who are sanctified in Christ Jesus, called to be saints (1 Cor 2:2)
>
> Including yourselves who are called to belong to Jesus Christ, to all God's beloved in Rome, who are called to be saints (Rom 1:6–7)
>
> [God] who saved us and called us with a holy calling (2 Tim 1:9)

The secondary use of *klesis* or *kaleō* is the invitation to service:

> Come to me, all you that are weary and are carrying heavy burdens, and I will give you rest. Take my yoke upon you, and learn from me; for I am gentle and humble in heart, and you will find rest for your souls. For my yoke is easy, and my burden is light. (Matt 11:28–30)
>
> As Jesus passed along the Sea of Galilee, he saw Simon and his brother Andrew casting a net into the sea—for they were fishermen. And Jesus said to them, "Follow me and I will make you fish for people." And immediately they left their nets and followed him. As he went a little farther, he saw James son of Zebedee and his brother John, who were in their boat mending the nets. Immediately he called them; and they left their father Zebedee in the boat with the hired men, and followed him. (Mark 1:16–20)

The calls to salvation and service are not wholly distinct aspects but complementary movements in the Christian life. To receive salvation is also to live out that salvation as a changed person. As we have seen, Paul characteristically follows his indicative descriptions of the nature of salvation with "therefore" or imperative statements of encouragement to "work out" that salvation in Christian ministry. Thus, the Pauline indicative and imperative reveal the complementary nature of the calls to salvation and to service:

> I [Paul] therefore, the prisoner in the Lord, beg you to lead a life worthy of the calling to which you have been called, with all humility and gentleness, with patience, bearing with one another in love, making every effort to maintain the unity of the Spirit in the bond of peace. There is one body and one Spirit, just as you were called to the one hope of your calling, one Lord, one faith, one baptism, one God and Father of all, who is above all and through all and in all. . . . The gifts he gave were that some would be apostles, some prophets, some evangelists, some pastors and

teachers, to equip the saints for the work of ministry, for building up the body of Christ. (Eph 4:1–6, 11–12)

Over the past two millennia, interpretations of the nature of calling have changed with the tides of church and society. We now turn to review those changes in order to see how they can help us understand the call to Christian ministry and ministry leadership today.

Calling in Christian History

The Latin Vulgate was the primary translation of the Bible for more than a thousand years in the remnants of the western Roman Empire, so vocation, the Latin word for "call" or "calling," became predominant in Western Christianity. Over the past two millennia, the idea of vocation has been defined and redefined according to varying understandings of church and society. For many centuries, the Roman Catholic Church viewed vocation as the call to the distinct religious roles of priest, monk, or nun. The Protestant Reformation changed the meaning of callings or vocations to be inclusive of all the "stations" or roles that God has created to give order to society. Through these stations, Christians are uniquely empowered by God to love their neighbors. In recent times, the idea of vocation has tended to lose its religious associations entirely. For many people today, to have a vocation simply means to have a job or a career. These changing views have clouded our understanding, so it is necessary to take a closer look at the development of calling in Christian history.

As we have seen, in the New Testament the language of vocation is used in two ways: as the call to salvation and as the call to service. In the earliest Christian centuries following the New Testament period, the primary emphasis was on the call to salvation itself. For the first three centuries, Christianity was illegal in the Roman Empire. Simply becoming a Christian was a decision fraught with risk and rejection. Christians were typically viewed as politically dangerous and socially deviant. In this hostile context, the early Christians understood calling in terms of the extreme personal sacrifice of simply becoming a true Christian. Ignatius of Antioch, around 107 CE on his way to martyrdom in Rome, describes this sentiment: "It is not that I want merely to be called a Christian, but actually to be one. . . . The greatness of Christianity lies in being hated by the world, not in its being convincing to it. . . . Let me be fodder for wild beasts—that is how I can get to God."²

With changing circumstances and the legalization of Christianity in the Roman Empire under Constantine, the ideal of becoming a true Christian shifted from the suffering of societal persecution to the suffering of self-denial. The self-induced practices of ascetic monasticism came to characterize a higher calling. Athanasius, in *The Life of Anthony*, describes Anthony's practices of living in isolation, sleeping on the ground, frequent fasting (even starvation), and praying incessantly as being especially valued by Christ: "And a voice [Christ's] came to him, 'Anthony, I was here but I waited to see your fight, because of which, since you have endured, and have not been defeated, I will ever be a help to you, and will make your name known everywhere.'"³ The ideal of self-sacrifice among the eremitic (solitary) monks and eventually those in cenobitic (communal) monasteries redefined and limited the view of religious calling only to those who could embark on such heroic self-denial for the sake of Christ. The development of a clergy class, separate and distinct from ordinary members or laity class, also contributed to a restricted view of calling.

In the earliest years of Christianity, church leaders and church members were distinguished more by functional roles than higher status. The formal distinction between clergy and laity developed only gradually in the second and third centuries when the status of clergy took on aspects of the Old Testament priesthood, and the meaning of the Lord's Supper took on sacramental connotations. In turn, the development of the sacramental Eucharist gave rise to a sacramental status of the clergy itself. Bishops, priests, monks, and nuns came to be seen as a higher order of Christians through their calling and ordination.⁴ This special order of Christians saw themselves as entering a distinctly spiritual or "religious" life as opposed to an ordinary or "temporal" life. The most prominent characteristic of this transition was the commitment to remain unmarried. Celibacy had become a significant defining act of personal sacrifice for those who entered the religious life. Hence, to have a calling or vocation meant the pursuit of a higher and holier life, dedicating oneself, even marrying oneself, to God and the church.⁵

2. Ignatius of Antioch, *Letters*, quoted in Placher, *Callings*, 237–38.
3. Athanasius, as quoted in Placher, *Callings*, 64.
4. Stevens, *Other Six Days*, 24–43.
5. Friend, *Rise of Christianity*, 411–12; Veith, *God at Work*, 18.

PART TWO: THE CALL TO MINISTRY LEADERSHIP

Vocation as a special calling to religious service prevailed in the Western church until the Protestant Reformation, but it remains a primary emphasis in the Roman Catholic Church today. Since the Second Vatican Council in the early 1960s, the Roman Catholic Church has expanded the idea of vocation to include both clergy and laity. Yet, this inclusion has not diverged from the basic view of vocation as relating to various "states" or levels of holiness. For Roman Catholics today, vocation means calling either to marriage, the priesthood, or the religious life. The clerics and the monastics are called to live in a state of celibacy, whereas the married are obviously not. It is clear, therefore, that for Catholics even today, marital status remains an essential factor in distinguishing vocations.[6] The Protestant Reformers of the sixteenth century reacted strongly to this view. Martin Luther, in particular, set forth a revolutionary reinterpretation of vocation. Luther, who himself had entered the religious vocation as a celibate Augustinian monk, came to reject this former life. Based on his study of the Greek New Testament, particularly the writings of Paul, Luther came to view salvation as produced solely by faith in God's forgiving grace. No human work could justify sinners or make them more acceptable to God. As a corollary to his new understanding of salvation, Luther developed his theology of vocation.

Luther found in Paul's writings not only the idea of justification by faith alone but also a new way to understand the meaning of calling. In 1 Cor 7, Luther perceived that Paul used the same Greek word for calling but in two different ways. The translation of 1 Cor 7:20 in the King James Version demonstrates the ambiguity: "Let every man abide in the same *calling* wherein he was *called*" (emphasis added). In the first instance, "calling" means a status or situation in life; in the second instance, "called" means the call to salvation. Luther's recognition of Paul's ambiguous usage in this text revolutionized his view of calling. Central to his new understanding was the idea that there are the two distinct realms in which the Christian lives: the spiritual and the physical. Calling is different in each realm. In the spiritual realm, a person is called to salvation. There, one deals directly and only with God through grace and faith. In the physical realm, a person is called to do the work of loving one's neighbor. One realm is governed by grace and the other by work. Christians, therefore, are free before God but bound by the law of love toward others.[7]

6. *Catechism of Catholic Church*, 439–46, 451–52.
7. Luther, *Commentaries*, 46.

Earthly callings for Luther, therefore, were not ways of working to please God but stations or roles through which *God works* to care for the world. God works through the callings of both Christians and non-Christians to order and preserve the creation.[8] God created all human callings and has ordered human life around the callings of family, state, and church. Callings are not extraordinary religious achievements but ordinary roles in society, e.g., father, mother, magistrate, soldier, pastor, etc.[9] Although Christians and non-Christians have callings, only Christians have the power of God truly to love their neighbors through their callings. A major consequence of Luther's revolutionary view was the elimination of any essential difference between clergy and laity.

> This is why all vocations are equal before God. Pastors, monks, nuns and popes are no holier than farmers, shopkeepers, dairy maids, or latrine diggers. In the spiritual kingdom, in a divine egalitarianism . . . peasants are equal to kings. . . . In God's earthly kingdom, though, Christians do have different callings, and their complex relationships with each other become occasions to live out the love of God. Again, Luther said that faith serves God, but works serve our neighbor. We often speak of "serving God," and this is a worthy goal, but strictly speaking, in the spiritual realm, it is God who serves us. . . . In our vocations, we are not serving God—we are serving other people.[10]

Whereas Luther insisted that earthly callings were ways to serve people but not God, John Calvin made no such distinction.[11] The result was that Calvin shifted the meaning of earthly callings toward pleasing God through work, rather than loving one's neighbor as in Luther. Calvin, like Luther, maintained the distinction between the spiritual realm and the physical realm, but he did not view these realms as entirely separate. Both were realms of God's "government." Grace and law went hand in hand for Calvin. Grace enabled obedience to the law, which meant that good works could be an indicator that a person was truly among the elect. This emphasis upon good works, in turn, shifted the focus of vocation from Luther's emphasis upon love for others toward diligent and productive work to please God.

---

8. Maxfield, "Luther and Lutheran Confessions," 30.
9. Luther, *Christians Can Be Soldiers*, 18–19.
10. Veith, *God at Work*, 39.
11. McGrath, *Life of John Calvin*, 160.

> Finally, this point is to be noted: the Lord bids each one of us in all of life's actions to look to his calling.... Therefore, lest through our stupidity and rashness everything be turned topsy-turvy, he has appointed duties for every man in his particular way of life. And that no one may thoughtlessly transgress his limits, he has named these various kinds of living "callings."... A man of obscure station will lead a private life ungrudgingly so as not to leave the rank in which he has been placed by God.... The magistrate will discharge his functions more willingly; the head of the household will confine himself to his duty; each man will bear and swallow discomforts, vexations, weariness, and anxieties in his way of life, when he has been persuaded that the burden was laid upon him by God. From this will arise also a singular consolation: that no task will be so sordid and base, provided you obey your calling in it, that it will not shine and be reckoned precious in God's sight.[12]

The distinction between Luther's and Calvin's views is subtle but significant. Luther's focus was on serving one's neighbor. Calvin's emphasis was on diligent performance for God and the demonstration of one's salvation. Calvin's view thus laid the foundations for the development of the "Protestant work ethic"[13] and, in more recent centuries, led to the reduction of vocation to mean little more than a kind of employment or occupation. Luther and Calvin had different emphases, but, at the end of the day, both were in essential agreement that all people have a calling. The radical wing of the Reformation saw things differently, however.

The radical wing of the Reformation refers to a collection of free church groups that rejected the authority of the state in matters of religion.[14] One of these groups, the Anabaptists, agreed with Luther and Calvin on the basic insight that salvation is strictly by grace and faith. They also agreed with the theology of the two realms or kingdoms, but the Anabaptists maintained that true Christians are citizens only of the spiritual realm and must separate themselves from the earthly or "political" realm. So, they viewed calling strictly as Christian discipleship and life in the community of Christ. Callings could not be found outside of the church. Although a few Anabaptists, like Balthasar Hubmaier, were more open to the world

---

12. Calvin, *Institutes of Christian Religion*, 724–25.

13. The Protestant work ethic was first described by sociologist Max Weber. See Weber, *Protestant Ethic*.

14. Estep, *Anabaptist Story*, 21–22.

outside their churches, as a whole, Anabaptists were not inclined to speak of vocation as a call to serve those outside of the church.[15]

The foregoing survey of views of calling from the Bible through the Reformation reveals a diversity of interpretations that creates the confusion we have inherited today. Table 3.1 provides a comparative summary of historical ways of understanding calling:

Table 3.1 Comparison of Historical Views of Calling

Biblical Emphases	Early Church	Roman Catholic	Martin Luther	John Calvin	Anabaptists
Salvation & service	True salvation that endures through societal rejection, persecution, or even martyrdom	A higher religious order of priests, monks, or nuns in which one serves God only and pursues spiritual perfection through celibacy and self-sacrifice	All the various life stations and roles through which God works to preserve the world and enable Christians, in particular, to love others	All the various duties of life through which Christians demonstrate their salvation and please God by the quality of their work	The gifts of the Holy Spirit given only to Christians for life in the church

Since the Reformation, theologians have developed various ways to understand the dynamics of calling through various classifications or typologies.

Classifications of Calling

William Perkins, an early Puritan theologian, was among the first to distinguish between general calling and particular calling in a way that differed from John Calvin. Calvin (reflecting Matt 22:14) had used the terms *general* and *special* to distinguish the non-elect from the elect, the lost from the saved. Perkins, however, more in line with Luther, used *general* and *particular* to distinguish the responsibilities incumbent on all Christians from the responsibilities God gives each particular person to perform in society: "The general calling is the calling of Christianity, which

15. Estep, *Anabaptist Story*, 82.

PART TWO: THE CALL TO MINISTRY LEADERSHIP

is common to all that live in the Church of God. The particular is that special calling that belongs to some particular men: . . . A personal calling is the execution of some particular office, arising of that distinction which God makes between man and man in every society."[16] The distinction between a general call to Christian life and a special call to a particular congregational or societal duty became standard, at least among Protestants. In recent years, however, there has been some helpful reflection and clarification of the various ways people hear and obey the general call and discern and pursue the individual call.

In the mid-twentieth century, the theologian H. Richard Niebuhr, who was particularly concerned with the theological education of Christian ministry leaders, distinguished four elements of calling to Christian ministry. These four elements included a general call to discipleship and three special or personal elements—secret, providential, and ecclesiastical:

> A call to the ministry includes at least these four elements: (1) the *call to be a Christian*, which is variously described as the call to discipleship of Jesus Christ, to hearing and doing the Word of God, to repentance and faith, et cetera; (2) *the secret call*, namely, that inner persuasion or experience whereby a person feels himself directly summoned or invited by God to take up the work of the ministry; (3) *the providential call*, which is that invitation and command to assume the work of the ministry which comes through the equipment of a person with the talents necessary of the exercise of the office and through the divine guidance of his life by all its circumstances; (4) *the ecclesiastical call*, that is, the summons and invitation extended to a man by some community or institution of the Church to engage in the work of the ministry.[17]

Niebuhr's typology reveals the dynamic nature of calling. Basic obedience to Christ, inward awareness, outward circumstances, and ecclesiastical affirmation are necessary for discernment of the call to ministry leadership.

While Niebuhr's analysis pertained to the call to professional or occupational Christian ministry, more recent typologies have sought to maintain the broader and more inclusive understanding of the Protestant Reformers. R. Paul Stevens delineates four kinds of calls that all Christians experience: the effectual call, the providential call, the charismatic call,

---

16. Perkins, *Treatise of the Vocations*, quoted in Placher, *Callings*, 264–65.
17. Niebuhr, *Purpose of the Church*, 64.

and the heart call.[18] The effectual call is the call to believe and follow Christ in discipleship; the providential call is the combination of circumstances and personality traits of an individual; the charismatic call is the gifting by the Holy Spirit for some particular role in the body of Christ; finally, the heart call is the inward compulsion to engage in a particular task. To these four types of calls, Stevens adds a fifth call, the ecclesiastical call, which is the call to leadership in Christian ministry. Steven's insists that this call is necessary for leadership. It is simply the recognition by the church that a person is suitable for such leadership in ministry. This call does not make a person any different than any other Christian.[19]

Another recent example is that by Doug Koskela in which he distinguishes three kinds of calling: general, missional, and direct. Koskela's primary contribution is the clarification of special calling. He subdivides the special call into the *missional call* and the *direct call*. According to Koskela, the missional call is "the specific guiding purpose God has given for her life that aligns with her gifts and passions."[20] The missional call transcends career or occupation and may be fulfilled in many ways throughout a person's life. To find one's missional call requires a process of discernment through the practice of prayer and other spiritual disciplines, intentional self-reflection, and interaction and conversation with other Christians.[21] The direct call, according to Koskela, is God's summons to a specific task. Not every Christian receives the direct call, but when it comes God makes it clear to a person. So, the direct call does not require a process of discernment, but it does require confirmation and obedience.[22] The typologies of Niebuhr, Stephens, and Koskela help to clarify the dynamic aspects of calling, but they also tend to muddy the waters by multiplying terminology. Therefore, a return to a basic distinction between the general call and the individual call helps to maintain clarity.

---

18. Stevens, *Other Six Days*, 80–83.
19. Stevens, *Other Six Days*, 152–55.
20. Koskela, *Calling and Clarity*, xiv.
21. Koskela, *Calling and Clarity*, 70–91.
22. Koskela, *Calling and Clarity*, 24–31.

4

General and Individual Calling

Consistent with the witness of the New Testament and the rediscovery by the Protestant Reformers, the general call is the summons by God for all people to believe and follow Christ. Anyone who thinks they may be called to leadership in Christian ministry must first and foremost live out the general call that goes out to all Christians, whether in leadership or not. The individual call is the personalizing and specializing of the general call. All people are called to believe and follow Christ, but all people have unique personalities, abilities, and situations through which they live out the call. As Koskela argues, it is through a process of discernment of the individual call that one finds God's individual calling and becomes obedient to his will. All those who would serve as leaders in Christian ministry must be obedient to the general call and have a strong conviction that their individual call is toward ministry leadership. In order to better understand and distinguish these two aspects of calling, we need to examine each one in depth.

Responding to the General Call

God's call goes out to all humanity through the gospel of Jesus Christ. God's summons requires a human response, a response that begins with hearing. Throughout the Bible, over and over again, hearing is commanded as necessary for believing God and doing God's will:

> Hear, O Israel: The LORD is our God, the LORD alone. You shall love the LORD your God with all your heart, and with all your soul, and with all your might. (Deut 6:4-5)

GENERAL AND INDIVIDUAL CALLING

> And he said, "Let anyone with ears to hear listen!" (Mark 4:9)

> Everyone then who hears these words of mine and acts on them will be like a wise man who built his house on rock. (Matt 7:25)

> My sheep hear my voice, I know them, and they follow me. (John 10:27)

> So faith comes from hearing, and hearing through the word of Christ. But I ask, have they not heard? Indeed they have, for "Their voice has gone out to all the earth, and their words to the ends of the world." (Rom 10:17–18)

God's call is not limited to a special group or class of people. All people are invited to hear, to repent, and to believe in the good news of the kingdom of God. This invitation includes the forgiveness of sins, the gift of eternal life, and the command to love God and neighbor. The primary issue is whether people will listen and heed this call.

The synoptic Gospels feature Jesus's allegorical "parable of the sower" in which various soils represent kinds of hearers and the responses they give to Jesus's proclamation of the kingdom. It is as if Jesus were saying, "Three out of four of you will fail to hear what I have to say, and, out of the quarter of you that do hear me, some will hear more effectively than others." We should note the word hear or listen (Greek, *akouō*) introduces and concludes this parable: "Listen! [*akouete*] A sower went out to sow. . . . And he said, "Let anyone with ears to hear listen [*akouein akouetō*]!" (Mark 4:3, 9; cf. Matt 13:3, 9, Luke 8:8). Through this parable, Jesus makes it clear that he is proclaiming the word of God to all people, but the different responses by each individual are due to the capacity and willingness to respond.

The full response to the call of God includes hearing, believing, and acting. The nature of this response is best understood as an ongoing process rather than a single act. This process begins with a first step toward Christ himself; he beckons us to come to him in surrender and trust: "Come to me, all you that are weary and are carrying heavy burdens, and I will give you rest. Take my yoke upon you, and learn from me; for I am gentle and humble in heart, and you will find rest for your souls. For my yoke is easy, and my burden is light" (Matt 11:28–30). Jesus calls us to surrender the false belief that we are self-sufficient and can make it through life on our own. By taking on Jesus's yoke (Jesus's authority, purpose, and work), we find our true calling and our own purpose. By working alongside Jesus as he restores and reconciles the world, our own lives take on the meaning that God intended for humanity. In finding this meaning, we also find rest. This rest is not the absence of doing, but it is the joy of fulfilling our true purpose and the knowledge that God is working with and through us:

> I am confident of this, that the one who began a good work among you will bring it to completion by the day of Jesus Christ. (Phil 1:6)

> For it is God who is at work in you, enabling you both to will and to work for his good pleasure. (Phil 2:13)

> For we are what he has made us, created in Christ Jesus for good works, which God prepared beforehand to be our way of life. (Eph 2:10)

The call to salvation, therefore, is far more than a transaction; it is the call to transformation. For too many Christians and even occupational ministry leaders, the call is simply a transaction of faith and forgiveness, belief and baptism, that gives us a trip to heaven. Far more than a single transaction, however, salvation is the call to transformation from meaningless to meaningful living. Jesus calls us to live abundantly now, not just eternally then. The abundant life is a restful life, because we finally are fulfilling the purpose for which we were created. As long as we live as *self-creators*, we serve a corrupt and powerless god. By trying to create our own meaning and purpose, work becomes endless toil to no clear end. Unfortunately, for ministry leaders who stray from the yoke of Christ, ministry itself becomes a burden of self-achievement. For this reason, the first step in the call is also a step that must be repeated continually. Every day, we are all called to come to Jesus and take on his yoke. Every day we must put aside striving for our own success. Every day we must acknowledge Jesus as Lord and submit to his word and will. In this process of daily faith and action, we find renewing energy, peace, and hope. We find rest.

Taking on the yoke of Christ involves two tasks. Using traditional theological terms, the ongoing task of personal transformation begins with justification and continues with sanctification. Justification literally means to be "made right" with God. This is the transactional aspect of salvation whereby God justifies the sinner through faith in Christ. Sanctification is the transformational aspect of salvation through which the believer gradually takes on the character of Christ in relation to others. The theological language gives the impression that there are distinct stages to the call, but in reality, the process of salvation is more organic and interrelated. Repeatedly the writers of the New Testament speak of the process of salvation:

> Therefore, my beloved, just as you have always obeyed me, not only in my presence, but much more now in my absence, work out your own salvation with fear and trembling; for it is God who is at work in you, enabling you both to will and to work for his good pleasure. (Phil 2:12-13)
>
> Rid yourselves, therefore, of all malice, and all guile, insincerity, envy, and all slander. Like newborn infants, long for the pure, spiritual milk, so that by it you may grow into salvation—if indeed you have tasted that the Lord is good. Come to him, a living stone, though rejected by mortals yet chosen and precious in God's sight, and like living stones, let yourselves be built into a spiritual house, to be a holy priesthood, to offer spiritual sacrifices acceptable to God through Jesus Christ. (1 Pet 2:1-5)

The same grace and faith that bring about justification also produce sanctification. The same hearing and believing needed to enter into the relationship with God are also required to continue in that relationship and extend it to others. We never get away from the need to hear and believe God's gracious voice. The same voice that called us and justified us is the voice that continues to call us and enable us to grow in the holiness of loving God and neighbor. Ministry leaders must always view themselves as engaged in this process. Ministry leaders are not finished products. The task of the call, the "working out" of salvation, is living in obedience to the commands of Christ. Primarily, Jesus has called us to love. The two great commandments sum up all the teaching of the Bible. We are to love God with our whole being and love our neighbors as we love ourselves:

> One of the scribes came near and heard them disputing with one another, and seeing that he answered them well, he asked him, "Which commandment is the first of all?" Jesus answered, "The first is, 'Hear, O Israel: the Lord our God, the Lord is one; you shall love the Lord your God with all your heart, and with all your soul, and with all your mind, and with all your strength.' The second is this, 'You shall love your neighbor as yourself.' There is no other commandment greater than these." (Mark 12:28-31)

When alone with his disciples on the night before the crucifixion, Jesus issued a single commandment as the primary identifier of the new Christian community: "I give you a new commandment, that you love one another. Just as I have loved you, you also should love one another. By this everyone will know that you are my disciples, if you have love for one another" (John

13:34–35). The two great commandments and the singular Johannine command are foundational to the general aspect of calling.

All Christians are called to love God and neighbor. The individual call extends the general call to others through personal gifts and specific tasks. If the general call is not heeded, then the individual call becomes futile. Through faith and obedience to the general call, the Christian gains the power to live out any special responsibilities and duties God may assign to the individual. Whatever responsibilities and duties these may be, they will always be extensions of loving God and loving others. They will reveal God's love and bestow God's love through the minister's feet and hands, voice and words.

Stemming from the great commands of the call are the great commissions to go, witness, and make disciples. Jesus's parting words to his disciples were assignments for action.

> And Jesus came and said to them, "All authority in heaven and on earth has been given to me. Go therefore and make disciples of all nations, baptizing them in the name of the Father and of the Son and of the Holy Spirit, and teaching them to obey everything that I have commanded you. And remember, I am with you always, to the end of the age." (Matt 28:18–20)

> Then he opened their minds to understand the scriptures, and he said to them, "Thus it is written, that the Messiah is to suffer and to rise from the dead on the third day, and that repentance and forgiveness of sins is to be proclaimed in his name to all nations, beginning from Jerusalem. You are witnesses of these things." (Luke 24:45–48)

> "But you will receive power when the Holy Spirit has come upon you; and you will be my witnesses in Jerusalem, in all Judea and Samaria, and to the ends of the earth." (Acts 1:8)[1]

Jesus gave these commissions to his disciples, but there is no indication that these commissions were limited to the twelve apostles or to a specially ordained group of his followers. In fact, the positioning of these commissions as the final, parting words of Jesus to his followers indicates their universal application to all believers. All Christians, as witnesses to the forgiving love of Christ, are called to go and to make disciples, disciples whose defining characteristics are love for God and love for others.

1. Additional biblical texts for the general call: Matt 6:33; John 14:21; Matt 25:34–40; Rom 12:1–2; 1 Pet 2:1–5; 1 Thess. 5:16–18.

Discerning the Individual Call

In harmony with the general summons for all people to hear, believe, and obey the commands and commissions of Jesus, the individual call is the expression and extension of the general call through the unique traits, circumstances, and community of each individual. The individual call fits each person for service to help meet the needs of others. In turn, the individual call gives rise to a personal sense of direction, purpose, and meaning within the general will of God. Contemporary writers describe the individual call in various ways. Some describe it as a place, others as a vision, a pursuit, a devotion, or as an awakening to God's purpose for one's life:

> The place God calls you to is the place where your deep gladness and the world's deep hunger meet.[2]

> A specific vision of how God wants us to use our time, energy and abilities to serve him in the world.[3]

> The pursuit of a life lived faithfully with God that includes the many dimensions of the good life.[4]

> Everything we are, everything we do, and everything we have invested with a special devotion and dynamism lived out as a response to God's summons and service.[5]

> Being raised from the dead, made alive to the reality that we do not merely exist, but we are 'called forth' to a divine purpose.[6]

The variety of descriptions of the individual call reveal the joy upon finding and following one's own calling.

Unlike the general call, however, which is clearly laid out in the commandments and commissions of the New Testament, the individual call requires a process of discernment. By examining and reflecting on spirituality, personality, gifts, and experiences, a person discerns his or her identity within the call of God. Discernment requires more than inward reflection, however. It also necessitates outward serving in and through the

---

2. Buechner, *Wishful Thinking*, 95.
3. Sittser, *Will of God*, 157.
4. Moser and Frankhauser, *Ready or Not*, 8.
5. Guinness, *Call*, 4.
6. Conyers, "Meaning of Vocation," 18.

community of faith. Through inward and outward self-exploration, therefore, one comes to see how God's call applies particularly to oneself.

The Process of Discernment

Discernment begins by asking the question "Who am I?" Most people have some basic sense of self-identity: gender, ethnicity, age, family background, etc. Yet, in many ways, people are a mystery to themselves. It is difficult to get a clear picture of one's personality, how one is perceived by others, and one's deep motivations. Awaiting execution in a Nazi prison, Bonhoeffer, a man of profound personal and spiritual insight, wrote of his own struggle with identity:

> Who am I? They often tell me
> I stepped from my cell's confinement
> Calmly, cheerfully, firmly,
> Like a Squire from his country house.
>
> Who am I? They often tell me
> I used to speak to my warders
> Freely and friendly and clearly,
> As though it were mine to command.
>
> Who am I? They also tell me
> I bore the days of misfortune
> Equably, smilingly, proudly,
> like one accustomed to win.
>
> Am I then really that which other men tell of?
> Or am I only what I myself know of myself?
> Restless and longing and sick, like a bird in a cage,
> Struggling for breath, as though hands were compressing
>   my throat,
> Yearning for colors, for flowers, for the voices of birds,
> Thirsting for words of kindness, for neighborliness,
> Tossing in expectations of great events,
> Powerlessly trembling for friends at an infinite distance,
> Weary and empty at praying, at thinking, at making,
> Faint, and ready to say farewell to it all.

Who am I? This or the Other?
Am I one person today and tomorrow another?
Am I both at once? A hypocrite before others,
And before myself a contemptible woebegone weakling? . . .

Who am I? They mock me, these lonely questions of mine.
Whoever I am, Thou knowest, O God, I am thine![7]

Evident in Bonhoeffer's words is his honest reflection on both positive and negative motivations and desires. This kind of reflection is at the heart of the discernment process. That process is best conducted by intentional actions of personal reflection: spiritual examination, assessment of personality, and evaluation of talents and gifts.

Spiritual Examination

Spiritual examination uncovers thoughts and actions, so that a person may make the changes necessary to better align with God's will. The Bible often speaks of the need for this kind of spiritual examination: "Examine me, O Lord, and try me; test my mind and my heart" (Ps 26:2 KJV); "Search me, O God, and know my heart; test me and know my thoughts. See if there is any wicked way in me, and lead me in the way everlasting" (Ps 139:23–24); "Examine yourselves to see whether you are living in the faith. Test yourselves" (2 Cor 13:5). The conduct of spiritual examination requires an intentional process of reflection. To reflect is to look back on our thoughts, feelings, motivations, and actions. Such reflection and recollection are at the heart of spiritual growth and spiritual formation. When we reflect on our lives and compare them with the life and teachings of Jesus, we can realign our spiritual lives accordingly.

All self-reflection involves this process of adjustment and readjustment. Perhaps the greatest writer in the history of the church on the process of spiritual examination was St. Ignatius of Loyola. Ignatius was a Spanish Christian who founded the Jesuit order within the Roman Catholic Church. In his famous work *Spiritual Exercises*, he laid out specific methods for reflection upon one's own conscience. These methods involved three primary steps: becoming aware, understanding, and acting. According to Ignatian scholar Timothy Gallagher, "'becoming aware'

---

7. Bonhoeffer, *Letters & Papers*, 347–48.

is the gateway to all spiritual discernment."[8] Such awareness requires psychological, moral, and spiritual reflection. Psychological reflection involves looking back at the feedback one receives from others and pondering her or his own thoughts and emotions generated by situations and social encounters throughout the day. Moral reflection is the examination of how faithful one's words, actions, choices, and relationships have been to the teachings of Jesus. Psychological and moral reflection in turn contribute to discernment, but spiritual reflection goes further. The primary task of spiritual reflection is to determine whether one is moving toward God or away from God in any particular thought or action:

> These two *fundamental directions* of the spiritual life . . . may be stated as follows: the *first* consists in movement *away from God* and *toward serious sin*; and *second*, the reverse of the first, consists in movement *toward God* and *away from serious sin*. . . . Ignatius thus highlights this all important fact: to discern correctly which spirit is working in a person's heart (and so to know what we should accept or reject), we must first *identify* the *fundamental direction* of that person's spiritual life.[9]

Determining whether one is moving toward or away from God requires honest, humble, and intentional reflection on thoughts, motivations, and actions. Although the spiritual exercises of St. Ignatius were originally intended for the monastery, there are simplified versions today that help all Christians practice the steps of the daily examen.

The daily examen can take place any time of the day, but the evening allows reflection over the entire day past. The examen is essentially a guided prayer that begins with noting how the grace of God was present during the day and giving thanks for those moments. One then reflects on the day's emotions. The highs and lows, joys and anxieties experienced during the day are particularly helpful for understanding oneself and where God may be working. The prayer continues with intercession as one focuses on a person, event, or issue of which he or she has become particularly aware. The prayer then concludes with a look forward to the challenges of the next day and a final request for help, guidance, and hope.[10] Spiritual practices like the daily examen of St. Ignatius enable people to see themselves more clearly and follow God's will more faithfully. The skill developed

---

8. Gallagher, *Discernment of Spirits*, 17.
9. Gallagher, *Discernment of Spirits*, 31 (emphasis in original).
10. Ignatian Spirituality, "How Can I Pray?"

through such intentional and regular self-reflection also helps one discern his or her individual call. Self-reflection increases one's ability to hear God and follow God's direction.

Assessment of Personality

Another step in the process of discerning the individual call is the assessment of one's own personality. Getting some handle on our own personality is not easy, however. It can be like a fish trying to describe water. We have difficulty finding a vantage point from which to view ourselves clearly. Personality refers to the multifaceted combination of temperaments, perceptions, and preferences displayed by every individual. Throughout history, there have been many attempts to develop classifications under which personalities may be described and understood. The earliest and perhaps most influential was the ancient typology of the Greek physician Hippocrates, which classified people by four kinds of personalities: choleric (intense and irritable), sanguine (enthusiastic and social), phlegmatic (calm and relaxed), and melancholic (analytical and quiet).

With the advent of modern psychology, many tools for self-assessment have been developed. Most of these consist of answering a series of questions that help to categorize one's personality type. Some of these are more evidenced-based than others. The Myer's Briggs Temperament Inventory (MBTI®) is perhaps the best known and most often used. The MBTI® is based on the psychological theories of C. G. Jung regarding preferred ways of perception and judgment. The MBTI® views personalities as various combinations of four basic preferences: the focus of attention (introverted or extraverted), the perception of information (senses or thoughts), the processing of decisions (thinking or feeling) and the preferred way of acting (planned or spontaneous).[11] Another assessment tool that has become popular in recent years, especially among Christians, is the Enneagram, which sets out nine personality types: the reformer, the helper, the achiever, the individualist, the investigator, the loyalist, the enthusiast, the challenger, and the peacemaker. These descriptions are viewed as "general patterns" rather than precise descriptions of any particular individual.[12] Unfortunately, the Enneagram has little supporting scientific evidence. Personality theorists are not generally favorable to the

11. Myers & Briggs Foundation, "MBTI® Basics."
12. Riso and Hudson, *Understanding the Enneagram*, 18–19.

instrument, arguing the Enneagram's interpretations of the personality types are subject to significant ambiguity.[13]

The labeling or even stereotyping that often flows from such personality typologies and inventories may not be as helpful for the exploration of the personal call as one might hope. A better approach is emerging with new research in personality science. Dan McAdams, a leading personality theorist, holds that personality consists of three layers: personality traits, personal values and habits, and personal stories (see fig. 4.1). The inner and most basic layer includes personality traits, which are a combination of genetic predispositions and learned interactions. The middle layer includes personal values and habits, which form a person's ideals and moral behavior. The outer layer includes the stories people construct about themselves and through which they view themselves. The inner layer, consisting of ingrained personality traits, is the most resistant to change. For example, a right-handed person has more difficulty doing tasks with the left hand. The middle layer is more malleable. A person can learn new values and develop new habits. The outer or story layer has both fixed elements and elements that continue to be added or revised. Ultimately, how people construct their own stories is what makes the biggest difference in their personal well-being and how well they can help others.

Figure 4.1 Layers of Personality[14]

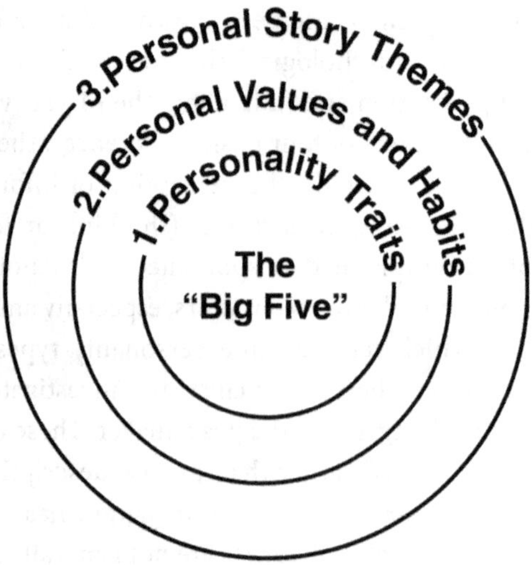

- 3. Personal Story Themes
- 2. Personal Values and Habits
- 1. Personality Traits
- The "Big Five"

13. Schnitker et al., "9 to 5."
14. Culled from information in Schnitker et al., "9 to 5."

Personality theorists have classified the personality traits of the inner or first layer into five dimensions, each expressing a spectrum of preferences (see fig. 4.2). Described as the "Big Five," the traits include: extraversion, neuroticism, conscientiousness, agreeableness, and openness to new experiences.

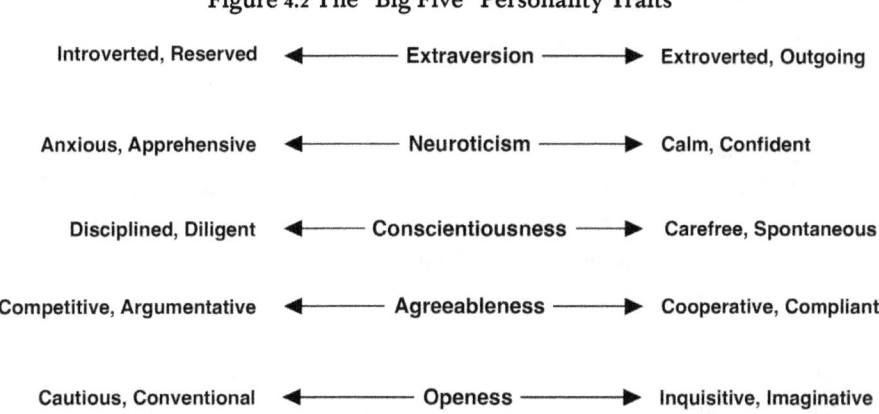

Figure 4.2 The "Big Five" Personality Traits

Extraversion refers to a person's capacity for social interaction or the degree to which a person is outgoing or more reserved. Neuroticism refers to the level of anxiety, whether easily worried and upset or usually calm. Conscientiousness refers to the level of competence, discipline, and sense of duty. Agreeableness refers to the level of competition or cooperation and compliance. Finally, openness to new experience refers to the level of imagination and exploration.[15] It is important to identify one's own personality traits through self-examination and reflection to gain insight as to how God may be leading in one's life.

Personality traits do not dictate one's calling, but they are good indicators of strengths and weaknesses relative to various roles, duties, and situations. A person who is socially outgoing may be more suited to ministry leadership than one who is more naturally aloof and introverted. A person who has a high degree of personal anxiety, especially when around other people or in difficult situations, may find ministry leadership to be a constant struggle of overcoming negative emotions. Also, people generally respond better to leadership by calm, non-anxious ministry leaders. Likewise, those who are well organized and disciplined self-starters tend

---

15. Schnitker et al., "9 to 5," 75–76.

to thrive in ministry leadership roles, because in many ministry leadership situations there is little external supervision and large amounts of discretionary time. Those who possess less self-discipline and need supervision to stay motivated may find ministry leadership difficult and boring. Team players, those who work well with others rather than competing or withdrawing, often make healthy and successful ministry leaders. Those who prefer to work alone and do things their own way, however, may find ministry leadership tedious and frustrating. Ministry leaders, therefore, who are naturally outgoing, calm, self-disciplined, cooperative, and creative have traits that are conducive to working with people. There are few people, however, who possess all of these more conducive traits. Most people's personality traits lie somewhere on a spectrum between extremes, and most have one or more strong traits for which they have to compensate to be effective in ministry leadership.

The second layer of personality, that of personal values and habits, is much more amenable to change and growth than basic personality traits. This layer of personality is where the general call is most applicable. All Christians are in need of the transformation of their basic selfish nature. This transformation requires both the indwelling of the Holy Spirit through conversion and the development of the habits of the spiritual life. The Christian virtues of faith, hope, love, joy, peace, patience, kindness, generosity, faithfulness, gentleness, and self-control (Gal 5:22) are developed through continual prayer and reflection as one interacts with others. The Christian values of reconciliation, promise-keeping, truth-telling, and peacemaking become habitual behaviors only as one internalizes the words of Jesus and attempts to live them out. Spiritual disciplines like the daily examen help in this process of growth in Christlikeness. Those who are trying to discern whether they are called to ministry leadership must examine their values and habits honestly and humbly. No ministry leader is perfect, but all ministry leaders must be growing in the values of the faith.

The third layer of personality includes the recurring themes of one's personal narrative or story. Perhaps no level of personality is more directly reflective of one's sense of individual calling. In the stories that we tell ourselves and others, it becomes evident how we put together all of the other elements of our personality traits, values, and experiences. McAdams describes this synthesis as one's narrative identity: "*Narrative identity is the internalized and changing story of your life that you begin to work on in the emerging adult years.*"[16] Through the construction of personal narratives, humans begin to make sense of their lives:

> Narrative identity reconstructs the autobiographical past and imagines the future in such a way as to provide a person's life with some degree of unity, purpose, and meaning. Thus, a person's life story synthesizes episodic memories with envisioned goals, creating a coherent account of identity in time. Through narrative identity, people convey to themselves and to others who they are now, how they came to be, and where they think their lives may going in the future.[17]

People begin to answer the question "Who am I?," therefore, by examining the stories they tell about themselves. Like all stories, personal narratives include characters, locations, and events woven into plots of hurt or healing, resentment or forgiveness, sorrow or joy. Indeed, the plots of human narratives are driven by some kind of difficulty or suffering.

Personal narratives not only relate information, but they help people find meaning in suffering. Observations by personality theorists indicate that psychological health and maturity are linked to the ability of people to describe their experiences of suffering and loss and also tell how they have learned and grown in positive and transformative ways through their suffering.[18] McAdams describes these kinds of narratives as "redemption" stories. "In the most general sense, redemption is *a deliverance from suffering to a better world.*"[19] McAdams's research discovered that people who could speak of overcoming their struggles in redemptive ways were more prone to be caring, nurturing, or generous people. According to Schnitker et al.:

> This suggests that one of the most important components of spiritual formation is constructing and reconstructing the stories of our lives and our communities to reflect the redemptive work of Christ. Christ's story of redemption is the essence of our faith. The traditional practice of telling the stories of our own redemption through testimonies should be the foundation of spiritual growth.[20]

---

16. McAdams, *Redemptive Self*, 83–84 (emphasis in original).
17. McAdams and McLean, "Narrative Identity," 233.
18. McAdams and McLean, "Narrative Identity," 234–35.
19. McAdams, *Redemptive Self*, 7 (emphasis in original).
20. Schnitker et. al., 76.

Those who sense that God may be leading them toward service in ministry leadership must honestly assess their own stories. Life stories void of a deep sense of personal redemption do not bode well for ministry leadership. Leaders in ministry must be people who have internalized God's mercy and grace. They must have a growing awareness that God has worked and is working through all the hurts and disappointments of their lives to bring about God's good purpose. Careful evaluation of one's personality, therefore, provides important clues toward discerning the individual call. Getting a clear picture of one's talents and gifts is also necessary in this process of discernment.

Evaluation of Talents and Gifts

Discerning how God may be calling an individual involves not only spiritual examination and assessment of personality but also the evaluation of one's talents and gifts. The word talent derives from Jesus's parable in Matt 25:14–30. In the parable, talents are sums of money that a property owner gives to his servants in varying amounts, "each according to his ability." In the context of Matt 25, the point of the parable is to recognize that each person has something God has given them to "invest" in the Lord's work. Unfortunately, there will be those who bury their talent, because they have little faith in God or themselves. A talent has since become synonymous with some special capacity or ability. Just as in the parable where people are given different sums of money, the abilities people possess vary from individual to individual, and the employment of these abilities varies as well. For Christians trying to discern individual calling, it is important to become aware of their abilities and to consider how they might be invested in ministry. Talents are not unrelated to spiritual gifts. Although talents can be seen as mere genetic attributes or trained abilities, when brought under the lordship of Christ, they are enhanced by the Holy Spirit for the building up of the body of Christ. As Paul worked with churches, he found it necessary to help individuals identify what he called *charismata*, or gifts of grace.

As Paul wrote to the new Christians in the churches he founded, he reminded them that each individual member had been uniquely gifted by the Holy Spirit to serve in the body of Christ in some way. This gifting of members was always for the purpose of promoting unity and love in the body. So, the gifts were not primarily for individuals to possess but for use in service for the greater good. These gifts were God-given abilities or capacities for service in God's work. In letters to the Corinthians and Romans, Paul explains that the Holy Spirit inspires each individual with different abilities or gifts. All gifts are equally good, and no particular gift is better than another. So, no individual Christian should be seen as more gifted or important than another. In this context of humility, therefore, gifts are identified and employed for the benefit of the whole body of Christ:

> Now there are varieties of gifts, but the same Spirit; and there are varieties of services, but the same Lord; and there are varieties of activities, but it is the same God who activates all of them in everyone. To each is given the manifestation of the Spirit for the common good. To one is given through the Spirit the utterance of wisdom, and to another the utterance of knowledge according to the same Spirit, to another faith by the same Spirit, to another gifts of healing by the one Spirit, to another the working of miracles, to another prophecy, to another the discernment of spirits, to another various kinds of tongues, to another the interpretation of tongues. All these are activated by one and the same Spirit, who allots to each one individually just as the Spirit chooses.... Now you are the body of Christ and individually members of it. And God has appointed in the church first apostles, second prophets, third teachers; then deeds of power, then gifts of healing, forms of assistance, forms of leadership, various kinds of tongues. (1 Cor 12:4–11, 27–28)

> For by the grace given to me I say to everyone among you not to think of yourself more highly than you ought to think, but to think with sober judgment, each according to the measure of faith that God has assigned. For as in one body we have many members, and not all the members have the same function, so we, who are many, are one body in Christ, and individually we are members one of another. We have gifts that differ according to the grace given to us: prophecy, in proportion to faith; ministry, in ministering; the teacher, in teaching; the exhorter, in exhortation; the giver, in generosity; the leader, in diligence; the compassionate, in cheerfulness. (Rom 12:3–8)

The context of Paul's discussion about spiritual gifts indicates that he is more interested in illustrating some of the diverse ways the Spirit works through individuals than in giving a precise and exhaustive typology of gifts. Paul's main goal is to foster unity and humility by showing that every church member has an important place and role in the body of Christ. For understanding one's personal call, therefore, it is necessary to get some sense of how the Spirit has gifted a person. While Paul emphasizes the egalitarian nature of the gifts, he also distinguishes certain leadership gifts for the equipping of the whole church for ministry: "The gifts he gave were that some would be apostles, some prophets, some evangelists, some pastors and teachers, to equip the saints for the work of ministry, for building up the body of Christ" (Eph 4:11–12). By distinguishing leadership or equipping gifts, Paul helps us understand how to distinguish the calling to leadership in Christian ministry from other callings. All calls come from God, and no one can take pride in one calling over the other; however, this does not mean that the various gifts work the same way. Paul lists many diverse gifts, so for clarity it is helpful to group the gifts under some general categories. The gifts can be gathered under three main functions of Christian ministry: proclamation, guidance, and care (see table 4.1).

Table 4.1 Spiritual Gifts

Proclamation	Guidance	Care
Apostleship	**Pastoring & Teaching**	**Serving & Helping**
apostolos, "one who is sent with a message"	*poimēn*, "to shepherd" Eph 4:11	*diakonia*, "service, ministry"
1 Cor 12:28	*didaskalos*, "one who instructs"	Rom 12:7
Eph 4:11	Rom 12:7	*antilepsis*, "helpful deeds"
	1 Cor 12:28	1 Cor 12:28
	Eph 4:11	
Prophecy	**Leading & Administrating**	**Encouraging**
prophētēs, "proclaim, preach"	*proistēmi*, "to supervise, to assist, to protect"	*parakaleō*, "called alongside, encourage, comfort"
Rom 12:6	Rom 12:8	Rom 12:8
1 Cor 12:10	*kubernēsis*, "to steer" (as a ship) or "to rule or govern"	
1 Cor 14:22–25	1 Cor 12:28	

GENERAL AND INDIVIDUAL CALLING

Proclamation	Guidance	Care
Evangelism *euangelion*, "good news" (to bring good news) Eph 4:11	**Wisdom, Knowledge, & Discernment** *sophia*, "wisdom" *gnōsis*, "knowledge" *diacríseis pneumatōn*, "discernment of spirits" 1 Cor 12:8, 10	**Giving & Mercy** *metadidōmi*, "to give" *eleos*, "mercy, compassion" Rom 12:8
Various Tongues *glōssa*, "tongue" (known or unknown with interpretation) 1 Cor 12:10, 28	**Faith** *pistis*, "faith, belief" 1 Cor 12:9	**Healing & Miracles** *iamatōn*, "healing" 1 Cor 12:9, 28 *energēmata dunameōn*, "works of power" 1 Cor 12:10, 28

Proclamation gifts are those that involve the verbal communication of the gospel of Jesus Christ in some way. The gift of apostleship is essentially that of carrying the gospel to another people group in another place. The English words mission or missionary are based on the Latin translations of the Greek word *apostolos*. Those who have a passionate concern for a people of another culture, the ability to be flexible and adaptable to other cultures, and possess unusual relational, organizational, and linguistic skills may find that they have the apostolic or missional gift. The gift of prophecy (Greek, *prophētēs*) is the ability to interpret and speak a timely word from God for a particular people in a particular circumstance. The word literally means to "forth-tell," not foretell, as is often assumed. Those who have a passion to preach the gospel, call people to repentance of personal sin and social injustice, and lead people to obedience to the commands of Christ may discern they have the prophetic gift. The gift of evangelism (*euangelion*) is the particular motivation and ability to speak the gospel message in a way that nonbelievers will understand and come to faith. The gift of tongues is the ability to learn, speak, or write other *known* languages. The miracle of Pentecost in Acts 2 was clearly the gifting of the ability to speak in the languages of various people groups. The Scripture also refers to "unknown" tongues (*glossolalia*), but Paul cautions that unknown tongues in public worship can create confusion. So he instructs that the use be in private as an expression of personal prayer, unless someone is able to interpret for the congregation (1 Cor 14:5–33). Those who are called to leadership in Christian ministry often find that they have some talent and ability for speaking. Whether that speaking talent is directed in more apostolic, prophetic, evangelistic, or linguistic ways can be determined only by participation and use in the community of faith. Whether one is gifted for leadership in these ways will become evident to the congregation and to the individual in combination with gifts of guidance.

The second category of spiritual gifts is those that involve leading or guiding people in some way. Guidance gifts are those that are associated particularly with equipping of other Christians for the work of ministry. The pastor or shepherd (*poimēn*) gift is often coupled with the gift of the teacher (*didaskalos*). The ability to provide spiritual nurture for others and teach others how to understand and practice the faith are essential gifts for ministry leaders. The pastor-teacher gift is often combined with either the gifts of caring supervision (*proistēmi*) or organizational administration (*kubernēsis*). Some pastor-teachers are better personal caregivers while some are better task managers, but they are not often equally gifted in both of these ways. So, effective pastor-teachers rely not only on their own gifts but also on complementary gifts of other ministry leaders.

Guidance gifts also include wisdom (*sophia*), knowledge (*gnosis*), and discernment (*diacrisis*). Any member of the body of Christ may have the gift to speak a word of wisdom, knowledge, or discernment, but these gifts are particularly necessary for those who lead others in Christian ministry. Leaders must have knowledge of the Bible, basic Christian beliefs, and basic human nature. Leaders also must have the wisdom to know *how* to use their knowledge for their own edification and for equipping others for the Christian life. The last guidance gift is the gift of faith (*pistis*). Certainly, all believers have the capacity for faith, but the spiritual gift of faith is the enhanced ability to rely on God's promises and to inspire others to trust God.

The caring gifts constitute the third category of spiritual gifts. These gifts are the various abilities Christians have to extend the love of Christ to others. The care of members for one another and the caring outreach to nonmembers of the body of Christ are essential to the work of the church. Both ministry leaders and followers may be gifted in any of these ways. These gifts include serving (*diakonia*), helping (*antilepsis*), encouraging (*parakaleō*), giving (*metadidōmi*), mercy (*eleos*), healing (*iamatōn*), and miracles (*energēmata dunameōn*). Whether a person is gifted in any of these ways will become apparent only through the actual practice of ministry in and through the church. As with all spiritual gifts, discovery comes only through the combination of one's inner awareness and the affirmations by others that one is gifted is any of these ways. The role of ministry leaders, therefore, is "to call forth" the gifts by teaching members about the general call, by helping them discern their own individual gifts, and by encouraging them to use their gifts in the work of the church.

The Call to Ministry Leadership

Discernment of individual calling, therefore, is a journey of self-discovery. In that journey one finds her or his identity in Christ. Spiritual examination, assessment of personality, and evaluation of talents and gifts are ways in which all Christians may clarify their particular purpose in the service of God. The case is the same for Christians who are called to leadership in ministry; yet, the call to ministry leadership also necessitates special *confirmation* by the Christian *community*. What Niebuhr and Stephens refer to as the "ecclesiastical call" is not actually an additional call, but it is the recognition and authorization by the body of Christ that a person's individual calling is to leadership of the body. That communal confirmation is necessary for ministry leadership speaks to the nature of calling itself. Calling is inherently relational. The general call is to relationship with God and relationship to others. We are called to love God and love one another. The individual call is also relational. Although the individual call has much to do with how the individual has been personally designed and equipped for ministry, the individual call is fulfilled only in ministry to others. The individual call to be a leader in ministry must therefore receive affirmation by people who know that person best and have witnessed the person's spiritual life, personal traits, and gifts for ministry leadership. Throughout Christian history that affirmation has come most often through the practice of ordination.

Ordination to Ministry Leadership

The word ordination is used to describe the way congregations authorize ministry leaders. From the earliest stages of Christian history, some form of ordination has been practiced by the church. Although Jesus did not use the word, he called and commissioned his apostles and disciples for ministry leadership (Matt 10:1–5 and parallels). In the book of Acts, we read of the church laying hands on individuals to commission them for ministry leadership (Acts 6:1–6, 13:1–3), and in 1 Tim 4:14, we read of Paul reminding Timothy that he had been set apart for ministry leadership: "Do not neglect the gift that is in you, which was given to you through prophecy through the laying on of hands by the council of elders." Paul also warns Timothy to be cautious in selecting others for ministry leadership, "Do not ordain [lit. "lay hands on"] anyone hastily," (1 Tim 5:22).

In the centuries after the New Testament period, the conduct of ordination became more formal, and the meaning of ordination became more sacramental and hierarchical. The earliest description of the rite of ordination is that by Hippolytus of Rome around 215 CE. He describes selection of the new bishop by "all the people" with the laying on of hands by the other bishops present. The ceremony is then followed by a prayer for the bestowal of the power of the Holy Spirit: "And now pour forth that Power which is from Thee of 'the princely Spirit.' . . . And that by the high priestly Spirit he may have authority 'to forgive sins.'"[21] Ordination was becoming a key ritual in the emerging authority structure of the church. The word ordain itself came from the Latin word for "order." To ordain meant, therefore, to raise a person to a higher order or higher status of holiness and authority. As we have already seen in chapter 3, views of calling began to change with the advent of the Protestant Reformation. As a result, Reformation groups came to reject ordination as a sacrament. Nevertheless, Reformers who retained sacramental views of communion tended also to retain some sense that ordination bestowed higher status, power, and authority on ministry leaders. Radical Reform groups (e.g., Anabaptists), on the other hand, rejected all sacramental connotations, even of the Lord's Supper and Baptism. So these groups also rejected hierarchical views of ordination. Although many radical Reformers continued to use the words ordain and ordination, they came to interpret these words in a functional or practical sense rather than an ontological or hierarchical sense.

Ministry leaders today, therefore, must understand the particular tradition of ordination and the theological point of view of the denomination or congregation in which they hope to serve. Thomas Oden, writing from the perspective of episcopal polity, says that ministry leadership is a gift of the Spirit, given through the rite of ordination: "Ordination combines an internal grace with an external act in which the inner reality is the reception of the divine gift and the external event is the laying on of hands in prayer. . . .

---

21. Quoted in Willimon, *Pastor*, 31–32.

It 'sets apart' the person for ministry by a formal rite of induction on behalf of the worldwide, intergenerational apostolic tradition."[22] Closely connected with the episcopal view is the question of what group does the ordaining. According to Oden, it is the whole church, but he quickly clarifies that the actual laying on of hands is by those who themselves have been ordained: "Most traditions, with few exceptions, have held that orders are conferred by the whole church through duly elected bishops or presbyters (elders) on behalf of the whole church, acting as successors to the apostles."[23]

In contrast to Oden's episcopal view, churches of confessional and congregational polity do not consider ordination to bestow a spiritual gift. Instead, ordination is the recognition and affirmation by the church that a person *already has been gifted* by the Spirit for ministry leadership. Ordination, then, is a solemn, public ceremony in which the individual commits herself or himself to faithfulness in ministry leadership, and the whole church commits the person and future leadership to God. It is not uncommon even in congregational churches to limit the laying on of hands only to those who themselves have been ordained (e.g., pastors and deacons). This practice, however, is inconsistent with congregational theology and polity. The more theologically consistent practice is for every confessing member to have the opportunity to lay hands on and pray for the new ministry leader. The question still remains, however, whether less prominent ministry leaders (e.g., Sunday school teachers, small group leaders, outreach ministry directors, etc.) should be ordained. A practical view would be that ordination should be limited to those ministry leaders who must bear responsibility for the care and equipping of the whole congregation.

---

22. Oden, *Pastoral Theology*, 27.
23. Oden, *Pastoral Theology*, 31.

Part Three

The Character of Ministry Leaders

FOR THOSE INDIVIDUALS WHO sense God's call to lead and equip others in Christian ministry, the utmost concern is that of their spiritual and moral character. Character includes the deepest thoughts, motivations, and values of a person—what Scripture calls the *heart*. In the Bible, the heart is the center of emotion, reason, and will, and the heart is the center of relationship with God.[1]

> But the LORD said to Samuel, "Do not look on his appearance or on the height of his stature, because I have rejected him; for the LORD does not see as mortals see; they look on the outward appearance, but the LORD looks on the heart." (1 Sam 16:7)
>
> Blessed are the pure in heart, for they will see God. (Matt 5:8)
>
> For where your treasure is, there your heart will be also. (Matt 6:21)
>
> But what comes out of the mouth proceeds from the heart, and this is what defiles. For out of the heart come evil intentions, murder, adultery, fornication, theft, false witness, slander. (Matt 15:18–19)

Leaders in Christian ministry are not perfect people, but they must be exemplary Christians. The confirmation by the church that one is called to ministry leadership depends to a large extent on a congregation's belief in the person's character. According to Stevens, "the *ecclesiastical call* means quite simply that a person's suitability for church leadership needs to be discerned by the church in two ways, first, in gifting, and second, in character."[2] Although character is centered deep within a person's heart,

---

1. Dentan, "Heart."
2. Stevens, *Other Six Days*, 155.

PART THREE: THE CHARACTER OF MINISTRY LEADERS

it is known to others by what a person says and does. Congregations have certain expectations of what should constitute the character of their leaders, and there are certain character traits that are especially conducive to ministry leadership. The next two chapters examine how moral character is formed, the character traits of ministry leaders, and the practices and habits that maintain moral integrity.

5

The Content of Character

A FEW YEARS AGO, it became popular to ask the question, "What would Jesus do?" Many Christian young people wore WWJD bracelets to remind them to ask this question before acting. The problem was and is that asking such a question in moments of confusion and in the heat of temptation is not likely to result in Christlike action. Good moral behavior is not the result of a momentary thought process. When we look at what Jesus actually taught about Christian morality, we find him speaking of a binding relationship.

The Easy Yoke

In Matthew's Gospel, Jesus spoke to his disciples about taking on his "yoke": "Come to me, all you that are weary and are carrying heavy burdens, and I will give you rest. Take my yoke upon you, and learn from me; for I am gentle and humble in heart, and you will find rest for your souls. For my yoke is easy, and my burden is light" (Matt 11:28–30). The purpose of a yoke is to join the power of two animals to pull a load. Dallas Willard understood that the "secret" of the easy yoke was the binding of oneself to Jesus: "The secret involves living as he lived in the entirety of his life—adopting his overall life-style.... The secret of the easy yoke is simple, actually. It is the intelligent, informed, unyielding resolve to live as Jesus lived in all aspects of life, not just in the moment of specific choice or action."[1] Taking on the yoke of Christ, according to Willard, means a continual way of living, not just an occasional way of thinking. Likewise, in John's Gospel, Jesus spoke to his disciples about their need to "abide" in him: "Abide in

1. Willard, *Spirit of the Disciplines*, 5, 10.

me as I abide in you. Just as the branch cannot bear fruit by itself unless it abides in the vine, neither can you unless you abide in me. I am the vine, you are the branches. Those who abide in me and I in them bear much fruit, because apart from me you can do nothing" (John 15:4–5). To abide means to dwell or remain. In other words, we are to consciously and intentionally live our lives in relationship with and in obedience to Jesus. To get a better picture of how ethical conduct is established and maintained, we need to turn to the work of Christian ethicists.

Formation of Moral Norms

Much good work has been done in recent years to uncover the nature of moral development. Since the dawn of the Enlightenment, philosophers in the Western world have proposed various theories of how to maintain ethical conduct based upon human reason alone (i.e., deontological ethics, utilitarian ethics, situational ethics, etc.). Recent Christian ethicists, however, demonstrate that ethical conduct depends upon the moral character formed within community.[2] Christian character is formed by *participation* in the biblical story as it is lived out in the Christian community. The defining values of this "story-shaped" community are found in the words and deeds of Jesus. Jesus walked with his disciples, preaching, teaching, and demonstrating the love of God and of people. According to Childs, "character is shaped in community where community has formed around a 'story' that binds people together . . . to be part of a community and the story of Jesus is to be formed in love, to have character imbued with the experience of God's love in Christ."[3] Character is shaped in community not only through the words of Jesus but also through the presence of the Holy Spirit. The new covenant brings with it the writing of the law upon the heart by the "Spirit of truth" who guides believers "into all truth" (Jer 31:33; John 16:13). The indwelling Spirit enables believers to know God personally and to be empowered to live faithfully.

Certainly, conversion to faith in Jesus Christ is a transformative moment, but Scripture also indicates that conversion is just the *beginning* of the Christian life. New Christians are forgiven of sin, but they still bear the tendency to sin. It takes living in the body of Christ to bring Christians to maturity. Those who participate deeply in a community built by

2. Stassen and Gushee, *Kingdom Ethics*, 99–124.
3. Childs, *Ethics in Business*, 72.

and around the teachings and example of Jesus have the best opportunity for the Christian story to become fully their own story. As they spend significant time in corporate worship, Bible study, prayer, fellowship, service, outreach, and witness, Christians can experience a deepening awareness of the grace and love of God that, through the presence and power of the Holy Spirit, gives birth to their own acts of mercy and kindness toward others. Moral principles and rules become the fruitful expressions of inward character and values, not externally-imposed requirements. Figure 5.1 illustrates the formation of moral norms according to Stassen and Gushee. Moral formation flows upward from basic convictions established in the story-shaped community, to the internalizing of general Christian moral principles (love of God and neighbor, fruits of the Spirit, etc.), which help one to know and understand how to apply the rules (commands) established by Jesus. Finally, these internalized convictions, principles, and rules enable a person to make momentary decisions that are more likely to be in line with the will of God.[4]

---

4. Although the four-level analysis of moral norms is taken from the work of Glen Stassen and David Gushee, the position that basic community narratives are most significant in moral reasoning is found in the thought of many Christian ethicists over the last several decades who have appropriated the renewed interest in the virtue ethics of Aristotle. Aristotle's view that virtues are learned through life in community has become a fruitful alternative to the more rationalistic, consequentialist, and deontological approaches of earlier twentieth-century views of Christian ethics. Consequentialism and deontology are still useful in describing biblical approaches, but the move toward character ethics by Alasdair MacIntyre, James McClendon, Stanley Hauerwas, James Childs, Stanley Grenz, Glen Stassen, and David Gushee (to name just a few among a large number) is much more helpful in understanding New Testament ethics in particular and the foundations of ethics in general. We should note, however, that the virtues of Jesus are not compatible with those of Aristotle, who judged virtues based on the ideal Greek male and the ideal Greek state, whereas the virtues of Jesus are defined solely by his example and his teaching, which demonstrate the renunciation of power through servanthood and self-sacrifice in a life dedicated solely to God.

Figure 5.1 Formation of Moral Norms

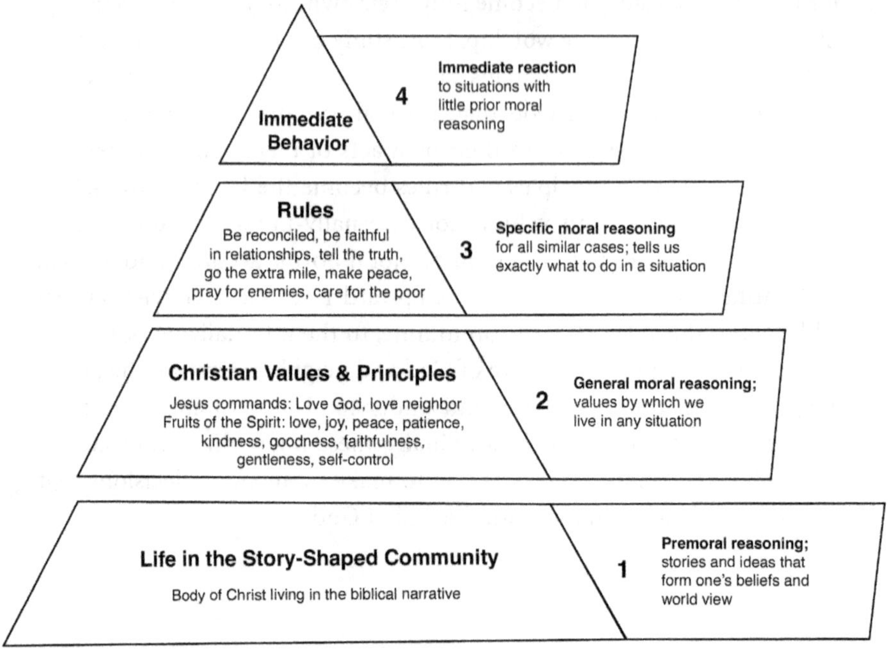

4 — Immediate Behavior: Immediate reaction to situations with little prior moral reasoning

3 — Rules: Be reconciled, be faithful in relationships, tell the truth, go the extra mile, make peace, pray for enemies, care for the poor. Specific moral reasoning for all similar cases; tells us exactly what to do in a situation

2 — Christian Values & Principles: Jesus commands: Love God, love neighbor. Fruits of the Spirit: love, joy, peace, patience, kindness, goodness, faithfulness, gentleness, self-control. General moral reasoning; values by which we live in any situation

1 — Life in the Story-Shaped Community: Body of Christ living in the biblical narrative. Premoral reasoning; stories and ideas that form one's beliefs and world view

Based on Stassen & Gushee's Analysis

Character Traits of Ministry Leaders

Ministry leaders, therefore, must be persons who have been shaped by the biblical story, by the indwelling Spirit, and by the community of Christ. The body of Christ looks to its leaders not only for what they know and do but, more importantly, for who they are. Ministry leaders embody in themselves the values of the church as a whole. In the mid-twentieth century, Wayne Oates described the influence of ministry leaders in terms of their "symbolic power." This power transcends the individual and evokes the very presence of God in the minds of those whom ministers lead.

> You represent and symbolize far more than yourself. You represent God the Father; you serve as a reminder of Jesus Christ; you follow the leading of the Holy Spirit; you are the emissary of a specific church; and you activate caricatures of the Christian faith to those who are hostile, suspicious, and/or detached from the Christian

> faith. Nevertheless, you are a shepherd to non-Christians as well as to those who are in the church.[5]

The prospect of possessing such symbolic power can be attractive, but it can also be overwhelming and even frightening. Although people may want ministry leaders to be reflections of God, the truth is that ministry leaders themselves are human sinners like everyone else. There is a disturbing discrepancy between the lofty role of ministry leaders and the reality of the persons themselves. It is important, therefore, to have realistic expectations, but living up even to realistic expectations is not easy.

In the same work cited above, Oates cites David S. Schuler's significant study conducted in the 1970s of congregational expectations of ministry leaders. Schuler's research revealed five traits most valued by congregations: unselfish service, personal integrity, kindness and generosity, acknowledgment of limitations, and builder of community.[6] Although this study is now very dated, Schuler's findings remain relevant for guiding ministry leaders today. What is especially informative about this list of expectations is that they have little to do with expertise in the skills and performance of ministry leadership, i.e., preaching, teaching, administration, or pastoral care. The list is primarily about humble and honest concern for others rather than self. Paradoxically, the symbolic power of ministry leaders is strongest in those who shun personal power for the sake of others. These leaders are effective because they know in their hearts that ministry is about bringing people to God, not promoting themselves.

It is not surprising, then, that the primary texts in the New Testament about the expectations of ministry leaders describe spiritual and moral attributes rather than sets of skills or duties. The most often cited texts are 1 Tim 3:1–7; Titus 1:5–9; and 1 Pet 5:1–6.

> The saying is sure: whoever aspires to the office of bishop desires a noble task. Now a bishop must be above reproach, married only once, temperate, sensible, respectable, hospitable, an apt teacher, not a drunkard, not violent but gentle, not quarrelsome, and not a lover of money. He must manage his own household well, keeping his children submissive and respectful in every way—for if someone does not know how to manage his own household, how can he take care of God's church? He must not be a recent convert, or he may be puffed up with conceit and fall into the

---

5. Oates, *Christian Pastor*, 65.
6. Oates, *Christian Pastor*, 67–68.

condemnation of the devil. Moreover, he must be well thought of by outsiders, so that he may not fall into disgrace and the snare of the devil. (1 Tim 3:1–7)

I left you behind in Crete for this reason, so that you should put in order what remained to be done, and should appoint elders in every town, as I directed you: someone who is blameless, married only once, whose children are believers, not accused of debauchery and not rebellious. For a bishop, as God's steward, must be blameless; he must not be arrogant or quick-tempered or addicted to wine or violent or greedy for gain; but he must be hospitable, a lover of goodness, prudent, upright, devout, and self-controlled. He must have a firm grasp of the word that is trustworthy in accordance with the teaching, so that he may be able both to preach with sound doctrine and to refute those who contradict it. (Titus 1:5–9)

Now as an elder myself and a witness of the sufferings of Christ, as well as one who shares in the glory to be revealed, I exhort the elders among you to tend the flock of God that is in your charge, exercising the oversight, not under compulsion but willingly, as God would have you do it—not for sordid gain but eagerly. Do not lord it over those in your charge, but be examples to the flock. And when the chief shepherd appears, you will win the crown of glory that never fades away. In the same way, you who are younger must accept the authority of the elders. And all of you must clothe yourselves with humility in your dealings with one another, for "God opposes the proud, but gives grace to the humble." (1 Pet 5:1–6)

The many words and phrases in the foregoing texts may be grouped into five primary character traits: reputable, self-disciplined, generous, humble, and spiritually mature (see table 5.1).

Table 5.1 Character Traits of Ministry Leaders

Character Traits	Words and Phrases in 1 Timothy, Titus, and 1 Peter
1. Reputable	Above reproach, one wife, blameless, respectable, well thought of by outsiders, a lover of goodness, upright, example to the flock, respectful and believing children, good manager of the household
2. Self-Disciplined	Temperate, sensible, not a drunkard, not violent but gentle, not quarrelsome, not debauched, not quick-tempered, not addicted to wine, prudent

Character Traits	Words and Phrases in 1 Timothy, Titus, and 1 Peter
3. Generous	Hospitable, not a lover of money, not greedy for gain, willing, eager, not under compulsion, not working for sorted gain
4. Humble	Not puffed up, not arrogant, does not lord it over, clothed with humility; "God opposes the proud but gives grace to the humble."
5. Spiritually Mature	An apt teacher, not a recent convert, devout, firm grasp of the word, able to preach with sound doctrine, tend the flock with oversight

Reputable

Ministry leaders gain respect by the ways that they embody the message of the gospel in every area of life; however, to be blameless or "above reproach" does not mean to be sinless. In fact, to be a healthy example of the Christian life, a person must be deeply aware of past sins and her or his potential to sin again. Ministry leaders must also have a profound awareness of God's forgiveness, so that they can lead others to find that same mercy and forgiveness. Likewise, ministry leaders must be both exemplary and realistic in regard to family life. Raising children is not easy, and there is no guarantee that children of faithful Christian parents will become believers themselves. Yet, it must be evident that ministry leaders love their families dearly and provide the care, time, and discipline needed for their marriage and children to flourish.

The phrase in 1 Tim 3:2 and Titus 1:6 that a minister must be "married only once" (*mias gunaikos andra*), literally "one-woman man," raises some additional issues regarding marriage and gender. How to interpret the phrase "one-woman man" is not entirely clear. A few English translations have opted for "married only once" (e.g., NRSV), but most have chosen, "the husband of one wife" (e.g., KJV). Hinson lists five ways the phrase has been interpreted: 1) faithful to one's wife; 2) monogamous, not polygamous; 3) never remarried; 4) never divorced; or 5) necessarily married.[7] Although any one of these views might be implied, only the first one clearly fits the context without conflicting with Paul's other teachings about marriage, remarriage,

7. Hinson, "1–2 Timothy and Titus," 317.

and singleness in 1 Corinthians and about the possibility of divorce in Matt 5:32. According to Lea and Griffin, "it is better to see Paul having demanded that the church leader be faithful to his one wife. The Greek describes the overseer literally as a 'one-woman kind of man.'"[8]

A corollary issue is whether ministry leaders necessarily have to be male, since the texts under review in 1 Timothy, Titus, and 1 Peter all appear to be addressed exclusively to men. The debate on whether women can serve as ministry leaders hinges on what texts one includes as evidence and the way one interprets those texts. In texts like 1 Tim 2:11–12 or 1 Cor 14:33–36, Paul appears to prohibit women from serving as ministry leaders. There are, however, considerable contextual and cultural reasons that these texts may be seen as time-bound rather than timeless teachings. The context of 1 Tim 2:11–12 indicates that Paul was trying to bring order to churches composed of new Christians who had taken Paul's teaching about freedom in Christ to an extreme. The status of women in particular had been greatly elevated by the gospel of Christ, but that elevation of cultural status and freedom clashed with the hierarchical and patriarchal cultural norms of the ancient Jewish and Greco-Roman world. To bring order, in 1 Corinthians, Paul states a general moral principle that preserves both individual freedom and responsibility to others: "All things are lawful, not all things are beneficial" (1 Cor 6:12, 10:23). Paul encourages the women, who are now free from the Jewish law and equal to men in Christ, to conform to the cultural norms of the first century for the benefit of the church and the surrounding community. Indeed, these texts have been interpreted in other ways, but it is always the responsibility of the biblical interpreter to try to understand any text within its literary, historical, and cultural context.

In contrast to these few texts in 1 Timothy and 1 Corinthians, there are many other Scriptures where women are described as serving in ministry leadership and even teaching men. Table 5.2 lists biblical examples of women serving in ministry leadership. In the Old Testament, Miriam, Deborah, and Huldah clearly were looked to as religious leaders and held authority over men. In the New Testament, women were prominent throughout Jesus's and Paul's ministries. In all four Gospels, but especially in the writings of Luke, there are many texts that are supportive of women in prophetic and instructional roles in ministry leadership. In the book of Acts, women equally received the Holy Spirit and are specifically described as being gifted to prophesy. Many women in the book of Acts and in Paul's

---

8. Lea and Griffin, *1, 2 Timothy, Titus*, 109–10.

letters are described as co-workers with him. Some are described as deacons, and one is even called an apostle. In fact, the core of Paul's theology is that salvation by grace levels all human distinctions in Christ: "As many of you as were baptized into Christ have clothed yourselves with Christ. There is no longer Jew or Greek, there is no longer slave or free, there is no longer male and female; for all of you are one in Christ Jesus" (Gal 3:27–28). If the Holy Spirit, then, is poured out equally on both men and women, then the church should not prohibit anyone who clearly demonstrates the Spirit's gifting and calling to ministry leadership, including women. Therefore, just as in the case with men, women who serve as ministry leaders must be reputable persons who are above reproach.

Table 5.2 Biblical Examples of Women in Ministry Leadership

Exod 15:20–21 Num 26:59 Mic 6:4	Miriam, the sister of Moses and Aaron, was a "prophet." Micah lists her as one of the three leaders of the Israelites: "I sent before you Moses, Aaron, and Miriam."
Judg 4:4–10, 5:1–31	Deborah was both a "prophetess" and a judge over Israel. She exercised religious, judicial, and military authority over Israel.
2 Kgs 22:14–20	The prophetess Huldah was consulted by the priests of King Josiah concerning the recently discovered "book of the law" (Deuteronomy). Huldah confirmed God's judgment upon Judah according to the words of the book.
Luke 2:36–38	Anna, the aged temple prophet, was the first person in the New Testament to proclaim publicly Jesus as the Messiah.
Luke 8:1–3	Women disciples Mary Magdalene, Joanna, Susanna, and many others traveled with Jesus and funded his ministry.
John 4:4–30	Jesus spoke publicly with a woman of Samaria, who then proclaimed Jesus to others.
Luke 10:38–42	Jesus instructed Mary and Martha as his disciples.
Mark 14:3 & parallels	A woman anointed Jesus as Messiah.
Matt 28:7–10 & parallels	Mary Magdalene, the other Mary, Salome, Joanna, and other women were the first to proclaim the resurrection.

Acts 2:16–18	The Holy Spirit was poured out on all, including men and women. Peter proclaimed that both men and women would prophesy.
Acts 16:14–15	Lydia, a businesswoman, was the first convert of Paul in Europe and hosted the Philippian church in her home.
Acts 18:24–26	Priscilla and Aquila both corrected and instructed Apollos.
Acts 21:8–9	Four daughters of Philip the Evangelist were prophets.
Rom 16:1–2	Phoebe, a deacon, carried Paul's Letter to the Romans. She was a supporter of Paul's ministry.
Rom 16:3	Priscilla and Aquila were co-workers with Paul in Corinth and were co-pastors in Rome.
Rom 16:6	Mary was a worker in the Roman church.
Rom 16:7	Junia was an apostle in the Roman church.
Gal 3:28	Paul's statement: "There is no longer male and female; for all of you are one in Christ Jesus."
1 Cor 1:11	Chloe was a host of a church in her house in Corinth.
1 Cor 11:5	Women were praying and prophesying at Corinth.
1 Cor 12–14 Rom 12 Eph 4	All church members, including women, possessed gifts of the Spirit.
Phil 4:2–3	Euodia and Syntyche were co-workers with Paul.

Self-Disciplined

A cluster of words and phrases in 1 Tim 3, Titus 1, and 1 Pet 5 indicates the need for ministers to have good habits of personal control: temperate, sensible, not a drunkard, not violent but gentle, not quarrelsome, not debauched, not quick-tempered, not addicted to wine, and prudent. The words describe a person who has a strong rein on emotions and appetites. All ministry leaders must know how to deal with feelings of frustration, hurt, and anger. They also must control lust and other cravings. Taking responsibility for one's behavior does not mean suppressing or ignoring our feelings and urges, however. Responsible leaders find healthy ways to deal with their base tendencies through prayer, confession, and counseling. Ministry leaders must come to recognize the stressors and triggers that throw them off balance, and they must cultivate positive habits that reflect the indwelling of the Spirit. Those positive habits, which are incumbent on all Christians, are especially important for ministry leaders. "By contrast, the fruit of the Spirit is love, joy, peace, patience, kindness, generosity, faithfulness, gentleness, and self-control" (Gal 5:2–23). Indeed, ministry leaders need most to exemplify the love of God: "Love is patient; love is kind; love is not envious or boastful or arrogant or rude. It does not insist on its own way; it is not irritable or resentful; it does not rejoice in wrongdoing, but rejoices in the truth" (1 Cor 13:4–6).

Generous

Generosity represents several phrases in 1 Timothy, Titus, and 1 Peter that indicate ministry leaders should not be in love with money or eager for unrighteous gain from their work. Instead, ministry leaders should be motivated by sincere desire to serve God and care for others. Their focus should be external to themselves and squarely on the needs and welfare of others. The word hospitable (from the Latin "to provide lodging") captures the essence of a person of generous character. Behind the Latin is the Greek word *philoxenos*, which literally means the love of strangers and is often used to mean the welcoming of guests. The core meaning is to provide space and shelter for another person. Making room for others by denying oneself is at the heart of Jesus's teaching and example. Ministry leaders are never more like Jesus than when they deny themselves for the well-being of others.

This requirement does not mean that ministry leaders should not have any concern for themselves, however. All ministry leaders have legitimate needs for their own well-being. Ministry leaders need some source of income that provides adequate if not ample support for self and family. Ministry leaders need to be careful to get the rest and rejuvenation necessary to be able to keep giving to others. Maintaining one's physical, mental, and emotional health is absolutely necessary in order to care for others. The point of generosity is not the sacrifice of one's own needs for others but the *motivation* one has for caring for others. When ministry leaders are motivated by the grace and mercy of God to extend that grace and mercy in love and care for others, generosity is present. When ministry leaders are motivated by what they can take from people—e.g., money, attention, praise, self-esteem, or pride—they become selfish manipulators rather than generous servants. Generosity requires, therefore, the ability to balance caring for one's personal needs while helping to meet the needs of others. The focus on needs is important, because ministry leaders cannot meet everyone's *wants*, even their own. Ministry leaders will quickly burn out trying to please others or trying make them happy. To be generous does not mean that a ministry leader takes on responsibility for other people's thoughts and feelings. The problem of over-helping by ministry leaders can become just as problematic as selfish greed. In fact, excessive helping can be a sign that ministry leaders are not truly generous. Trying to make oneself feel good by pleasing others is just a subtle form of self-indulgence. Generosity, therefore, requires careful and constant self-examination and reflection. It also requires humility.

Humble

Humility is among the most highlighted character traits in the Bible. Both 1 Pet 5:5 and Jas 4:6 quote Prov 3:34, "God opposes the proud but gives grace to the humble." In Peter's statement, "clothe yourselves with humility," many commentators have heard the echo of John 13:1–5, where Jesus clothed himself with a towel and washed his disciples' feet.[9] The towel and basin themselves have become symbolic of the humility and service required of ministry leaders. The care and equipping of other Christians necessitate humility, yet humility is a most difficult trait to cultivate. Although the disciples followed Jesus every day for three years, toward the end of his earthly ministry they were still competing for rank and honor: "Then they came to Capernaum; and when he was in the house he asked them, 'What were you arguing about on the way?' But they were silent, for on the way they had argued with one another who was the greatest'" (Mark 9:33–34). In any age, humans naturally desire respect and influence, but for the disciples, living in the midst of the first-century "honor–shame" culture, the appeal of prestige and power was pervasive and compelling. In this culture, it was a sign of blessing by the gods to have wealth, health, prestige, and power, and it was a sign of disfavor by the gods to be poor, ill, humble, and weak. Jesus's life and work were the great reversal of this culture of pride and power.

---

9. Marshall, *1 Peter*, 165.

The sin of pride is the oldest human failing. The desire "to be like God" has characterized humans since the serpent dazzled Adam and Eve with the prospect of having divine knowledge of good and evil. The propensity to believe a lie in the pursuit of power has been with humanity ever since. Jesus counteracted the human bent toward deceit and thirst for power through the self-denial of the incarnation and crucifixion. Paul wrote, or quoted, the great "kenotic hymn" of Philippians in response to the disagreement and prideful self-assertion by members of the church of Philippi. The verb "emptied" (Greek, *ekēnōsen*) and the hymn in which it is embedded capture the humble attitude and action of Jesus in the incarnation:

> Do nothing from selfish ambition or conceit, but in humility regard others as better than yourselves. Let each of you look not to your own interests, but to the interests of others. Let the same mind be in you that was in Christ Jesus, who, though he was in the form of God, did not regard equality with God as something to be exploited, but emptied [*ekēnōsen*] himself, taking the form of a slave, being born in human likeness. And being found in human form, he humbled himself and became obedient to the point of death even death on a cross. Therefore God also highly exalted him and gave him the name that is above every name, so that at the name of Jesus every knee should bend, in heaven and on earth and under the earth, and every tongue should confess that Jesus Christ is Lord, to the glory of God the Father. (Phil 2:3–11)

The incarnation of Jesus was the supreme act of humility by our Creator for the sake of the creation. We are never more like God than when we humble ourselves in obedience to God for the care and well-being of others. Jesus restores the meaning of honor to that of God's original design. Honor is found in humility rather than in prideful selfishness. Ministry leaders must not be puffed up, not be arrogant, and not lord it over others. As Peter instructed ministry leaders old and young, "humble yourselves therefore under the mighty hand of God, so that he may exalt you in due time" (1 Pet 5:6). God honors ministry leaders who humble themselves.

Spiritually Mature

Ministry leaders equip others only to the degree that they themselves have been equipped. A number of the descriptions in the leadership texts refer to spiritual maturity: not a recent convert, devout, a firm grasp of the word, able to preach with sound doctrine, and an apt teacher. New Christians are just that; they are new to the faith and have only a beginner's awareness of the dynamics of the Christian life. Enthusiasm comes and goes. Awareness of God is clear and then cloudy. Relationships run warm and then cold. Feelings and thoughts are in constant flux and subject to many internal and external influences. There are no substitutes for time and experience in spiritual formation and growth. A maturing Christian has to find spiritual equilibrium through the undulating experiences of life.

Spiritual maturity is a combination of heart, head, and hands. Spiritually mature people are *hosiōs*, "devout" or "holy" (Titus 1:8). The description is most often used in the New Testament of Christ himself (Acts 2:27, 13:35, Heb 7:26, Rev 15:4, 16:5). Christ always demonstrated a deep love of the Father and devotion to the Father's will. Indeed, ministry leaders must themselves exemplify significant growth in conformity to the character of Christ, even if that growth is far from complete. Their outward behavior in words and deeds must reveal that their heart is committed to God; they must demonstrate a deep love for God in a growing personal relationship. Yet, a devout person does not necessarily exude some otherworldly aura or speak in stilted religious jargon. Truly devout ministry leaders can be down-to-earth sinner/saints who have learned and are learning how to walk with God through thick and thin. They have lived in this world long enough to understand both the grace of God and the grind of the day, the joy and suffering that characterize living as a Christian in this fallen world. They have gained resilience, toughness, and endurance.

Spiritual maturity is reflected not only in the heart of devotion but also in the head of understanding. Ministry leaders must have a good grasp of Scripture and the ability to help others understand the Christian faith. As we have seen in the first part of this book, ministry leaders must understand and be able to explain the story of the Bible and how each particular verse, paragraph, chapter, and book fits within that story. All ministry leaders must be students of the word, and this means that they must seek out those who can explain the word correctly. All of us at some point are in the same position as the Ethiopian in the book of Acts: "Then the Spirit said to Philip, 'Go over to this chariot and join it.' So Philip ran up to it and heard him reading the prophet Isaiah. He asked, 'Do you understand what you are reading?' He replied, 'How can I, unless someone guides me?'" (Acts 8:29–31). The Ethiopian demonstrated humility and wisdom that day in his awareness of his need for instruction.

Spiritual maturity flows from the humble willingness to learn. Some would-be ministry leaders, however, are "puffed up" with pride and are unteachable. They think they know everything and do not believe that God can use other Christians to help them toward a better understanding. Ministry leaders must listen to and learn from the wisdom of the Christian community past and present, because the Holy Spirit indwells and speaks through the body of Christ. Sound biblical interpreters stand on the shoulders of the long line of interpreters from the first century until today. Idiosyncratic views, unique interpretations that have no support or agreement outside a single individual, are almost always flawed or false. Ministry leaders who become competent interpreters gladly receive formal and informal education provided by faithful and competent scholars, teachers, and mentors. Such education should include the study of the Bible, Christian history, theology, and the practice of Christian ministry. Those who sense God's call to ministry leadership should be hungry to learn all they can, so that they will be true interpreters of the faith and competent guides for the saints.

Along with heart and head, the hands must be engaged in ministry for spiritual maturity to be evident. People may be passionate believers and appear to understand the faith, but if they are not engaged in some form of hands-on service, they are not ready to become leaders in ministry. When a person expresses interest in becoming a leader in ministry, among the first questions should be "What are you doing at the moment? How are you currently serving Christ?" Ministry leadership is only one form of all the ways Christians can serve. In fact, most ministry roles and tasks should be conducted by people who are *not* in ministry leadership positions. Ministry leadership as a voluntary or paid occupation should be preceded by significant time spent serving others in various ways. The examples are endless: guiding another person in discipleship, visiting the sick in the hospital or elderly in their homes, teaching a Bible class or life group, reading Scripture or giving testimony in a worship service, giving devotionals in a nursing home, participating in short-term missions with youth, serving on a homeless ministry team, serving on a church committee, working in a crisis pregnancy center, handing out food at a local pantry, singing in a choir or worship band, developing a prayer ministry at one's job or in one's home, or participating in an outreach ministry to a neighborhood, local school, or apartment complex. The truth is that ministry leaders find and confirm their calling through actually *doing* ministry, and congregations that see ministers in action have the evidence they need to call them as leaders. These five character traits, therefore, typify those who should lead in ministry. These traits define good character, but they do not necessarily guarantee good conduct.

6

The Integrity of Conduct

ONE OF THE MOST distressing things about ministry leaders is that sometimes their actions do not live up to their words. Even leaders of exemplary character can have moments or seasons of moral failure. Consistent ethical conduct does not just happen. Moral integrity is based in one's character, but it is maintained through habitual practices that give rise to sound moral living. The process of character formation is no different for ministry leaders than for any other Christian. Yet, the *role* of ministry leadership in the moral formation of the community is distinctive. The body of Christ looks to its leaders to be moral examples and to provide instruction in Christian ethical behavior. Ministry leaders do not have higher ethical standards than other Christians, but they do have greater obligations to exemplify those ethical standards for the sake of the growth of other Christians. For this reason, ministry leaders must be trustworthy. People's ability to trust their leaders is produced by their integrity. In the literal sense, integrity means "wholeness." We refer to whole numbers as "integers." The Latin root of integrity means "intact" or "undivided." In the moral sense, to have integrity means to be a person whose beliefs, words, and actions are undivided; they are consistent with each other. The consistency and depth of one's personal devotional practices are the most important aspects for maintaining the integrity of a ministry leader.

Making Space for God

The integrity of ministry leaders is directly related to the quality of their personal devotional life. Congregations eventually become aware that their leaders are either spending more time listening to God or playing video games, reading the Scripture or looking at their social media feed. Ministry leaders who ignore their constant need for God allow the cares of the world to destroy their integrity. To maintain integrity, ministry leaders must actively and intentionally engage in spiritual practices that keep them in relation with God and his will. Henri Nouwen says that "making space" for God is key in spiritual formation and spiritual growth.[1] The practice of making space is the setting aside of time and establishing a place to get alone with God. When God created the world he lovingly created time and space in which humans could thrive and have fellowship with God. After the fall into sin, the fellowship with God was broken. Humans now filled space and time with their own idolatrous creations and selfish desires. In establishing the old covenant, God began the process of carving out sacred space and time once again. He commanded the people to make a tabernacle and to set aside the Sabbath as physical and temporal "spaces" in which to pray and commune with God. The religious practices of bringing sacrifices to the tabernacle and suspending work on the Sabbath were powerful ways to keep the people conscious of God and in relationship with God. Yet, in the old covenant, tabernacle and Sabbath were spaces limited to the people of Israel. In the new covenant, God provided meeting spaces accessible to all humanity. The person of Jesus and the indwelling Holy Spirit became the "places" where all people could meet with God. "And the Word became flesh and lived [*eskēnōsen*, "pitched his tent"] among us, and we have seen his glory, the glory as of a father's only son, full of grace and truth" (John 1:14); "and I will ask the Father, and he will give you another Advocate, to be with you forever. . . . You know him, because he abides with you, and he will be in you" (John 14:16–17).

Ministry leaders of integrity, therefore, engage in spiritual practices each day. To create space in one's day requires pushing aside everything that competes for attention. Finding a quiet place and a sufficient period of time are absolutely necessary. Jesus is the example: "In the morning, while it was still very dark, he got up and went to a deserted place, and there he prayed" (Mark 1:35). "Now during those days he went out to the mountain to pray; and he spent the night in prayer to God" (Luke 6:12). "He was praying in a certain place, and after he had finished, one of his disciples said to him, 'Lord, teach us to pray, as John taught his disciples'" (Luke 11:1). Private, personal prayer is at the very heart of the Christian life.

---

1. Nouwen, "Moving from Solitude."

Prayer is more than asking God for things, however. The true object of prayer is relationship. As with intimate human relationships, simply being together with God is most important. Sitting in silence with the mind and heart focused on God allows the Spirit of God to speak. Such speaking can be in words, but often it is a deeper awareness: "Likewise the Spirit helps us in our weakness; for we do not know how to pray as we ought, but that very Spirit intercedes with sighs too deep for words. And God, who searches the heart, knows what is the mind of the Spirit, because the Spirit intercedes for the saints according to the will of God" (Rom 8:26–27). Knowing that the Holy Spirit is praying for us produces a powerful sense of God's grace. Our praise and thanksgiving become more than perfunctory exercises. They become expressions of love for our merciful Creator, our daily Sustainer, and powerful Savior. When we have a deep awareness of God's grace, we then freely bring our petitions and requests to God. We also humbly defer to the will of God. There are many different ways to pray and many resources to help with prayer, but most important for ministry leaders is to find the space and the time to *do* it. In concert with the practice of prayer is the practice of meditating on Scripture.

Ministry leaders deal with Scripture all the time. At the heart of their work is the proclamation and teaching of the word of God. The Bible can, however, become a dull sword in the hands of a leader who reads and studies it *only* for the sake of explaining it to others. Ministry leaders of integrity must engage Scripture deeply and devotionally to be trustworthy interpreters themselves. Traditional Christian devotional practice has followed two approaches: *lectio continua*, the "continuous reading," and *lectio divina*, the "divine reading" of Scripture. Continuous reading is sequential reading of whole chapters of Scripture. We certainly should engage in continuous reading of the Bible for study, but it is even more important to immerse ourselves in the biblical story to the extent that it reorients our worldview. In the words of Bonhoeffer,

> consecutive reading of Biblical books forces everyone who wants to hear to put himself, or to allow himself to be found, where God has acted once and for all for the salvation of men. We become a part of what once took place for our salvation. Forgetting and losing ourselves, we, too, pass through the Red Sea, through the desert, across the Jordan into the promised land.... We are torn out of our own existence and set down in the midst of holy history of God on earth.... It is in fact more important for us to know what God did to Israel, to His Son Jesus Christ, than to seek

what God intends for us today.... Our salvation is "external to ourselves." I find no salvation in my life history, but only in the history of Jesus Christ.[2]

Alongside *lectio continua* is *lectio divina*, which is the personal reading of select texts of Scripture in private devotions. In the individual's time alone with God, one reads and listens to the Scripture to hear a personal word from God. For his students studying to be ministry leaders, Bonhoeffer described the difference between *lectio continua* and *lectio divina*:

> Whereas in our devotions together we read long consecutive passages, in our personal meditation we confine ourselves to a brief selected text, . . . here we go into the unfathomable depths of a particular sentence and word.... In our meditation we ponder the chosen text on the strength of the promise that it has something utterly personal to say to us for this day and for our Christian life, that is not only God's word for the Church, but also God's Word for us individually.... And when we do this, we are doing no more than the simplest, untutored Christian does every day; we read God's Word as God's Word for us.[3]

The classical practice of *lectio divina* proceeds through four movements: *lectio* (reading), *meditatio* (meditation), *oratio* (prayer), and *contemplatio* (contemplation). Slow and thoughtful reading of a brief biblical text is followed by meditation on the words. Meditation has been described as the "mind descending into the heart."[4] It is dwelling on the words to the point that one senses how the words address her or his own life. The prayers (*oratio*) that follow arise naturally from the feelings and impressions generated by reading and meditation. Prayers of praise, thanksgiving, repentance, petition, or intercession are deeply felt expressions of the heart, rather than routine utterances. *Lectio divina* then concludes with contemplation, which is simply resting in God's presence and peace. Pennington describes it this way: "As we listen to the Word (*lectio*), a word, a phrase, a sentence may strike us, and we let it reverberate within, opening and expanding, forming and shaping (*meditatio*), calling forth varied responses (*oratio*) until finally we simply rest in the Reality to which it all leads (*contemplatio*)."[5]

---

2. Bonhoeffer, *Life Together*, 53–54.
3. Bonhoeffer, *Life Together*, 81–82.
4. Pennington, *Lectio Divina*, 61.
5. Pennington, *Lectio Divina*, 66.

Actions of Integrity

Personal devotional practices are the internal glue of integrity. Character traits, moral judgments, and momentary actions are held together by the quality and depth of a leader's personal relationship with God. The external fruit of internal integrity is what the people of God see in their ministry leaders. Based upon the life and teachings of Jesus, ethicists have derived general rules of love that enable ministry leaders to demonstrate integrity. James Childs has highlighted two of these—promise-keeping and truth-telling—as especially important for maintaining integrity.[6] Promise-keeping is essential to integrity. No action is more harmonious with God's own covenant-making character. God is a promise-making and promise-keeping God. Assuming the role of a ministry leader carries with it explicit or implicit promises to love and care for the people, to work to the best of one's ability, to plan and prepare well, and to carry through on those plans. The extent to which ministry leaders fulfill their promises is the measure of their integrity.

Truth-telling is closely related to promise-keeping, but the emphasis here is on what one says. Jesus taught that speech needs to be direct and to the point: "And do not swear by your head, for you cannot make one hair white or black. Let your word be 'Yes, Yes' or 'No, No'; anything more than this comes from the evil one" (Matt 5:36–37). Lies destroy trust and relationships. Ministry leaders have a heavy responsibility to guard their tongue (Jas 3:1). Nothing can destroy integrity more quickly than the loss of confidence that a person is telling the truth.

Wayne Oates describes three additional actions that are particularly conducive to integrity—durability of relationships, day-to-day face-to-faceness, and greatness of heart. Durability in relationships is closely related to promise-keeping and truth-telling, but in this case the focus is on relationships in particular.[7] Jesus challenged his listeners to be faithful in their marriages, rather than seeking easy divorces. His great command to love one another could be fulfilled only by faithfulness. Faithfulness in all relationships requires seeing others as ends in themselves rather than as means to an end. The well-being of people is the ultimate purpose of ministry leadership.

---

6. Childs, *Faith, Formation, and Decision*, 135–49.
7. Oates, "Settling," 145–48.

To durability in relationships, Oates adds what he calls "day-to-day face-to-faceness."[8] Jesus could hardly have been more critical of the hypocrisy of the religious leaders of his day. The religious leaders claimed to see, but they were blind; they claimed to serve God, but they served their own interests. Hypocrisy literally means to wear a false face. Ministry leaders must be open and honest people. They embody a serious message, but they must not take themselves too seriously. A good sense of humor about one's faults can go a long way toward maintaining integrity. Candor allows people to see the real person underneath. When a person trusts fully in God, there is no need to hide oneself from others.

Finally, Oates describes the quality of "greatness of heart" as indicative of integrity.[9] Greatness of heart means means that a person displays a broad graciousness and mercy toward others. Instead of pettiness or vengefulness, a greathearted person accepts others without judgment and condemnation. Jesus, who had every right to pass judgment on others, said that he did not come to condemn the world but to save it. When ministry leaders follow the example of Jesus, they leave the judging up to God and extend the same grace and forgiveness to others that God has given to them. Perhaps there is no greater integrity in ministry leaders than when people encounter the grace of God in them.

Self-Management

An additional aspect of integrity is what some people call time management. No one can manage time, however. The only thing we can truly manage is ourselves and how we conduct ourselves in the time we have. So, a better and more comprehensive term is *self-management*, which consists to a great extent of the habits one develops for daily work. Ministry leadership is characterized by a large amount of discretionary time. Most ministry leaders do not punch a time clock, and they do not have someone constantly supervising their work. So what they choose to do during the day is mostly up to them alone. It is not uncommon to hear of ministry leaders who are rarely in the office or seldom make a home or hospital visit. There are some even who choose to play golf five days a week. Some ministry leaders are lazy, but many others just have a hard time dealing with discretionary time. It is absolutely necessary, therefore, for ministry leaders to adopt practices

---

8. Oates, "Settling," 146.
9. Oates, "Settling," 147–48.

and develop habits of self-management. Those practices and habits include setting clear goals and meeting expectations, establishing priorities, developing a regular weekly schedule, adhering to daily routines, anticipating interruptions and crises, and cultivating self-starting habits.

Setting Goals and Meeting Expectations

The old saying is true: "When you aim at nothing, you hit it every time." Ministry leaders must have clear goals and expectations of what they are supposed to do (and not do). These goals and expectations are generated from two sources: external and internal. Examples of external expectations include job descriptions and congregational oversight. Congregations that employ ministry leaders part-time, full-time, or even as unpaid interns or volunteers should give them a written job description. Job descriptions contain the expectations of the congregation for the work of the ministry leader. It is also important that ministry leaders meet with a supervisor or church committee and go over the job description to make sure that the ministry leader understands what is stated or unstated in the job description. Alongside the external, congregational expectations, ministry leaders should also develop their own internal goals for themselves and for their ministry.

Establishing Priorities

Knowing one's own goals enables ministry leaders to set priorities. Ministry leaders can waste a lot of time doing things that can wait and avoiding things that should be done immediately. The problem with priorities is that they often are more difficult, require more thought, or are just not as appealing at the moment as other things. Daily prayer can easily be pushed aside by other activities, especially since no one else will ever know. In fact, much of what ministry leaders do is not visible to others. So, focusing on priorities like sermon preparation or visiting a homebound member requires ministry leaders to be more intentional about getting these kinds of things done. Ministry leaders also must be careful to give attention to priorities outside of their occupational duties. Spending time with one's family is often neglected if not prioritized and scheduled.

PART THREE: THE CHARACTER OF MINISTRY LEADERS

Developing a Weekly Schedule

A weekly schedule is one of the most important aids for keeping focused on priorities. One helpful approach is to create a weekly schedule by dividing each day into three periods, morning, afternoon, and evening. This division creates twenty-one periods for scheduling. Ministry leaders should try to schedule no more than ten to twelve periods for occupational duties and at least two to four for family duties each week. The rest should be for personal recreation and rest, including a day off with no preset schedule (see fig. 6.1).

Figure 6.1 Example of a Twenty-One Period Schedule

	Sunday	Monday	Tuesday	Wednesday	Thursday	Friday	Saturday
Morning	Devotional Greet Church Members Troubleshoot Problems Lead Worship/ Deliver Sermon	Devotional Sermon Prep Worship Planning	Devotional Sermon Prep Staff Meeting	Devotional Sermon Prep Wednesday Evening Bible Study Prep	Devotional Day Off	Devotional Finalize Sermon Finalize Sunday Prep	Devotional Review Sermon Home Activities
Afternoon	Lunch with Family Call Guests/Rest Committee or Church Council Meeting	Lunch at Home Counseling Appointment Write Letters, Emails, Newsletter, or Blog	Lunch with Staff Individual Meetings with Leaders or Counseling Appointment Physical Exercise	Lunch with Church Member Visit/Call Hospitals/ Nursing Homes/ Prospects	Day Off Physical Exercise	Lunch with Staff or Church Member Discipleship with Individual Evangelistic Appointment	Home Activities Family Time Physical Exercise
Evening	Family Time	Meetings or Calls/Visits to Church Members or Prospects	Family Time	Lead Wednesday Prayer Meeting	Day Off	Family Time	Review Sermon/Rest

Ten to twelve periods for church work, nine to ten periods for family or personal time

Adhering to Daily Routines

Those who play golf are taught to develop a routine for approaching each shot. The routine (stepping up to the ball, positioning the feet and hands, taking the same number of practice swings, etc.) creates the muscle memory that enables a golfer to consistently hit the ball well. In a similar way, ministry leaders should develop a routine for approaching each day. A regular sleep schedule, a good breakfast, a habitual morning devotional, regular exercise are basics for a healthy routine. Whatever happens during the course of a day, ministry leaders need to be mentally and physically capable of handling the stress and the decision-making involved in working through the day. So, among the most important priorities for ministry leaders is self-care. Getting enough sleep, eating nutritional meals, and getting regular exercise are not optional for ministry leaders, if they are to be effective. God made humans to function a certain way, and ministry leaders who do not pay attention to their personal health are damaging what God created. Humans are a combination of flesh and spirit, and both must receive care and attention in order to serve God and others. Daily self-care and accomplishing necessary tasks are facilitated best by a routine of creating and adhering to a daily to-do list of some kind. Some ministers use 3x5 cards that fit in a pocket, some use legal pads, some use multi-section notebooks, and some use electronic devices. Whatever the method, writing down specific tasks to be accomplished during the day goes a long way to getting things done and providing a sense of accomplishment when each task is crossed off the list.

Another reason for the development of a daily routine is that it is likely to be interrupted. Any number of things can interfere with a well-planned schedule. A church member can call with a personal crisis, a homeless family can show up at the church, or someone in the fellowship can die. When events like these happen, all attention gets diverted to the crisis moment. By having a regular daily routine and a weekly schedule, however, the ministry leader is in a much better position to cope with the interruption. In fact, without a routine and weekly schedule, there is nothing to be interrupted. With a regular schedule, priorities can be put on hold to address the interruption, and then regular work can resume.

Learning to Self-Start

Finally, in order to make it all work, ministry leaders must develop effective self-starting habits. Ministry leaders do not punch time clocks, and there are no supervisors to enforce start times or set deadlines for most tasks. Those who become ministry leaders simply have to motivate themselves and develop ways to begin tasks. Self-starting can be learned through intentional training and practice. "Lazy" people have developed habitual ways of putting off or avoiding work. Self-starters are those who have learned ways of getting started on a task and getting into the work at hand. One of these ways is to arrive early for any task or for any meeting. Arriving early gives oneself enough time to think through the day, make final preparations, greet people when they arrive, and have a few moments to oneself before the action starts. A second way to develop the habit of self-starting is to focus on the beginning of a task. The saying "Once begun, half done" may be a bit of an exaggeration, but there is much truth in the fact that getting started is half the battle of accomplishing any task. To focus on the beginning does not mean that one does not have in mind the whole task, but no one can do a whole task at once. All anyone can do is to start, and start, and start again. To make a trip of a thousand miles, one has to drive a mile, and, to drive one mile, one has to get in the car, start it up, and put it in gear. By breaking big tasks down into small steps, things get done. Preparing a sermon does not begin with a completed manuscript but with writing of a single word. Making a visit does not begin with entering the hospital room but by getting out of one's own chair. Self-starters accomplish large tasks, but they never do everything at once. The old adage rings true: "How do you eat an elephant?—One bite at a time."

A third way of developing the habit of self-starting is to think through the process of a task. This sounds like a direct contradiction of focusing on the beginning of a task, but it actually is a great stress reliever and enables you to focus on the beginning. In making that thousand-mile drive it is helpful to look at a map and determine the best route. Once you have an idea of where you are going, you can relax and follow the plan. Many people who have difficulty getting started with a task have not thought through the task, so they are paralyzed by confusion. Confusion is the enemy of effective action. Planning leads to focus, and focus is the secret to getting started with any task.

To this point, we have examined the spiritual and practical actions that enable ministry leaders to serve with integrity. Yet, integrity in ministry leadership also depends on the larger context of meaning within which one views her or his work. For ministry leaders, that larger context is always found in the biblical story, and within that story the primary metaphor for the integrity of a ministry leader is that of the shepherd.

Becoming a Shepherd Leader

It is common today to hear of "servant leadership." Although the idea certainly has Christian roots, servant leadership models have been adopted by all manner of nonreligious organizations and institutions. In the description above of the character trait of humility, it is clear that leaders of Christian ministry must be servants at heart, but servanthood is not a broad enough idea to describe the purpose of ministry leadership. When we turn to the Bible, leadership is most often associated with the role of the shepherd. The English word pastor, often used to describe ministry leaders, is from the Latin word for "herdsman," which in turn is a translation of the biblical words for shepherd (*rohi* in Hebrew, *poimēn* in Greek). The ancient Israelites were shepherds, so it is not surprising that the shepherd became the primary metaphor to describe the leaders of Israel. Abraham, Isaac, Jacob, Moses, and David were all shepherds. David, the most revered of Israel's leaders, wrote the finest description of shepherd leadership in Ps 23. In the psalm, God is the Shepherd who leads David in ways that he knew well from his own days caring for sheep:

> The LORD is my shepherd, I shall not want.
>
> He makes me lie down in green pastures;
>
> he leads me beside still waters; he restores my soul.
>
> He leads me in right paths for his name's sake.
>
> Even though I walk through the darkest valley, I fear no evil;
>
> for you are with me; your rod and your staff—they comfort me.
>
> You prepare a table before me in the presence of my enemies;
>
> you anoint my head with oil; my cup overflows.
>
> Surely goodness and mercy shall follow me all the days of my life,
>
> and I shall dwell in the house of the LORD my whole life long.

David's wonderful psalm of trust in God shows that the purpose of shepherd leadership is to lead others to a secure and abundant life. A thriving human, just as a thriving sheep, must have nourishment, safety, and loving care. In verse 1, David identifies the Lord as his personal Shepherd who provides all David needs to live. Ministry leaders do not have the power and resources within themselves to meet the needs of their people, so their role is to lead the people to the same Shepherd of life that David knew. In verse 2, the Shepherd begins to lead the sheep on a journey to safe, quiet places where there is plenty of food, water, and rest. Likewise, it is a ministry leader's work to lead people to the Source of spiritual nourishment that gives abundant and eternal life. In the third verse, the Shepherd, for the sake of his own good name, leads the sheep in the right ways and to good places. Ministry leaders, as well, for the sake of God's good name, lead people in right ways and toward good behavior. In verse 4, the Shepherd walks with the sheep through dangerous places, calms their fears, and defends them against all threats. Ministry leaders also walk with people through difficult and fearful moments of life, pointing them to the only One who can carry them through. These leaders help people find security in God, and they guard against false teachings and destructive conflicts. In verse 5, the image of the shepherd is enhanced by mixing the metaphor with that of a host who displays gracious hospitality, provides a place of safety, lays out a sumptuous meal, and pours soothing ointment on the head. Ministry leaders too are gracious hosts who bless people by being a refuge from threats and leading them to the Word that satisfies spiritual hunger and quenches spiritual thirst. In the last verse, the Shepherd leads the sheep back home to the protection of the sheepfold. The sheep have learned to trust in the loving care of the Shepherd as they journey out and in through all of their days. People who follow caring ministry leaders also come to trust that they are being led well, and they look forward to dwelling one day in the house of the Good Shepherd.

David's depiction of God as the ideal Shepherd stands in sharp contrast to the harsh criticisms by the Hebrew prophets of the leaders of Israel. Jeremiah and Ezekiel described the failure of Israel's leaders in terms of the failure of the basic responsibilities of the shepherd:

> My tent is destroyed,
> > and all my cords are broken;
> my children have gone from me,
> > and they are no more;
> there is no one to spread my tent again,
> > and to set up my curtains.
> For the shepherds are stupid,
> > and do not inquire of the Lord;
> therefore they have not prospered,
> > and all their flock is scattered. (Jer 10:20–21)

> Woe to the shepherds who destroy and scatter the sheep of my pasture! says the Lord. Therefore thus says the Lord, the God of Israel, concerning the shepherds who shepherd my people: It is you who have scattered my flock, and have driven them away, and you have not attended to them. So I will attend to you for your evil doings, says the Lord. (Jer 23:1–2)

THE INTEGRITY OF CONDUCT

> The word of the Lord came to me: Mortal, prophesy against the shepherds of Israel: prophesy, and say to them—to the shepherds: Thus says the Lord God: Ah, you shepherds of Israel who have been feeding yourselves! Should not shepherds feed the sheep? You eat the fat, you clothe yourselves with the wool, you slaughter the fatlings; but you do not feed the sheep. You have not strengthened the weak, you have not healed the sick, you have not bound up the injured, you have not brought back the strayed, you have not sought the lost, but with force and harshness you have ruled them. So they were scattered, because there was no shepherd; and scattered, they became food for all the wild animals. My sheep were scattered, they wandered over all the mountains and on every high hill; my sheep were scattered over all the face of the earth, with no one to search or seek for them. (Ezek 34:1–6)

Jeremiah and Ezekiel saw the destruction of Judah and the exile to Babylon as the failure of rulers who were supposed to ensure the well-being of their people. The failures of the shepherds of Israel are the reverse of Ps 23. These shepherd leaders ignored their responsibility for those in their care. The people became a means to an end rather than the end themselves. These evil shepherds actually preyed on their own sheep, eating and clothing themselves from the fat and the wool of the sheep. The leaders failed to care for the weak and the sick, and they did not look for the lost. In the end, these shepherds abandoned their posts, and the people were scattered.

In response to the failure of Israel's shepherd leaders, God declared that he would replace these false shepherds with himself.

> Then I myself will gather the remnant of my flock out of all the lands where I have driven them, and I will bring them back to their fold, and they shall be fruitful and multiply. (Jer 23:3)

> For thus says the Lord God: I myself will search for my sheep, and will seek them out. As shepherds seek out their flocks when they are among their scattered sheep, so I will seek out my sheep. I will rescue them from all the places to which they have been scattered on a day of clouds and thick darkness. I will bring them out from the peoples and gather them from the countries, and will bring them into their own land; and I will feed them on the mountains of Israel, by the watercourses, and in all the inhabited parts of the land. I will feed them with good pasture, and the mountain heights of Israel shall be their pasture; there they shall lie down in good grazing land, and they shall feed on rich pasture on the mountains of Israel. I myself will be the shepherd of my sheep, and I will make

them lie down, says the LORD God. I will seek the lost, and I will bring back the strayed, and I will bind up the injured, and I will strengthen the weak, but the fat and the strong I will destroy. I will feed them with justice. (Ezek 34:11-16)

The promise of God to be the Shepherd of the people was fulfilled in Jesus Christ. When Jesus described himself in John 10 as the Good Shepherd, he was contrasting himself with the former and current leaders of Israel. What makes this Shepherd good is his concern for the well-being of the sheep to the point of giving his own life for them: "I am the good shepherd. The good shepherd lays down his life for the sheep" (John 10:11). The shepherding role of ministry leaders, then, is that of assistants to the Good Shepherd.

Peter had to go through many difficult experiences before he was able to submit his will to the will of God. He wanted to rule with Christ in his kingdom, but he did not want to follow Christ to the cross. After Peter had denied Jesus three times, the risen Jesus met him in Galilee. Peter had returned to fishing. Jesus, the Good Shepherd, was coming for his lost sheep. After three years with Jesus and even seeing the risen Jesus, Peter still did not understand his purpose. So, Jesus took Peter aside and matched Peter's three denials with three restorative questions and three commands:

> When they had finished breakfast, Jesus said to Simon Peter, "Simon son of John, do you love me more than these?" He said to him, "Yes, Lord; you know that I love you." Jesus said to him, "Feed my lambs." A second time he said to him, "Simon son of John, do you love me?" He said to him, "Yes, Lord; you know that I love you." Jesus said to him, "Tend my sheep." He said to him the third time, "Simon son of John, do you love me?" Peter felt hurt because he said to him the third time, "Do you love me?" And he said to him, "Lord, you know everything; you know that I love you." Jesus said to him, "Feed my sheep." (John 21:15-17)

It was painful to hear Jesus repeatedly ask the same question, but it was necessary for Peter to understand that his primary role from now on was to assist Jesus in caring for his sheep. That Peter got the message and, with the help of the Holy Spirit, came to understand the purpose of his leadership in ministry is evident in Peter's later writing: "I exhort the elders among you to tend the flock of God that is in your charge, exercising the oversight, not under compulsion but willingly, as God would have you do it—not for sordid gain but eagerly. Do not lord it over those in your charge, but be examples to the flock. And when the chief shepherd appears, you will win the crown of glory that never fades away" (1 Pet 5:1–4).

Peter came to understand that God in Christ through the power of the Spirit is the "Chief Shepherd" who has entrusted his flock to "under-shepherds." It is the sole responsibility of the under-shepherds to lead the people to the Chief Shepherd through whom they will find life. Paul also, in his final words to the leaders of the Ephesian church, reminded them of their role as shepherds: "Keep watch over yourselves and over all the flock, of which the Holy Spirit has made your overseers, to shepherd the church of God that he obtained with the blood of his own Son" (Acts 20:28).

Ministry leaders who serve with integrity, therefore, view themselves and their ministry within the larger context of the ministry of the Good Shepherd whose sole object is to provide for the well-being, the shalom, of the sheep. We who serve as shepherd leaders do so as those who tend the flock of Jesus. To have integrity as ministry leaders means that we are deeply aware of that responsibility and, like Christ himself, lay down our lives for the sake of the sheep.

Part Four

The Practices of Ministry Leadership —Proclamation, Care, and Guidance

MINISTRY LEADERSHIP REQUIRES A variety of skills to perform a diverse set of tasks. No single individual is equally gifted in all the ways required, and no one can perform all areas of ministry leadership equally well. That said, ministry leaders still need to understand all that leading others in ministry entails and do their best to make sure all of the bases are covered—by themselves or with help. One way to view the areas of ministry leadership is to look at the life and work of Jesus.

Jesus preached the message of the kingdom, cared for sinners, and led his disciples to do the same. Christian commentators throughout history have seen in Jesus's actions the fulfillment of the three leadership roles of the Old Testament: prophet, priest, and king. Eusebius of Caesarea, writing in the fourth century CE said that in Jesus these three Old Testament roles came together and exceeded all earthly precursors: "the divine and heavenly Word, who is the only High Priest of the universe, the King of creation, and the only supreme Prophet."[1] Long before Eusebius, the book of Revelation described Jesus as "the faithful witness" (Prophet), the "first born of the dead" (Priest), and "the ruler of the kings of the earth" (King) (Rev 1:5). As the Prophet, Priest, and King, Jesus's work was to reveal, to restore, and to rule. At least since the time of the Reformation, the "threefold office" of Christ has been a standard way to think of the person and work of Jesus, and, by association, the practices of Christian ministry leaders.[2]

---

1. Eusebius, quoted in Moody, *Word of Truth*, 366.
2. Calvin, *Institutes of Christian Religion*, 2.15.

PART FOUR: THE PRACTICES OF MINISTRY LEADERSHIP

The practices of ministry leadership naturally divide into the three functions of proclamation, care, and guidance, which correspond to Christ's work of revelation, restoration, and rule. It is not a coincidence that Israel developed the leadership roles of prophets, priests, and kings. These roles correspond to the basic spiritual needs of humans as God has created us. We all need to hear a word from God, we need God's forgiveness and healing, and we need guidance and direction to do the work of God. Figure 7.1 illustrates the interrelation of these three areas and the task and actions of each. That the spheres are overlapping circles illustrates that the areas of ministry leadership are not separate silos or independently functioning roles. They are thoroughly integrated tasks and processes, each sphere contributing to the work of the other.

Ministry leaders must resist the temptation to view themselves as *the* prophet, *the* priest, or *the* king of a congregation. Only Jesus fills those roles. The ultimate goal, therefore, of the proclaiming, caring, and guiding work of ministry leaders is to bring the people to Christ as their true Prophet, Priest, and King. In the next six chapters we examine two aspects of each these three areas: proclamation—witness and preaching; care—counsel and comfort; and guidance—worship and work. Although our study divides these practices into distinct functions, the reader must keep in mind that in actual practice these functions are never entirely separate. Each area contributes to the effectiveness of the other, and ministry leaders do well when they develop proficiency in each area.

Figure 7.1 The Practices of Ministry Leaders—Proclaim, Care, and Guide

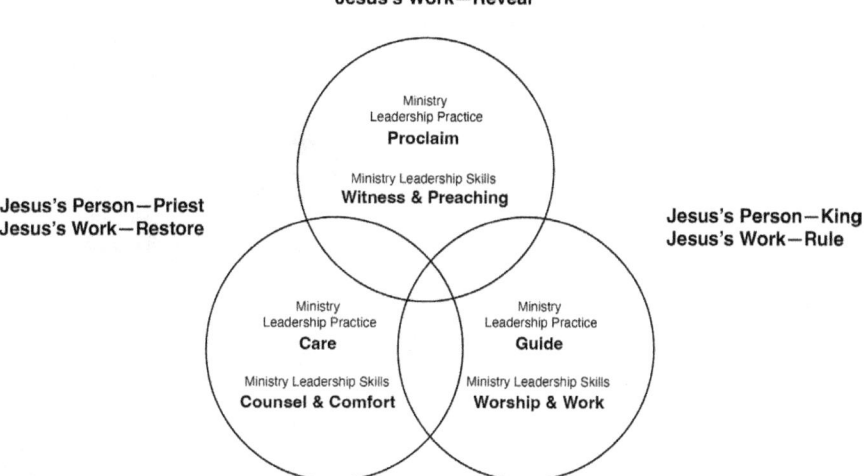

7

Proclamation as Witness

PROCLAMATION IS VITAL FOR ministry leadership. Jesus came bearing witness and preaching the coming of the kingdom of God. Likewise, ministry leaders witness and preach the word. Through the inspiration of the Scriptures and the illumination of minds and hearts by the Holy Spirit, God convicts and convinces people of the truth of the gospel, but the words of witness are communicated through human mediators. Ministry leaders are not God, and their words are human words. God, however, uses those humble, human words to speak his truth. Ministry leaders speak with "fear and trembling," believing that their words can be illumined by the Spirit, but those words are always utterances from "clay jars":

> For we do not proclaim ourselves; we proclaim Jesus Christ as Lord and ourselves as your slaves for Jesus' sake. For it is the God who said, "Let light shine out of darkness," who has shone in our hearts to give the light of the knowledge of the glory of God in the face of Jesus Christ. But we have this treasure in clay jars, so that it may be made clear that this extraordinary power belongs to God and does not come from us. . . . But just as we have the same spirit of faith that is in accordance with scripture—"I believed, and so I spoke"—we also believe, and so we speak, because we know that the one who raised the Lord Jesus will raise us also with Jesus, and will bring us with you into his presence. (2 Cor 4:5-7, 13-14)

Communicating the Gospel

The most basic and necessary ability of ministry leaders is to communicate the gospel in ways that people can understand and come to faith in

Christ. The early Christians understood that their primary ministry was that of witness. Jesus called and commissioned his disciples to be witnesses who would convey his message to the world, "And he said to them, 'Follow me, and I will make you fish for people'" (Matt 4:19); "but you will receive power when the Holy Spirit has come upon you; and you will be my witnesses in Jerusalem, in all Judea and Samaria, and to the ends of the earth" (Acts 1:8). Peter, in the book of Acts, repeatedly describes the primary role of the disciples to be that of witness. When the disciples cast lots to determine who will replace Judas as a member of the twelve, the prime qualification is that of being a witness, "one of these must become a witness with us to his resurrection" (Acts 1:22). In his sermons, Peter repeatedly calls attention to the fact that the disciples were witnesses of Jesus's resurrection: "This Jesus God raised up, and of that we are all witnesses" (Acts 2:32); "and you killed the Author of life, whom God raised from the dead. To this we are witnesses" (Acts 3:15); "and we are witnesses to these things, and so is the Holy Spirit whom God has given to those who obey him" (Acts 5:32); "we are witnesses to all that he did both in Judea and in Jerusalem" (Acts 10:39). Paul, as well, describes his conversion and calling to be that of witness: "for you will be his witness to all the world of what you have seen and heard" (Acts 22:15).

The English word witness translates the Greek word *martus*, which, even in the New Testament, began to take on the meaning of our word martyr—to witness unto death, or to die for one's faith. It is Paul himself who uses the word witness to describe the first martyr of the church: "And while the blood of your witness [*marturos*] Stephen was shed, I myself was standing and approving" (Acts 22:20). Then and now, witness carries risk. In the ancient world and in the modern world, Christian witness can bring rejection, persecution, and even death. So ministry leaders must be realistic about the cost of witness while also realizing that witness is essential. Thankfully, many people are receptive to a humble, thoughtful, and caring word of personal witness.

Witness comes from the Old English root *wit*, which meant "to know." A witness, therefore, is someone who has personal knowledge of something. The first disciples were witnesses to the life, death, and resurrection of Jesus, and it was by believing their witness, "the gospel," that people received the Holy Spirit and came to know the risen Christ personally. To witness, in a Christian sense, therefore, is to tell what one knows of the gospel and of one's own experience with the Person revealed through the gospel. A witness today tells both the gospel story *and* his or her own story of believing and knowing Jesus. In order to give a witness, three elements are necessary: relationship, testimony, and the gospel message itself.

Relationship

It is common to view witness as going out to tell strangers about Jesus—e.g., sharing the gospel with a passerby on a street corner, going door to door in a neighborhood, or distributing gospel tracts in a busy shopping mall or on a crowded beach. Certainly, we must be prepared to witness to those we do not know, but comparatively few people actually are led to Christ in this way. Most people come to Christ through existing relationships. Those who become believers are usually introduced to the gospel by someone they already know and trust. When a person comes to believe in the gospel, he or she is placing their trust not only in the message but also in the messenger. It is hard to trust a witness who just walks up and starts a very personal conversation about the person's sins and need for salvation. Oscar Thompson, one of the great teachers of witness, used the image of concentric circles to describe the closeness or distance of the relationships that surround a person.[1]

> The most important word in the English language is *relationship*. The gospel always moved on lines of relationship—Jerusalem, Judea, Samaria, the uttermost parts of the earth—in seemingly out-moving waves. Acts 20:20 says that they went "from house to house." Andrew went to Peter; Philip, to Nathaniel; the woman at the well, back to her city. Cornelius went to his household; the Philippian jailer to his household; . . . the natural thing to want to do is share it with those we know. . . . Life-style evangelism in the New Testament did not begin with Person X. It worked through relationships that had already been established.[2]

Like the waves from a rock tossed into a pond, the priorities of sharing Christ should move outward to family, friends, acquaintances, and finally to strangers.

---

1. Thompson, *Concentric Circles of Concern*, 13–27.
2. Thompson, *Concentric Circles of Concern*, 20.

Figure 7.2 Priorities of Witness Based on Thompson

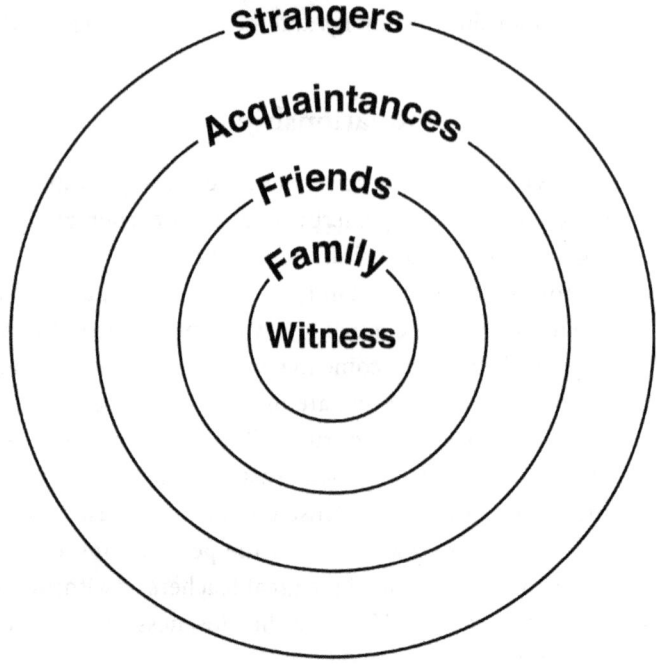

According to Thompson, in each circle, witness is cultivated through genuine interest and concern for the other person. The ground is broken by learning about the person and engaging in intercessory prayer for his or her needs. Sometimes, just asking the simple question "How can I pray for you?" can open the door for the sharing of the gospel. The soil is nourished by being with the person, especially during moments of joy (births, weddings, celebrations) and suffering (illness, financial setback, death). Finally, when the time is right, the seed of the gospel is ready for planting, and the person is ready to hear and hopefully receive the message. By being present with others, listening to them, and praying for them, they see the love of God. When the love of God is embodied and exemplified in a relationship, the soil is well prepared for planting.

Testimony

At some point in the development of a relationship, there comes the moment the witness needs to move from indirect to direct. That movement is best made by telling one's personal testimony. To testify is just another way of saying to witness. The words testify or testimony are based on the Latin root *testis*, meaning "witness." The telling of one's own story so that others might believe has strong support in the New Testament. Jesus commanded the former demon-possessed man to "go home to your friends, and tell them how much the Lord has done for you, and what mercy he has shown you" (Matt 5:19). John, following Jesus's encounter with the Samaritan woman at the well, reported that "many Samaritans from that city believed in him because of the woman's testimony ["word of witness" in Greek]'" (John 4:39). The testimony of one's faith in Christ, according to the book of Revelation, has the power to defeat even Satan himself: "But they have conquered him by the blood of the Lamb and by the word of their testimony, for they did not cling to life even in the face of death" (Rev 12:11). Luke records the testimony of Paul's conversion no less than three times, once from a third person perspective and twice as Paul himself telling his testimony. Also, in Galatians 1 and Philippians 3, Paul reiterates his testimony of conversion to Christ. John also testifies of his and the other disciples' experience with Christ:

> We declare to you what was from the beginning, what we have heard, what we have seen with our eyes, what we have looked at and touched with our hands, concerning the word of life—this life was revealed, and we have seen it and testify ["witness" in Greek] to it, and declare to you the eternal life that was with the Father and was revealed to us—we declare to you what we have seen and heard so that you also may have fellowship with us; and truly our fellowship is with the Father and with his Son Jesus Christ. (1 John 1:1-4)

The power of one's testimony should not be underestimated. In chapter 3, we saw that moral formation begins in the story-formed community. One way to understand salvation is the moment when the biblical story becomes our own story. We come to believe that the God of the Bible not only created the world but also created us individually. We come to believe that this God who loves the world also loves us personally, and we are convicted that we too have sinned against this God. We believe that we are one of the lost sheep that Jesus came to save, and we believe in the resurrection of Jesus and that we too have abundant and eternal life through Jesus. We believe that the Holy Spirit has taken up residence within us personally to guide us and empower us to witness. When we relate our testimony to others, we demonstrate how the biblical story has become our own story, and we invite others to enter into that story themselves.

The power of testimony also lies in the fact that people will usually listen to a personal story. Testimony changes the beginning of the conversation from "You need to believe in Jesus" to "Can I tell you how I have found meaning and hope for my life?" Many people would naturally resist the first approach, whereas it is hard to say no to someone who simply asks to tell their own story, especially when that story offers something as attractive as hope. Peter describes witness in this way: "Always be ready to make your defense to anyone who demands from you an accounting for the hope that is in you; yet do it with gentleness and reverence" (1 Pet 3:15–16). Notice that Peter describes witness in terms of an explanation of one's personal hope ("in you"). Testimony is always incarnational. The word of the gospel takes on the flesh and blood of the believer. Witness is not the mere relating of information but the sharing of one's life. Also, notice Peter's final instruction, "do it with gentleness and reverence." Sharing one's testimony is a deeply personal and vulnerable act of self-revelation intended to help others drop their own defenses and allow their own deepest needs and desires to come to the surface. Telling one's testimony gives others the personal space and safety they need to listen and think. When witness becomes blunt confrontation, we back others into a corner, and the consequence may be that they do not hear a message of grace and love but of condemnation and rejection. When we share a testimony of our own deep need for grace and love and our finding forgiveness and acceptance in Christ, we reflect the God who "so loved the world that he gave his one and only Son" (John 3:16).

When, in our testimonies, we humbly speak of finding God's love and forgiveness for ourselves, we encourage others to believe the truth of the gospel. Faith is contagious; it is caught rather than taught. Most people believe something not because they have completely verified it or reasoned it out for themselves, but because other people they trust strongly believe and have been changed by that belief. This fact of human nature can be troubling, because there are many things that people believe that are simply not true. We cannot change this situation. All human knowledge begins with some kind of step of faith into the unknown. Truth is verified after a step of faith, not before. In the classical illustration of the chair, we can see how this works. We see a chair and examine it closely, but to verify that it can support our weight we must sit in it. Sitting in the chair is analogous to the exercise of faith. We do not know until we try. In the words of St. Augustine, *credo ut intellegam,*

"I believe that I may understand." The sharing of a testimony invites others to see for themselves if what we are saying is true.

So, what does a testimony entail? It is unfortunate that the idea of testimony is often reduced to the three-step formula of a conversion story, e.g., my life before Christ, how I came to Christ, and my life with Christ. In this approach, the emphasis is placed on the second step, the transaction from unbelief to belief or from lost to saved. The second step is seen to be important, because it lays the groundwork for leading the other person through a similar transaction. Yet, conversion is much more than a transaction of repentance and forgiveness. It is the ongoing *transformation* of life from rebellious sinner to obedient saint, and it is the story of this transformation that is most attractive and powerful in one's testimony. Testimonies do not have to be linear progressions. They should not be formulas into which all stories must fit. The best testimonies answer transformational questions in personal and creative ways. Testimonies should answer questions like these: "What difference has my faith in Jesus made in my life?" or "How has my relationship with God changed me?" or "How does my faith in Jesus give me hope?" (or joy, peace, security, life, grace, mercy, meaning, purpose, etc.) or "Why does my faith in Jesus make sense to me?" (or help me make sense of the world). The answers to these questions should be as personal as appropriate. Talking in sweeping generalities (e.g., God loves everyone; Jesus forgives sinners) is not as helpful as a specific situation (e.g., I felt so weak, afraid, and unloved, but I met a friend, Kim, who had a peace and confidence I did not have. Then one day, Kim told me about Jesus . . . today I can still feel lonely at times, but now that I know that God loves and cares for me, I know in my heart that I am never alone . . ."). The sharing of one's personal testimony can open doors to the heart that nothing else will, but at some point, testimony must give way to leading the person through the message of the gospel itself.

Gospel

The first chapter described the biblical story of God's purpose and work from creation to the kingdom of God. When we share the gospel, we are sharing the essential truths of this long and complex history of salvation. It is common today to condense God's work of salvation to a core set of themes to make it easy to share and easy to understand and believe. Simplification is especially needed when one is talking to a young child or when one has little time to go into much depth. However, ministry leaders must keep the breadth and depth of the biblical story in mind even as they try to make it easier for others to understand. The gospel message can be summarized, but it will always be more than a simplistic formula.

The word gospel is from Old English *godspell*, meaning "good tale" or "good story." The underlying Greek word, *euangelion*, literally means "good news." In the New Testament, gospel is used in multiple ways. For Jesus himself, the gospel was his proclamation of the arrival of the kingdom of God. "Now after John was arrested, Jesus came to Galilee, proclaiming the good news [gospel] of God, and saying, 'The time is fulfilled, and the kingdom of God has come near; repent, and believe in the good news'" (Mark 1:14–15). In Paul's writings, the meaning of gospel shifts focus from the kingdom to the King. The gospel for Paul is the salvation that comes by faith in the crucifixion and resurrection of Jesus:

> Now I would remind you, brothers and sisters, of the good news [gospel] that I proclaimed to you, which you in turn received, in which also you stand, through which also you are being saved, if you hold firmly to the message that I proclaimed to you—unless you have come to believe in vain. For I handed on to you as of first importance what I in turn had received: that Christ died for our sins in accordance with the scriptures, and that he was buried, and that he was raised on the third day in accordance with the scriptures, and that he appeared to Cephas, then to the twelve. Then he appeared to more than five hundred brothers and sisters at one time, most of whom are still alive, though some have died. Then he appeared to James, then to all the apostles. (1 Cor 15:1–7)

> Paul, a servant of Jesus Christ, called to be an apostle, set apart for the gospel of God, which he promised beforehand through his prophets in the holy scriptures, the gospel concerning his Son, who was descended from David according to the flesh and was declared to be Son of God with power according to the spirit of holiness by resurrection from the dead, Jesus Christ our Lord. . . . For I am not ashamed of the gospel; it is the power of God for salvation to everyone who has faith, to the Jew first and also to the Greek. For in it the righteousness of God is revealed through faith for faith; as it is written, "The one who is righteous will live by faith." (Rom 1:1–4, 16–17)

Paul understood the gospel as the preaching of Christ's crucifixion and resurrection, and he understood salvation as forgiveness and life through faith in Christ.

A complete view of the gospel message, then, brings together Jesus's preaching of the kingdom and Paul's preaching of the King. When ministry leaders share the gospel, they are inviting people to believe in the resurrected Jesus, to enter the kingdom of God, and to serve Christ as their King. We must not reduce the gospel to simplistic formulas for getting to heaven. Salvation is not transaction but transformation. Indeed, in salvation we receive eternal life, but more importantly we are reconciled and restored to relationship with our Creator. We are delivered from a sinful, self-centered, and perishable life to a righteous, Christ-centered, and imperishable life. We are enabled through the power of the Holy Spirit to love others and become useful servants in God's work of restoring the creation.

When we understand the gospel in this way, we are able to make skillful and wise use of a thematic outline of the gospel. Many find a four-point outline works well: God's purpose, our problem, God's gift, our response. These four themes introduce the most important truths of the Christian faith, and they are best shared using texts of Scripture. It is very important to bring others to the Bible when sharing the gospel. They need to understand where the gospel message comes from, and they need to be able to explore it for themselves. Table 7.1 includes Scripture texts beside each theme and truth of the gospel.

Table 7.1 Four Themes of the Gospel with Biblical References

Gospel Theme	Gospel Truth	Supporting Bible Texts
God's Purpose	Life & Love	John 10:10b: "I came that they may have life, and have it abundantly."
		John 3:16: "For God so loved the world that he gave his only Son, so that everyone who believes in him may not perish but may have eternal life."

PART FOUR: THE PRACTICES OF MINISTRY LEADERSHIP

Gospel Theme	Gospel Truth	Supporting Bible Texts
Our Problem	Sin & Death	Isa 53:6: "All we like sheep have gone astray; we have all turned to our own way, and the Lord has laid on him the iniquity of us all.
		Rom 3:23: "Since all have sinned and fall short of the glory of God."
		Rom 6:23: "For the wages of sin is death, but the free gift of God is eternal life in Christ Jesus our Lord."
		Heb 9:27: "And just as it is appointed for mortals to die once, and after that the judgment."
God's Gift	Jesus: Cross Resurrection King/Kingdom Forgiveness Eternal Life	Rom 6:23: "For the wages of sin is death, but the free gift of God is eternal life in Christ Jesus our Lord."
		Rom 5:8: "But God proves his love for us in that while we still were sinners Christ died for us."
		1 Pet 3:18: "For Christ also suffered for sins once for all, the righteous for the unrighteous, in order to bring you to God. He was put to death in the flesh, but made alive in the spirit.
		Phil 2:9–11: "Therefore God also highly exalted him and gave him the name that is above every name, so that at the name of Jesus every knee should bend, in heaven and on earth and under the earth, and every tongue should confess that Jesus Christ is Lord, to the glory of God the Father."
		Rev 11:15: "The kingdom of the world has become the kingdom of our Lord and of his Messiah, and he will reign forever and ever."

Gospel Theme	Gospel Truth	Supporting Bible Texts
Our Response	Repentance & Belief	John 1:12, "But to all who received him, who believed in his name, he gave power to become children of God,"
		Eph 2:8–9, "For by grace you have been saved through faith, and this is not your own doing; it is the gift of God—not the result of works, so that no one may boast."
		I John 5:13, "I write these things to you who believe in the name of the Son of God, so that you may know that you have eternal life."
		John 5:24, "Very truly, I tell you, anyone who hears my word and believes him who sent me has eternal life, and does not come under judgment, but has passed from death to life."

There are many other methods of organizing and sharing the gospel (e.g., the Roman Road, the illustration of the bridge, storying the gospel, etc.), but a more recent and helpful approach is that of James Choung and his method of explaining the *True Story*. Choung emphasizes the fact that Jesus preached the kingdom of God as his primary message. So, the gospel is more about the transformation of the world than individuals making it to heaven. He believes that the current generation is hungry to hear this bigger message, because it addresses concerns for the restoration of world systems and for the restoration of relationships between people and between humans and God.

> If we present a faith that's only concerned about the eternal destination of a soul after death, then perhaps we've missed the mark. And if we share a faith that ignores broken relationships and societal injustices, then we've done our Christian faith a disservice. Jesus' message is about so much more than most of us realize, and it seems right to share the good news he came to offer.[3]

Choung's approach uses a diagram of four circles to relate the *True Story*. The circles show the progression from the good creation, to the corruption of creation, to the restoration of people by Jesus, and finally to the sending out of Christians to heal the world. It is in the third and fourth circles that Choung's

3. Choung, *True Story*, 10.

approach is most innovative. The restoration by Jesus brings humans into the kingdom of God, "where what God wants to happen actually happens." Salvation, therefore, transforms individuals so that they can transform the world. Restored Christians are then sent into the world to further the process of restoring the whole creation. "Jesus wants us to join this resistance movement, against evil, to go out and heal the planet."[4]

The Evangelistic Conversation

Our review of the main elements of witness and the content of the gospel is not complete without some guidance as to how a ministry leader might actually engage a person in a conversation that leads to the sharing of the gospel. If time and circumstance allow, approaching someone to share the gospel or to have an "evangelistic conversation" is best done with as few distractions as possible. Setting up an appointment to talk in a confidential setting is ideal; however, ministry leaders often have to work with the situation as best they can. To get started, it is best to ask some questions. Good, open-ended questions raise interest without putting the other person on the defensive. Questions also make the sharing of the gospel more of a dialogue than a monologue. People are more willing to listen to others when they themselves feel they have been heard and that the witness cares about what they have to say. The initial questions should move the conversation toward personal and spiritual matters. Here are some examples:

> Where do you find meaning and purpose in your life?
>
> What would you say is most important to you?
>
> In times like these, what resources do you depend on?
>
> How do you cope with the challenges of life?
>
> Do you ever think much about spiritual things?
>
> Have you ever thought much about God?
>
> Where do you find hope?

If possible, the questions should relate to something the person has already said or to some situation in her or his life. Also, the question should be asked with genuine interest in hearing the answer. Following up answers with additional questions can be helpful, especially if the person's answers reveal personal struggles or suffering of some kind.

4. Choung, *True Story*, 212–13.

The sharing of one's testimony is the next step in the conversation. A request for permission should precede the testimony, e.g., "Can I tell you where I have found meaning in purpose in my life?" or "May I tell you about the difference God has made in my life?" or "Can I tell you about my relationship with Jesus Christ?" By requesting permission, the witness is showing respect for the other person and indicating that the witness has something special to say and wants the other to listen. Following the sharing of one's testimony, it is time to make another request: "I would like to share with you the same message that changed my life, is that okay with you?" The person may say no, because they are not ready for some reason. If this happens, then it is best to end the conversation by saying something like "I can tell you need some time to think about what I have shared with you, but I would like to meet with you again when you are ready. Is that okay with you?" If, on the other hand, the person responds positively to the testimony and indicates a desire to hear the message of the gospel, then go right into one of the approaches described above. If possible, lead the person through the Scripture texts using a marked Bible or a smartphone. If you are using a diagram approach, just use whatever paper is at hand—even a restaurant napkin. After explaining the four gospel themes or some other approach, then it is time to ask two more questions, "Does this make sense to you?" and "Do you want to ask Jesus to forgive you and become your King right now?" If the answer to the first question is no, then the witness may need to give further explanation of something. If the answer to the second question is no, then the witness should be sensitive to the objection and determine whether or not it is best to continue the conversation. If the answers to both questions are yes, then the next step is to lead the person through a prayer of repentance and faith in Jesus.

> Repeat after me: "Lord, Jesus, I know that I have sinned against God and that I cannot save myself. I repent of my sin and ask for your mercy and forgiveness. I believe that you died and rose again to deliver me from sin and death. Please receive me into your kingdom and become the King and Lord of my life. Please send your Holy Spirit to dwell in me, and help me now to love you and love others. Thank you, Lord, for your grace and love. I pray these things in Jesus's name, amen."

In the midst of an evangelistic conversation, a person may raise objections. Although a full discussion of dealing with theological questions is beyond the scope of this book, there are some simple responses one can make that bring the conversation back around to the gospel. Randy

Newman describes a useful method based on Jesus's own method of responding to objections. Jesus often responded to objections by answering a question with a question. By responding with a question rather than an argument, the dialogue may keep going rather than letting the objection derail or end the conversation. Here are some examples:

Objection: "I don't believe in God."

Response: "Really?" "What do you believe in?" "Can I tell you why I believe in God?"

Objection: "Why should I believe the Bible?"

Response: "Have you ever read the Bible?" "Can I tell you how reading the Bible has changed my life?"

Objection: "Why does a good God allow so many people to suffer?"

Response: "I wish I knew." "How do you deal with suffering?" "What helps you to cope with it?" "Can I tell you how my faith in Christ has helped me cope with suffering?"

Objection: "What about those who have never heard about Christ?"

Response: "What do you think?" "Why do you care about those who have not heard?"[5]

All through the process of talking to someone about Jesus, it is absolutely necessary to focus on the person and not only on sharing a message. Sharing the gospel must never be reduced to a sales pitch with the goal of "soul winning." When we share the gospel, first and foremost, we are introducing the person to the love of God. That love is always demonstrated by genuine caring for the other person's needs. The only way we can address those needs is by listening and helping the person to know they have been heard by us. It is not so much about what we have to say but whether the other person believes that we really care about them. It is evident, therefore, that proclamation as witness requires forethought, preparation, and practice. The same is the case with the ministry of proclamation through preaching.

---

5. Newman, *Questioning Evangelism*. The examples are compilations and extrapolations from examples throughout Newman's book. Some but not all of the questions are direct quotations.

8

Proclamation as Preaching

NO OTHER MINISTRY LEADERSHIP task is more conspicuous than preaching. In fact, some people think that preaching is the only thing that ministry leaders do. It is not uncommon to hear "I wish I had your job. You work only one day a week." However false such a statement may be and no matter how much it stings the ego, there is a kernel of truth in it. The weekly sermon, especially in Protestant churches, is at the heart of the life of the community. If people are changed by anything that ministry leaders do, it is likely to occur as they hear the word preached and put into practice what they hear. The Scriptures attest to the importance of preaching:

> For since, in the wisdom of God, the world did not know God through wisdom, God decided, through the foolishness of our proclamation, to save those who believe. (1 Cor 1:21)

> But how are they to call on one in whom they have not believed? And how are they to believe in one of whom they have never heard? And how are they to hear without someone to proclaim him? And how are they to proclaim him unless they are sent? As it is written, "How beautiful are the feet of those who bring good news!" But not all have obeyed the good news; for Isaiah says, "Lord, who has believed our message?" So faith comes from what is heard, and what is heard comes through the word of Christ. (Rom 10:14–17)

In the texts above, the words proclamation or proclaim translate various conjugations of the Greek verb *kērusso*, meaning to announce a message. Scholars use the corresponding Greek noun, *kērugma*, to describe the content of the earliest preaching in the New Testament, in particular, the sermons of Peter and Paul in the book of Acts. The earliest preaching was essentially the public proclamation of the gospel to non-Christians. The content of this early *kērugma* focused on the life, death, and resurrection of Jesus and the need to believe in him. Later in the New Testament period and throughout the development of Christian history, preaching came to be directed not only to those outside the church but also to those within.

In the early church, preaching within the body consisted primarily of comments by a ministry leader on the Scripture reading for the day's worship. Justin Martyr, writing around 150 CE, described the reading of Scripture and role of the presider or "president" (an early word for a ministry leader) in applying the text: "When the reader has finished, the president in a discourse urges and invites [us] to the imitation of these noble things."[1] By the third century CE, formal Jewish and Greek principles of literary interpretation or *hermeneutics* began to be used to aid the preaching of biblical texts, and by the fourth and fifth centuries, principles of classical rhetoric were being applied to the development of sermons. Rhetorical principles like those of Aristotle and Cicero enabled preachers to persuade minds and hearts more effectively. During the medieval period, the importance of preaching diminished with the dominance of the sacrament of the Eucharist (Lord's Supper) as the focal point of worship. The Reformation restored the prominence of the sermon, at least in Protestant churches. Since the Reformation, myriads of books have been devoted to the subject of preaching and the development of sermons.

The Authoritative Source

The Bible is the authoritative source for all Christian preaching. Preachers may bring in all manner of insights and illustrations from personal experience, life situations, literature, or media, but the only *primary* subject matter for their sermons must be the biblical text. Sermons expose the truths within Scripture texts and persuade minds and hearts to believe and obey those truths. Preachers should not use the Bible as a tool to support their own ideas. In the words of Bonhoeffer, "it is not our heart that determines our course, but God's Word."[2] The Bible is not a reference book to be consulted selectively and cited for whatever the preacher wants to say. As the authoritative source of God's word to humanity, the Bible must be allowed to speak on its own terms. Karl Barth called this entering "the strange new world within the Bible":

1. Martyr, "First Apology," 287.
2. Bonhoeffer, *Life Together*, 55.

> It is not the right human thoughts about God which form the content of the Bible, but the right divine thoughts about men. The Bible tells us not how we should talk with God but what he says to us; not how we find the way to him, but how he has sought and found the way to us; not the right relation in which we must place ourselves to him, but the covenant which he has made with all who are Abraham's spiritual children and which he has sealed one and for all in Jesus Christ. It is this which is within the Bible. The word of God is within the Bible.[3]

Faithful preachers go to Scripture to listen to what God is saying, and they hear his word as a word spoken to themselves before they proclaim it to others. Preaching, then, requires faith that God speaks through Scripture and that what God has to say is more important than anything the preacher wants to say.

Preachers, therefore, believe that the Spirit of God has inspired these writings in the past and illumines the meaning in the present. The fact that the text is inspired and illumined by God must not be in doubt, although knowing exactly *how* the text is inspired and illumined will always be a mystery. The Bible clearly says that God has inspired Scripture: "All scripture is inspired by God and is useful for teaching, for reproof, for correction, and for training in righteousness, so that everyone who belongs to God may be proficient, equipped for every good work" (2 Tim 3:16–17). The phrase "inspired by God" translates the single Greek word *theopnuestos*, which literally means "God-breathed." The use of the word inspire echoes the Genesis account of the creation of Adam: "Then the LORD God formed man from the dust of the ground, and breathed into his nostrils the breath of life; and the man became a living being" (Gen 2:7). A lifeless mound of dust was animated by the Spirit of God to bring about human life. Likewise, in the Bible the Spirit transforms inert human thoughts and words to life-giving divine revelation. The fact of inspiration is clearly stated in the Bible, but the process of inspiration is never explained. Many theories have been generated to explain how the words of the text are both human and divine. The views run from one end of the spectrum to the other. At one extreme are the views that stress the full divinity of Scripture. The words of Scripture are dictated by God with little human input. At the other extreme are views that see the words of Scripture as essentially human words that describe divinely inspired events. In between these extremes is a range of views

---

3. Barth, *Word of God*, 44.

that maintain the human and divine in the words of Scripture to greater or lesser degrees. The approach here is to see the inspiration of Scripture as analogous to the full humanity and full divinity of Christ himself. This "dynamic" view of inspiration allows for the personalities and limitations of the human writers while maintaining that God speaks through their human words. Such a view preserves the mystery of inspiration and allows for faith in the text and the critical work of interpretation.

Hermeneutics

If we are convinced that God speaks through Scripture, then we must do everything we can to make sure we are interpreting the Bible correctly. The English word hermeneutics is derived from the Greek *hermēneuō*, meaning to explain, interpret, or translate.[4] At the end of Luke's Gospel, Jesus walked with the two disciples on the road to Emmaus. There he interpreted the Old Testament Scriptures to them: "Then beginning with Moses and all the prophets, he interpreted [*diermēneusen*] to them the things about himself in all the scriptures" (Luke 24:27). Hermeneutics, in our current usage, is the systematic study of how the original meaning of a text can be recovered and communicated in a different historical and cultural context. In the words of Perry Yoder, "we see that the task of hermeneutics is to teach us how we may tell a valid explanation from an invalid one—what constitutes a correct understanding of the passage. . . . But hermeneutics is not only interested in deciding what is a valid interpretation; it is also concerned with how interpretations are used—how we may apply our understanding of Scripture to the problems of our life today."[5] Theories of hermeneutics have a long history of development and draw from many areas of study, e.g., philosophy of language, linguistics, literature, and theology. So, one must keep in mind that hermeneutics is a challenging and complex field of study. That said, since the Reformation, theologians have established basic assumptions and principles for deriving the meaning of biblical texts.

Protestant biblical hermeneutics rests on three basic principles: progressive revelation, the interpretation of Scripture by Scripture, and Jesus Christ as the ultimate criterion of interpretation. The first principle of sound hermeneutics, progressive revelation, refers to the fact that God has *gradually* and *increasingly* made himself known in history. Primitive human

4. Humphreys, "Hermeneutics," 373.
5. Yoder, *Understanding the Bible*, vii.

beings, embedded tribal cultures and polytheistic religions of the ancient world, had little ability to understand this mysterious God. God had to communicate like an adult speaking with a small child, laying down basic commands. Only in "the fullness of time" (Gal 4:4) was humanity ready for the full revelation of God in Jesus Christ. In the words of Bernard Ramm, "by progressive revelation we mean that the Bible sets forth a movement of God, with the *initiative* coming from *God and not man, in which God brings man up through* the theological infancy of the Old Testament to the maturity of the New Testament."[6] The principle of progressive revelation fits well with the view of dynamic inspiration described above. Dynamic inspiration allows room for what we actually find in the Bible itself—a story of increasing depth and clarity about who God is and what God is doing. The Bible cannot be read in a "flat" way as if revelation in the Old Testament was equal to that of the New Testament. Instead, the revelation of God in Scripture should be seen as steadily rising through the dynamic undulations of low and high, soft and loud, hazy and clear moments of disclosure until it reaches the heights of the words and deeds of Jesus in the Gospels.

The second principle of sound hermeneutics holds that Scripture interprets Scripture. In other words, any particular part of Scripture must be interpreted within the context of the *whole* of Scripture. Since the Bible is an unfolding story that culminates with the revelation in Jesus Christ, then every part of the story must eventually be understood within the ultimate outcome of the story. Like reading a mystery novel, the pieces do not all come together until the moment of full disclosure; only then does any earlier piece of the mystery finally make sense.

The third principle of sound hermeneutics is the most important—Jesus Christ is the ultimate criterion of interpretation. Scripture is correctly interpreted only in light of the revelation of Jesus. These three hermeneutical principles—progressive revelation, the interpretation of Scripture by Scripture, and the criterion of Jesus Christ—form the framework for the principles of biblical exegesis.

Biblical Exegesis

Exegesis is the study of a particular text of Scripture with the intent to extract and explain the meaning of that text. General principles of exegesis include context, comparison, and emphasis. The most basic principle of

---

6. Ramm, *Protestant Biblical Interpretation*, 102 (emphasis in original).

biblical exegesis is to interpret any text within its context. A biblical text is, at a minimum, a complete sentence.[7] Individual words are the building blocks, but it is only as they are used in a sentence that the meaning and function of words can be determined. If I were to ask "What is the meaning of *it*?" without context, the most that anyone could answer would be a dictionary definition, e.g., "that thing." If given the context of a sentence, paragraph, chapter, book, Testament, and entire biblical canon, the word *it* takes on very specific and rich meaning. For example, Paul uses the word *it* in Romans: "I am not ashamed of the gospel; *it* is the power of God for salvation" (Rom 1:16). The context clearly indicates that *it* refers to "the gospel," which is a major subject in the writings of Paul and the entire the New Testament. Understanding what Paul means by "the gospel" requires examining his use of "the gospel" in the context of the entire book of Romans, by making comparisons with Paul's descriptions of the gospel in his other writings and by examining Luke's accounts of Paul's speeches in the book of Acts. Examination of context does not end with the biblical text, however. Context also includes the historical, cultural, and religious settings in the first-century world. Interpreters need to ask, "How was the word 'gospel' (*euangelion*) used outside of the New Testament?" A full examination of context also includes the way the text has been understood throughout Christian history, e.g., "What did the word 'gospel' mean in Roman Catholicism, the Reformers, or among the early Baptists?," etc. Finally, the examination of context extends to the views of recent scholars in their commentaries on the text.

Two corollary principles of context are comparison and emphasis. The study of context usually reveals other biblical texts by the same writer or other writers that parallel the way a word or phrase is used in the current text under review. If, however, comparisons cannot be found, then the interpreter must be cautious about determining meaning. Interpreters must give priority to ideas that are repeated and clear and be careful with texts that are rare and obscure. In 1 Cor 15:29, Paul speaks of baptism for the dead: "Otherwise, what will those people do who receive baptism on behalf of the dead?" Nowhere else in Paul's writings does he refer to "baptism on behalf of the dead." The immediate context does not give any help either. In 1 Cor 15, the entire discussion is about the nature of resurrection, not baptism.

---

7. According to Vanhoozer, "J. Barr and P. Ricoeur agree, the basic unit of meaning is not the individual sign or word but the sentence. For words are ambiguous until they are used in concrete instances of discourse" (Vanhoozer, "Exegesis and Hermeneutics," 58).

When interpreters take this verse out of context, they may read into it a meaning that was never intended. Based on this single verse, the Latter-Day Saints (the Mormons) developed a major practice of baptizing people for their deceased ancestors, whereas no major Christian denomination has ever interpreted the verse as promoting such a practice.

The second corollary principle of context is that of emphasis. The study of context helps the interpreter to distinguish what is the main emphasis or core meaning from what is a tangential or spurious idea. Words are multivalent, so they mean different things in different contexts. The goal of exegesis is to determine the main point of emphasis in a particular text. Unfortunately, many biblical interpreters read into texts what they want to find there. When this happens, the interpreter has gone from proper exegesis (reading meaning out) to erroneous *eisogesis* (reading meaning in). By determining the emphasis of a text, one can make a judgment about what is descriptive or prescriptive, time-bound or timeless in Scripture. Christians look to Scripture for guidance for living in the modern world. Not everything in Scripture, however, is instructive for Christian living in the present day. The Bible contains descriptions of historical circumstances and events that are strange and foreign in the modern world. Descriptions of animal and grain sacrifices, prophetic warnings against making alliances with Assyrians, eating food sacrificed to idols—these are clearly descriptions of practices and issues from another time and place than our own; they are time-bound. Other texts are clearly intended to be timeless. Jesus's teaching that we are to love God and love our neighbor is prescriptive; it is instruction that was intended for Jesus's audience in the first century and for the readers of the twenty-first century. Paul's instruction for slaves to obey their masters is clearly descriptive and time-bound, but an underlying principle of faithful service by Christians in any circumstance may be seen as timeless. Distinguishing between descriptive and prescriptive biblical texts can be difficult and even controversial, but it must be done. Studying the context, comparison, and emphasis are the only ways to do so.

These three exegetical principles are then applied to a text through a number of steps. Although these steps are described here in sequence, in actual practice the exegete may revisit the steps repeatedly, proceeding more in a circular fashion rather than in a straight line. In other words, exegesis is a messy process. Nevertheless, developing skill in this process is necessary for all who preach. Exegesis begins with the reading of the text in several English translations. If the interpreter has knowledge of the

Hebrew and Greek, then she or he should translate the text for themselves. No other single aspect of exegesis is as helpful and informative as the ability to translate a text from the biblical languages. Yet, much can still be gained by reading various English translations, whether one can translate from Hebrew and Greek or not. Translations fall into two basic kinds, formal equivalence and functional equivalence. Formal equivalence translations attempt to preserve as much of the syntax and words of the underlying Hebrew or Greek as possible while rendering the meaning into English. Functional equivalence translations, to varying degrees, adhere less to the syntax and words of the original languages in order to render the meaning in the idiom of contemporary readers.[8] Exegetes should read the text in two or more formal equivalence translations and follow up with one or more functional equivalence translations. Examples of formal equivalence English translations include the New American Standard Version (NASB), the New Revised Standard Version (NRSV), and the King James Version (KJV); examples of moderate, functional equivalent translations include Today's New International Version (TNIV) and the New Living Translation (NLT); examples of looser, functional translations (paraphrases) are the Message and the Contemporary English Version (CEV). Based on the multiple readings of the text in various translations, the exegete should gain a basic understanding of the meaning of the text and make note of words, phrases, and sentences that are unclear or vary in translation.

The next steps include the study of particular words and of the grammar of the text. While one must keep in mind that the precise meaning of individual words cannot be determined outside the context of a sentence, it is still important to study the background, range of meanings, and uses of significant words in a text of Scripture. Words are studied both etymologically and comparatively.[9] Etymology is the study of the origins of words and the history of development and use. Comparative study is the study of the occurrences of the word throughout the Bible or in nonbiblical literature of the ancient world. Etymological and comparative study employ Bible concordances, Bible dictionaries, Hebrew and Greek lexicons, special word study texts, and Bible commentaries to determine both the English translations and the underlying Hebrew or Greek words. One must be cautious, however, not to read possible definitions into a word that the context will not support.

8. Fee and Strauss, *How to Choose Translation*, 26–27.
9. Ramm, *Protestant Biblical Interpretation*, 129–33.

The grammatical study of the text follows the study of the words. Grammar has to do with the structure or syntax of a language. The exegete who does not know Hebrew or Greek will have to rely on reference works like those listed above to show out how particular grammatical constructions affect the meaning of the text. By studying good formal equivalence translations, sometimes an exegete can see differences in how grammar is being translated. Specifically, a study of grammar includes the relationship of the subject of a sentence to a predicate, the declension of the nouns (subject, object, indirect object, gender, number), the conjugations of the verbs (tense, mood, participle), and the use of prepositions. Grammatical study is assisted by the diagramming of a text, which can be done in the original language or in English. A diagram makes clear what words and phrases are the subject, verb, and object of the text and what words and phrases modify or explain the primary words.

Examination of the kind of literature or *genre* builds on the study of words and grammar. Knowing the genre provides an important contextual clue to meaning. Brief figures of speech, larger literary units within chapters, and comprehensive genres of biblical books must be taken into account. Brief figures of speech (e.g., metaphor, simile, or hyperbole) are used all through the Bible, and they require particular study to avoid taking what is figurative in a literal way. Jesus described himself as a gate or door, but we do not really believe he was made of wood and hinges. Jesus told his disciples to cut off their hands and pluck out their eyes to avoid lust, but we do not really believe that the disciples were blind and had no hands. Larger literary units include parables, pronouncement sayings, extended metaphors, sermons, and dialogues. By studying the parables, for example, the exegete learns that parables usually explain a single point at issue and that they confront as well as explain. Parables call for the listener to get involved and respond personally to the truth that confronts him or her. Determining the genre of an entire book of the Bible is also essential for understanding a text. Biblical books fall into a number of literary genres: narrative, poetry, prophecy, wisdom, Gospel, letter, sermon, or apocalypse. If a text is contained in a narrative, then one knows to look for characters, plot, and dramatic action. If a text is contained in poetry, then one looks for varying kinds of repetition and the emotions being expressed: praise, thanksgiving, lament, trust. If the text is contained in apocalyptic literature, one studies to see how the symbols encourage faithfulness and hope through difficulty and suffering.

The next step in the process of exegesis is to study the historical, cultural, and sociological background of the text. Biblical interpreters must always keep in mind that they are reading an ancient set of writings from locations, languages, customs, and values that are vastly different than those of the interpreters themselves. Geography, political divisions, rulers, economic systems, philosophies, cultural and religious practices, social norms, and values—all must be studied to understand a text properly within its ancient context. For example, Paul says in 1 Corinthians that "'All things all lawful for me,' but not all things are beneficial" (1 Cor 6:12). A proper exegesis of this text would involve all of the things we have spoken about above. Exegesis would require a study of the city of Corinth in the first century. Corinth was a major port of call on the Mediterranean, midway between Rome and the great trading centers at the eastern end of the empire. Corinth was a cosmopolitan, multicultural, pluralistic, and morally corrupt city. So, it is not surprising that Paul had to address so many different social and moral issues in 1 Corinthians. The background study would not only examine the external setting of the text but also the internal issues of the transmission of the text (textual criticism), authorship, date, and occasion for the writing. In the case of the 1 Corinthians text above, proper exegesis would uncover the fact that 1 Corinthians was not the first letter Paul had written to the church, and the writing of 1 Corinthians touched off some sort of argument between Paul and the church that resulted in a "painful visit" and a harsh letter (2 Cor 10–13?) before finally coming to a peaceful resolution (2 Cor 1–9). Also, the study of Greco-Roman social values and practices helps to understand why Paul struggled to come up with a moral principle that preserved the gospel message of freedom while also helping the Corinthians understand their Christian responsibility toward others. Making sense, therefore, of a text like 1 Cor 6:12 cannot be done without a thorough study of the historical, cultural, and sociological context of Corinth and Paul's correspondence with the church in that city.

The final step in the process of exegesis is to take all of the information gleaned from the various steps and make some conclusions about the meaning of the text as a whole. The interpreter should identify the main themes and the subthemes. In doing so, the interpreter needs to ask what theological truths are being communicated. What is the text saying about God, humans, faith, sin, Christ, salvation, etc.? Once preachers have a good grasp of the meaning and theological implications of the text, then they are ready to prepare a sermon.

Basic Sermon Types

If preachers have done good work in the exegesis of a text, they have already made significant process toward preparing a biblical sermon. The structure or form of biblical sermons traditionally has fallen into three basic types: topical, textual, and expository.[10] The topical sermon begins with a topic or a subject and then enlists a biblical text or texts to explain the topic. The advantage of the topical sermon is that a single idea drives the message from the start. If a sermon is on the topic "Forgiveness," then supporting texts and points of the sermon will all explain, illustrate, or apply some aspect of forgiveness. The disadvantage of topical sermons is that preachers may choose topics more for what they want to say than what the Bible has to say. There is a tendency also to pull biblical words out of context or to use biblical texts in ways that the context does not support.

A second general type of sermon is the textual sermon. Unlike the topical sermon, the textual sermon begins with a biblical text and derives the form of the sermon directly from the structure of the text itself. Textual sermons may be either deductive or inductive. A deductive sermon moves from general truths to explanation and application. An inductive sermon moves from "evidence" toward general conclusions. Brief biblical texts with clearly expressed ideas make the best deductive, textual sermons. In the example below, notice that each of the points simply restate the main clauses in the same order of Prov 3:5-6, "Trust in the Lord with all your heart, and do not rely on your own insight. In all your ways acknowledge him, and he will make straight your paths." A textual sermon on Prov 3:5-6 might look like this:

1. Put all your trust in the Lord.

2. Do not depend on your own viewpoint.

3. Listen to God in everything you do and wherever you go.

4. God will show you the way.

Another example of a textual sermon on John 3:16 might look like this:

---

10. This sermon typology has a long history and is described in many of the classical sermon preparation textbooks, e.g., Broadus, *On Preparation and Delivery*, 54-61; Blackwood, *Preaching from the Bible*, 36-44. The narrative sermon is sometimes listed as a fourth type; however, it is more accurate to consider narrative sermons as subtypes of either the textual or expository types.

1. God loved the world.
2. God gave his only Son.
3. Whoever believes in Jesus receives eternal life.

A deductive, textual sermon is a good choice for an inexperienced preacher. If one selects a brief and clear text, sermon preparation is relatively simple and straightforward.

An inductive, textual sermon in narrative form also works well for those who are just beginning to preach. This kind of sermon should also cover a relatively brief and clear biblical narrative, e.g., a parable of Jesus, Jesus's encounter with an individual, an event in the book of Acts, moments in the life of an Old Testament character, etc. For example, a narrative textual sermon on the story of Zacchaeus (Luke 19:1–10) might look like this:

1. Description of the setting—city of Jericho. Jesus on his way to Jerusalem and the crucifixion. Crowds building in anticipation that Jesus would finally declare himself to be the Messiah, etc.

   Inductive point—People get excited about Jesus, but they often do not understand his true purpose.

2. Description of the main character—Zacchaeus was a notorious tax collector, etc.

   Inductive point—No matter who we are or what we have done, our lives can change the moment we turn to Jesus.

3. Description of the dramatic action—Zacchaeus climbing the tree. Jesus stopping and speaking to Zacchaeus. The reaction of the crowd.

   Inductive point—When we turn to Jesus, we find that Jesus has already been searching for us.

4. Description of the resolution—Zacchaeus's repentance and salvation. Jesus's pronouncement.

   Inductive point—Jesus's ultimate purpose is to find the lost and bring them back to himself.

Textual preaching, whether deductive or inductive, helps the preacher to stick to the biblical text and bring out the meaning for the hearers. The logic or the "flow" of thought is already contained in the text. All the preacher has to do is rethink and understand that flow of words and ideas and then explain them to the people. All too often, however, inexperienced preachers choose texts that are much too long and complex. It is not uncommon to hear a young preacher try to cover multiple paragraphs, an entire chapter, or even multiple chapters of Scripture in a single sermon. When this happens, the sermon usually becomes a tedious and incoherent cluster of ideas rather than a unified message. When preachers attempt to cover too much text, it is because they have not done the hard work of exegesis. Diligent exegesis forces preachers to focus on smaller, coherent units of thought and not get lost in a maze of words and ideas.

The third general type is the expository sermon. The word expository can be used in a very broad sense to refer to any kind of preaching or teaching that intends to *expose* the meaning of a text. In the more limited sense, expository describes a particular type of sermon designed to reveal the thesis or main idea of a biblical text and convert that idea into language and concepts that make sense to people in the present day. An expository sermon is designed especially to bridge the "hermeneutical arch" from the *then* to the *now* (see fig. 8.1).

Figure 8.1 The Hermeneutical Arch

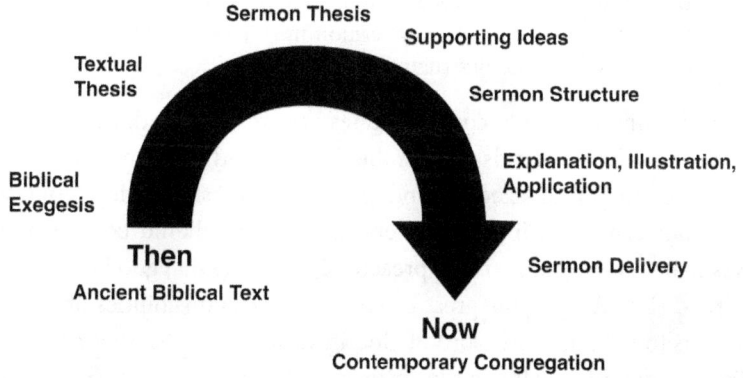

The heart of the expository sermon is the disclosure, through exegesis, of the main idea expressed in the text. Based on this main idea or "textual thesis," the expositor develops a single timeless statement or "sermon thesis" that can make the journey over the hermeneutical arch from the then to the now. Haddon Robinson argues that the single idea of the expository sermon is what gives the type its rhetorical strength: "Students of public speaking and preaching have argued for centuries that effective communication demands a single theme. . . . Terminology may vary—central idea, proposition, theme, thesis statement, main thought—but the concept is the same: an effective speech 'centers on one specific thing, a central idea.'"[11] Once this idea is discovered, the preacher then can reword and reorder the supporting ideas from the biblical text in ways that better communicate with a modern audience.

Like textual sermons, expository sermons can be either deductive or inductive, but the key to the expository sermon is that from beginning to end it is governed by a single, main idea. In a deductive, expository sermon, the main idea is stated, examined, illustrated, and applied through the logical flow of supporting points. In an inductive, expository sermon the posing of a series of questions or the examination of a narrative leads eventually to the conclusion of a single thesis. Broadus states that the primary characteristic that distinguishes an expository sermon from other kinds of biblical sermons is unity and order:

> What, then, is the prime requisite for effective expository preaching? The answer must be unity. Unity in a discourse is necessary to instruction, to conviction, and to persuasion. . . . But unity in an expository discourse is never the goal of many preachers. They conceive it as a mere series of disjointed remarks upon the successive verses. . . . An expository sermon may have, and must have, both unity and orderly structure.[12]

Preaching that truly communicates the word of God, therefore, is a difficult task that demands faith in the Bible, sound hermeneutical principles, thorough biblical exegesis, and knowledge and skill in developing and delivering sermons. Ministry leaders who preach should commit themselves to be life-long students of preaching, knowing that good preaching is a learned skill. Among the great privileges and responsibilities of ministry leaders is to proclaim the word of God in various ways, so that people will believe God, find new life in the Spirit, and follow Christ in serving others. An equal privilege and responsibility of ministry leaders is the providing of care for people through counsel and comfort.

---

11. Robinson, *Biblical Preaching*, 17.
12. Broadus, *On Preparation and Delivery*, 60.

9

Care as Counsel

SHIFTING OUR FOCUS FROM one sphere of ministry leadership to another, we must remember that all three spheres—proclamation, care, and guidance—are interdependent. Through proclamation, ministers are certainly caring for and guiding their people, and, without the proclamation of the word of God, the practices of care and guidance have no context and no clear purpose. The ministry of care extends the priestly work of the Good Shepherd through the under-shepherd work of ministry leaders. Jesus came to seek and to save the lost. He looked for the hurting and grieving, he challenged the prideful and powerful, and he gave his life for all.

Congregational leaders are listeners, not just speakers. When people need to sort out their personal struggles, they often seek out those from whom they hear a word from God. So ministry leaders need to be able to "switch hats" from getting attention to giving attention. Jesus made this switch well. Although his primary mission was to proclaim the kingdom of God, he responded quickly to people who came to him with personal crises or questions. Jesus listened carefully to their words, but he also listened to their hearts. When Nicodemus came to Jesus seeking theological answers, Jesus perceived that Nicodemus had a deeper crisis of faith. Jesus "cut to the chase" and addressed Nicodemus's need to believe in something beyond his own comprehension, to suspend his traditional perspective, and to surrender his self-righteousness in order to be born of the Spirit (John 3:1–16). On another occasion, when a young man came to Jesus inquiring about eternal life, Jesus listened carefully to his words and perceived that the man's struggle was not with knowledge but with faith. Being a "good" religious person and obeying the law came easy to the man, but he still did not have assurance of eternal life. There was an emptiness deep in his heart, so he came to Jesus. What Jesus told him went beyond anything he had anticipated:

> As he was setting out on a journey, a man ran up and knelt before him, and asked him, "Good Teacher, what must I do to inherit eternal life?" Jesus said to him, "Why do you call me good? No one is good but God alone. You know the commandments: 'You shall not murder; You shall not commit adultery; You shall not steal; You shall not bear false witness; You shall not defraud; Honor your father and mother.'" He said to him, "Teacher, I have kept all these since my youth." Jesus, looking at him, loved him and said, "You lack one thing; go, sell what you own, and give the money to the poor, and you will have treasure in heaven; then come, follow me." When he heard this, he was shocked and went away grieving, for he had many possessions. (Mark 10:17–22)

Jesus's counsel astounded the man, but that counsel was born of Jesus's love and his desire for the man to know the fullness of God's righteousness, not just the emptiness of being a rich "good" man.

Ministry Leaders as Counselors

People come to their ministry leaders with all manner of concerns, and, like Nicodemus and the rich young man, the issues they present often mask deeper struggles of faith and trust. Ministry leaders, however, do not have Jesus's power to see directly into people's minds and hearts. So, the role of ministry leaders is to point people to Jesus, the one who truly knows their hearts. It is not the ministry leader's job to "diagnose" the spiritual and emotional conditions of people, no matter how evident their problems may appear. It also is not the job of ministry leaders to be professional psychologists. Most ministry leaders do not have the education and training to be considered professional counselors. Although professional counselors, especially Christian professional counselors, can help people in ways similar to ministry leaders, their primary focus is on treating mental disorders or correcting dysfunctional behaviors. Professional counselors, whether faith-based or secular, typically have at least a master's degree in psychology and counseling. They have been supervised through hundreds of hours of counseling, and they have passed exams for state licensure in some specific area of counseling, e.g., marriage and family, depression, children's therapy, etc. Professional counselors are networked with resources in the medical community to help people cope with long-term psychological issues. They are trained to deal with neuroses (depression, anxiety, obsessive behaviors, phobias, anger management, etc.) and psychoses (breaks with reality, schizophrenia, bipolar disorder, hallucinations, etc.). No one would go to a ministry leader to set a broken bone or to remove a brain tumor (unless that leader was also a qualified physician); nor should one go to a ministry leader to treat bipolar disorder or schizophrenia. That said, ministry leaders have some significant advantages in helping their people that professional counselors do not. They can make a significant difference in their people's lives by the kind of counsel they *can* provide.

Unlike professional counselors, ministry leaders share congregational life with the people they counsel. Most any time and place, ministry leaders may find themselves with someone who seeks their counsel. Accessibility in informal settings is one of the major differences between ministry leaders and professional counselors. People already know and trust their ministry leaders, and they can approach them in various settings, e.g., in a hallway before worship, while cooking breakfast for a church gathering, or leaning against the hood of a truck in the church parking lot. Another major difference is that ministry leaders can *initiate* conversations of counsel. In their role as ministry leaders, they have implicit permission to approach their people in appropriate ways that professional counselors never would or could do. Before or after a worship service, Bible study, or prayer meeting, ministry leaders routinely may ask "How are you doing?," and the response often is about struggles with health, family, work, or grief. Telephone calls, visits to homes, dropping by places of business, scheduling a breakfast or lunch meeting—all of these and more are ways ministry leaders can take the initiative for counsel. A third major difference is that people come to their ministry leaders to get help from God. Professional counselors are not primarily spiritual guides, but ministry leaders are.

The work of ministry leaders as counselors, therefore, is to help people cope and grow spiritually through the crises of their lives. The word crisis comes from the Greek, meaning an "act of separating." Crises are decisive moments that separate what was from what is and will be. They are not always negative, but they are all challenging. Charles Gerkin defines a crisis as "a boundary situation between human aspirations and finite possibilities that become visible and demand attention."[1] Crises are moments when people's hopes and expectations meet the realities of life. In these moments,

---

1. Gerkin, *Crisis Experience*, 32.

ministry leaders may find greater access to the personal lives of their people. Some crises may be welcome moments that indicate successful progress in life. Cultures have developed "rites of passage," celebrations around the birth of a child, entering school, adolescence, graduations, and marriage. These decisive moments indicate growth, that one period of life has been completed and a new one has begun. They also can be bittersweet moments, for, alongside the joys, there can be longing for the past and anxiety about what is to come. In between these welcome moments, there are many other unwelcome crises with no celebratory rites. These kinds of crises bring confusion, worry, pain, and despair. Often these unwelcome crises involve some kind of loss, e.g., loss of property, health, security, relationship, or life itself. Whether in welcome or unwelcome crises, in informal or formal settings, the counsel of a faithful ministry leader can be of great help.

Brief Pastoral Counseling

Ministry leaders are busy people with many responsibilities for leading their people in the work of ministry. So, they usually have only a few hours in any week to devote to counseling. "Brief pastoral counseling" describes the kind of counseling that most ministry leaders are able to do well and that most people actually want. The word "brief" indicates that the number of counseling sessions is few and is geared to solving a particular problem, not providing long-term therapy. According to Howard Stone, "brief counseling methods help resolve people's problems faster than open-ended counseling. This more closely accommodates the desires of most counselees—rapidly resolving their troubles."[2] In brief counseling, the goal is to help a person in as few sessions as possible. One to three sessions is typical. The counselor's role is to listen to a person describe their problem, help them clarify their thoughts and feelings, explore alternative solutions, help them form goals, and then act on those goals. If at any point in the counseling process the counselor believes that the person needs more expert help than he or she can give, then they must *refer* the counselee to an appropriate professional counselor.

---

2. Stone, *Brief Pastoral Counseling*, 8.

Active Listening

Although most congregational leaders have not had professional training in counseling, there are some basic skills that all counselors need to know and be able to do. These are "active listening" skills, which include attending, clarifying, sorting, explaining, exploring, and deciding.

Attending to the Person

All effective counseling begins with attending. To attend means to focus completely on another person. The act of attending is itself a ministry of grace; freely giving someone undivided attention bestows value and significance. Jesus attended to people. He focused his attention on an undeserving woman of Samaria (John 4), on a notorious tax collector named Zacchaeus (Luke 19), and on a thief dying next to him on the cross (Luke 23). Jesus's disciples also learned from him the grace and the power of attending to people:

> One day Peter and John were going up to the temple at the hour of prayer, at three o'clock in the afternoon. And a man lame from birth was being carried in. . . . When he saw Peter and John about to go into the temple, he asked them for alms. Peter looked intently at him, as did John, and said, "Look at us." And he fixed his attention on them, expecting to receive something from them. But Peter said, "I have no silver or gold, but what I have I give you; in the name of Jesus Christ of Nazareth, stand up and walk." And he took him by the right hand and raised him up; and immediately his feet and ankles were made strong. Jumping up, he stood and began to walk, and he entered the temple with them, walking and leaping and praising God. (Acts 3:1–8)

When Peter focused his attention on the man, the man returned that attention in expectation and hope. This hope is not unlike the hope that arises in people's hearts when their counselors focus their attention on them.

To attend also means that *the other person is aware of the attention.* So attending is more than mental focus; it requires the involvement of the body, the eyes, and the ears. According to Carkhuff, attending is the precondition of helping. The basic principle of attending is reciprocity; people to whom we attend will, in turn, attend to us.[3] Physical attending

---

3. Carkhuff, *Art of Helping*, 55–78.

involves the positioning of the body by squaring, leaning, and establishing eye contact (see fig. 9.1).

Figure 9.1 Attending Posture[4]

Counselors must "square" their bodies, fully facing the other person without being turned to one side or the other. If sitting, the chairs may have to be moved in order to square up. The actual distance apart is not as important (although it should be a comfortable, noninvasive distance, e.g., two or more feet). Counselors also must have a slight body lean toward the counselee. The counselors' arms and legs should be uncrossed, which indicates an openness to the other person. Leaning away, turned to one side with arms or legs crossed, is a defensive posture and may communicate disapproval, rejection, or disinterest. Finally, eye contact conveys, above all, that one is paying attention to another. Eye contact is looking into the eyes of another, but it is not intense or unbroken staring. Lowering or even closing one's eyes briefly to think or talk is normal, but the general demeanor is that of giving continual attention to the other person with one's eyes. Eye contact also includes observing the broader picture of a person's behavior as she or he talks. Humans communicate verbally and nonverbally. We "hear" with our eyes as well as ears, and we are instantly comparing the content of the words with the contextual

---

4. Drawing by Esther Crawford, based on descriptions from Carkhuff, *Art of Helping*, 64–65.

cues of volume, tone, facial expressions, hand gestures, grooming, posture, movements of the body. By attending to all of these cues, counselors can make inferences about the counselee's emotional state. Counselors are particularly observant of *incongruities* between what people say and what they are communicating with their bodies. People often say things they do not really mean, because they are not ready to deal with what they are feeling. By attending carefully to words, appearance, and movements, counselors are ready to respond to what they are hearing and seeing.

Clarifying Content

The principle of reciprocity kicks in when counselees begin to respond positively to the attention of the counselor. Counselors are consciously and intentionally attending to all that people say and how they say it, but it is also the case that counselees too are observing the responses and behaviors of the counselor. Counselees want to know that they are being understood. When they feel that counselors are accurately hearing what they are saying, they begin to trust the counselor. The establishment of trust is the basis for the help that counselors provide. Counselors must first make sure they are clearly hearing what counselees are saying. Counselors want to make sure of the facts. They want to know who, what, when, where, and why.[5] So, they respond with brief summary statements of what they have heard the counselees say and then allow the counselees to affirm, correct, or reject the counselors' summary. The summary statements often take the following form: "I hear you saying _____" or "In other words, _____." Here is an example:

> **Counselee:** I have not slept in two days. We don't know where our son is. I called him on the phone and he answered, but he did not tell me anything. I talked to the dean of students at his university, but they have no way of tracking him down. I think he got overwhelmed with his school work and just left. He is probably staying with a friend.
>
> **Counselor's Response:** I hear you saying that you and your wife don't know where your son is and that you have not been able to sleep. You think he may have gotten overwhelmed with school and left, and you think he may be staying with a friend. Is that correct?

---

5. Carkhuff, *Art of Helping*, 100–101.

> **Counselee:** Yes! I don't know what to do! I am so worried about him.

The near word-for-word response of the counselor may seem strange or awkward, but in a real conversation the repetition communicates clearly that the counselee is being heard. Repeating the counselee's words back to her can be met with agreement or with correction and clarification. In the example of above, the counselee's response shows that the counselor's summary allowed the counselee to express more openly the depth of worry he was feeling. In doing so, the counselor has laid the foundation for the next step in the process.

Sorting Feelings

If a counselor is attending well and responding accurately to the content of what the counselee is presenting, it is likely that the emotions that accompany the information are coming to the surface. Emotions are nonrational; they are feelings, not thoughts. So, to be able to think about their feelings, people must "reflect" on them, and to reflect they must have a "mirror" (a counselor) to help them "see" the volume and tone of their voice, the wringing of their hands, the strong words they use, or the little laugh at something that isn't funny. Active listening by counselors now must move up a step from responding to content to responding to feelings. Their response to feelings often takes the following form: "You feel _____" or "You must be very _____."[6] Here is an example:

> **Counselee:** My wife and I are so worried about our son. I can't understand what he's thinking. Why doesn't he just come home? I don't know why he is doing this to us? We care so much about him, but I don't think he cares much about us!
>
> **Counselor's response:** You feel worried and confused and hurt. You must be a little upset with him too.
>
> **Counselee:** Upset? No, I am more than upset, I am angry! I am so mad at him, I could wring his neck!

The counselor in this example has simply reflected the feelings of what he or she heard and observed. By suggesting words to describe the counselee's feelings, the counselor has helped the man become more aware of the intense

---

6. Carkhuff, *Art of Helping*, 104–15.

anger that underlies his worry and confusion. Gaining awareness of his emotions is the beginning of gaining some control over himself in this situation. Knowing that he is angry does not locate his son, but it enables the man to work constructively for his son's return. Matching words to feelings is an important job for the counselor. To do so, counselors need a large stock of feeling words that span a spectrum from mild to intense (see table 9.1).

Table 9.1 Words for Clarifying Various Emotions

Basic Emotion	Mild	Medium	Intense
Happy	happy, feeling good, pleased, glad, content	delighted, elated, joyful	ecstatic, overjoyed, over the top, on cloud nine
Sad	sad, unhappy, down, blue, gloomy	despondent, dejected, depressed	miserable, sorrowful, wretched, desolate
Worried	worried, concerned, anxious, apprehensive, uneasy, dread	afraid, nervous, scared, troubled, alarmed	terrified, horrified, frightened, in a panic
Confused	confused, puzzled, baffled	mystified, muddled, mixed up	lost, bewildered
Angry	upset, irritated, annoyed, indignant	angry, heated, cross, incensed, infuriated	mad, furious, enraged, outraged, livid

Identifying and labeling feelings raises them from nonrational sensations to rational thoughts. When people can recognize their emotions and verbalize them (e.g., "I am angry," "I am miserable," "I am frightened," etc.), they are moving in the direction of making sense of themselves and their situation.

Explaining the Problem

People seek counseling because they are having difficulty dealing with their problems. A good bit of that difficulty is confusion. People lose their bearings in a sea of emotions. Counselors help people make sense of all they are feeling so that they can begin to work constructively toward a solution of the *real* problem. The fourth step in active listening is to lead the counselee to be able *to explain* their problem. An explanation connects an effect with a cause. At an appropriate moment in the process of listening and responding, the counselor needs to offer an explanation that the counselee may accept or reject. Either way, by moving toward explanation counselors encourage counselees to see a broader picture that will help them get their bearings and begin to deal with their problems. A typical counselor's response that ventures an explanation takes the following form: "You feel _____ *because* _____."[7] Here is an example:

> **Counselee:** I am so mad at my son! How can he do this to us? He just leaves school and goes who knows where without one word to us. We love him so much and would do anything for him, but he never wants our help, he always pushes us away.
>
> **Counselor's response:** You are so mad at your son *because* he never wants your help and pushes you away.
>
> **Counselee:** Well, yes. Why does he refuse to let us help him? When he was younger, we did so many things together. I was always helping him, and he always listened to me. But in these last couple of years, it's like he just won't let me in to his life. We helped him get into this fine university, and we helped him to decide on a good degree plan that will prepare him for a good job, and now he has thrown it all away. Sometimes I think he resents our help and just wants to live as if we don't exist.
>
> **Counselor's response:** You must be frustrated and hurt, *because* you used to be able to help your son, but now that he is older he does not want your help.
>
> **Counselee:** Hmm. I guess I should not be surprised. When I was his age I wanted to get as far away from my parents as could get. So, I went off and joined the army. I never thought how my parents must have felt when I took off. I just needed to get some distance and find out who I was and what I wanted to do. Maybe my son just feels the same way.

The connecting of feeling with a cause in the responses of the counselor did not give full explanations of the man's problem, but the responses moved him in the direction of thinking about a cause for his son's actions. The breakthrough came when the man began to realize why his son may be acting the way he is. The real problem is that the parents and their son have moved into a new stage of life, and their relationship must change

---

7. Carkhuff, *Art of Helping*, 117–23.

and grow. Now the son must begin finding his own way and making his own decisions, and the parents need to learn how to love him but also give him space and freedom.

In the first four steps of active listening, counselors focus entirely on getting the counselees to think more clearly about their situation. When counselees begin to understand how their own behavior has given rise to their problem, they are beginning to find a way forward. It is at this point that ministry leaders can begin to move from active listening to more active guiding.

Exploring Options

When people understand a problem, then they can work toward a solution. That work involves thinking through various options. The counselor might simply say something like this: "You seem to have a good grasp of the problem now; how do you think you might go about solving it?" In the example above of the man with the missing son, the counselor might also bring into the conversation Jesus's parable of the lost or "prodigal" son in Luke 15. The counselor might even assign the text as "homework" for reading and study between one session and the next. It is certainly appropriate for ministry leaders to refer to Scripture at this stage in the counseling process, but it is important not to invoke Scripture before the counselor has helped the counselee understand his or her emotions and gain some sense of the real problem. The ministry leader is often able to relate a person's problem to some helpful aspect of the biblical story. In the case of the example above, by reading the story of the lost son, the man might gain insight for what he is to do now. The father in the story let his son go and had to wait for him to return. When the son did return, the father welcomed him with open arms and threw a party. One alternative, therefore, may be simply to calm down and wait. If the parents can call their son, they might just let him know that they understand that he needs time, and that they know he will find his way. One other insight the man may gain from the story of the lost son is that God also suffers when his people go away from him. Suffering is often the occasion for spiritual growth and gaining insight into the nature of God and God's love for us.

PART FOUR: THE PRACTICES OF MINISTRY LEADERSHIP

Deciding on a Course of Action

The process of brief counseling concludes when the counselee decides on a direction to take to overcome or at least cope with the problem. At this point, it is the counselor's job to encourage and release the counselee to put his or her plan into action. Since counseling by ministry leaders is brief, it does not (or should not) allow for counselees to become dependent on the counselor or the counseling. In fact, the purpose of brief counseling is to help people get back on their feet to live their own lives. By keeping the number and length of counseling sessions brief, counselors help counselees move on with their lives.

10

Care as Comfort

THE SECOND ASPECT OF the practice of care is providing comfort to people who are suffering illness or grief. Some of the counseling skills described in the previous chapter, especially the skills of attending, are also employed by ministry leaders when they give comfort to others; however, the object of comfort is not the same as counsel. When comforting people in the throes of illness or grief, ministry leaders are not in "problem-solving" mode. The word comfort comes from the Latin word *confortare*, which means "to strengthen." People who are ill or grieving are in a weakened state, and they need spiritual and emotional support. They need to be lifted up through the prayers of the congregation and the presence of ministry leaders. The "ministry of presence" is perhaps the single most effective aspect of giving comfort to another. People draw strength from the presence of others, especially from those whom they trust and respect as their spiritual leaders. Job's friends may not have known the right things to say, but they did know that they had to go and be present with Job in his suffering.

> Now when Job's three friends heard of all these troubles that had come upon him, each of them set out from his home—Eliphaz the Temanite, Bildad the Shuhite, and Zophar the Naamathite. They met together to go and console and comfort him. When they saw him from a distance, they did not recognize him, and they raised their voices and wept aloud; they tore their robes and threw dust in the air upon their heads. They sat with him on the ground seven days and seven nights, and no one spoke a word to him, for they saw that his suffering was very great. (Job 2:11–13)

Like Job's friends, congregational leaders need to go and "suffer with" their people. The ministry of presence is more than just being in the room; it is actually entering into the suffering of another. It would be shocking today for ministry leaders to go to someone's home weeping loudly, tearing their clothes, and throwing dust on their heads, but, within our more reserved twenty-first-century Western culture, the quiet presence of a spiritual leader communicates the same thing: "I am here to suffer with you." More importantly, the presence of ministry leaders communicates that *God is also present* and suffering with the person. Given the significance and strength of the comfort provided by ministry leaders, they need to think through their own understanding of suffering and death.

Thinking Theologically about Suffering

All Christians who think about their faith are thinking theologically. "Theology is a seeking after understanding—a process of thinking about life in the light of the faith that Christians engage in because of their calling."[1] In this definition by Stone and Duke, notice the connection of faith and life. When ministry leaders reach out to provide comfort to those who are suffering pain or grieving death, faith is encountering life in its most challenging form, and it can be disorienting. Pain and loss bring confusion and loss of meaning. The old ways of making sense of the world no longer work. If ministry leaders are to bring real comfort to people and not just react in the moment, they need to think long and hard about how to make sense of suffering and death. It is not that they need to come up with a bunch of theological explanations to satisfy hurting people; it is that ministry leaders need a sound Christian theology of suffering and death *for themselves*.

Ministry leaders are those who bring hope through proclaiming the good news of the gospel. They are used to telling people that God loves them and has a wonderful life for them if they will believe and trust in God. So it is difficult for these leaders to know what to say when life is not so wonderful. Ministry leaders can be at a loss for words in the presence of those who are overcome with physical or emotional pain. Some spiritual leaders avoid being around suffering altogether. Others try to "cheer up" suffering people. A few come up with absurd explanations for tragedy. Many years ago, I myself attended the funeral of a young girl tragically killed in a car accident. The pastor tried to offer comfort by saying, "God wanted your child to be with him, so he reached down and took her to heaven." This appalling

---

1. Stone and Duke, *How to Think Theologically*, 2–3.

statement not only failed to provide comfort but also revealed a profound lack of understanding of the situation and of God.

So what does a healthy Christian theology of suffering and death look like? In order to think theologically about suffering, people have to think about both their life situations and about their beliefs about God. A common life situation of those who suffer is isolation and loneliness. When people are in pain, their ability to interact with others is diminished. An illness may isolate them physically in their home or in a hospital room, and it may separate them mentally and emotionally within their own weakness and misery. Death separates the survivors from one who brought meaning and purpose to their lives. Death also separates the grieving from others who cannot fully understand that grief. The isolation of illness or death can produce deep loneliness or even a sense of abandonment. A person may even feel that God is punishing them. In the laments of the Psalms, we can hear the turmoil that illness brings:

> O Lord, do not rebuke me in your anger
> > or discipline me in your wrath.
> Be gracious to me, O Lord, for I am languishing;
> > O Lord, heal me, for my bones are shaking with terror.
> My soul also is struck with terror,
> > while you, O Lord—how long?
>
> Turn, O Lord, save my life;
> > deliver me for the sake of your steadfast love.
> For in death there is no remembrance of you;
> > in Sheol who can give you praise?
>
> I am weary with my moaning;
> > every night I flood my bed with tears;
> > I drench my couch with my weeping.
> My eyes waste away because of grief;
> > they grow weak because of all my foes.
>
> Depart from me, all you workers of evil,
> > for the Lord has heard the sound of my weeping.
> The Lord has heard my supplication;

> the LORD accepts my prayer.
> All my enemies shall be ashamed and struck with terror;
> they shall turn back and in a moment be put to shame. (Ps 6)

The lament psalms express pain, sorrow, cries for mercy, and cries for healing. It is remarkable that the Bible contains songs that give words to the painful emotions people experience. The biblical writers were not afraid to express the unvarnished truth of human feelings. Jesus himself found in the Psalms the words to express what he was feeling. Dying on the cross, Jesus uttered the first verse of Ps 22, "My God, my God, why have you forsaken me?" Although the opening of Ps 22 speaks of God's abandonment, the latter verses of the psalm proceed to affirm the help and presence of God:

> You who fear the LORD, praise him!
> All you offspring of Jacob, glorify him;
> stand in awe of him, all you offspring of Israel!
> For he did not despise or abhor
> the affliction of the afflicted;
> he did not hide his face from me
> but heard when I cried to him. (Ps 22:23-24)

Ministry leaders help people walk through the same journey expressed in the lament psalms, the journey from isolation to consolation, from feeling that God is distant to knowing that God is near. When we turn to the larger biblical story, we can better understand why this journey is necessary and where the journey ends. The Bible reveals God to be the good Creator of a good creation, but that creation has been corrupted by human sin. We now live in a fallen world under the curse of suffering and death, but God has never stopped working to restore the creation from the curse. God has long suffered throughout the history of Israel down to the present moment, and he has entered directly into this world of human suffering in the incarnation of Jesus. God has overcome sin, suffering, and death through Jesus Christ. He loves us so much that, in Christ, he suffered for us even to the point of death on the cross.

The kingdom of God has arrived in Jesus, but God's work of restoration is still in process. We still suffer and die in this world, but our hope is in the God who knows and understands our suffering. God cares deeply for us and is leading us to the kingdom in which he "will wipe every tear from their eyes" (Rev 21:4). Suffering and death will be overcome in the resurrection to eternal life. In the present, we who comprise the body of Christ complete his sufferings: "I am now rejoicing in my sufferings for your sake, and in my flesh I am completing what is lacking in Christ's afflictions for the sake of his body, that is, the church" (Col 1:24). As we wait for Christ's return, we comfort one another with the hope that awaits us: "And after you have suffered for a little while, the God of all grace, who has called you to his eternal glory in Christ, will himself restore, support, strengthen, and establish you" (1 Pet 5:10).

Christians cannot escape suffering in the present moment, but we can transform it by finding meaning and hope in the new life beyond the suffering. Through suffering, we can grow as Christians and be better able to understand and help others who suffer. In suffering we come face to face with our weakness and our mortality. The illusion of self-sufficiency and independence are stripped away. We come to know that our life is fully in God's hands, and only he can sustain it and renew it. Of all people, Christians can be present with others in their suffering, because they know that suffering and death are the realities of this present life. They also know that suffering and death are not the final word.

Indeed, God heals in this present life, and we certainly can pray for healing. All healing is from God who created our bodies to heal themselves and provides physicians to assist the healing process. Miraculous healing, or healing that we cannot explain, is something God does as God chooses. Jesus healed people and raised the dead, but he did not heal everyone then and he does not heal everyone now. Jesus's miracles were strategic actions that gave credence to his authority and his message of the good news of the kingdom. In John 9, Jesus and his disciples come upon a man born blind. The disciples' question reveals the common theology of the day: "His disciples asked him, 'Rabbi, who sinned, this man or his parents, that he was born blind?'" (John 9:2). The disciples, along with almost everyone else, believed that suffering was caused by the direct punishment of God for some specific sin. To be blind from birth presented a challenge to this theological view. Jesus's response is even more challenging: "Neither this man nor his parents sinned; he was born blind so that God's works might be revealed in him" (John 9:3). Jesus challenges the whole idea that individual suffering is divine retribution for personal sins. He indicates that the man's blindness is not the *result of* God's work but the *occasion for* God to work. God is not against us; God is for us. Our individual suffering is one small part of the suffering of the whole creation, but God is working in and through the creation to set things right. God is not imposing suffering but working to relieve it. So Jesus proceeds to give the man sight, something only the Creator could do.

Yet, even Jesus's healings in the first century were temporary. The man born blind eventually died. Lazarus also died, as did everyone else Jesus healed or raised from the dead. The ultimate healing of Jesus is not of our perishable bodies but of the resurrection of our imperishable bodies in the kingdom of God (1 Cor 15:42–44). So the role of ministry leaders is not to run from suffering, to fix suffering, or to explain suffering. Our role is to enter into the suffering of others with the comfort of the good God who understands suffering and will eventually bring it to an end in this life or in the life to come. The ultimate comfort in suffering comes from the Holy Spirit who comes alongside us in our pain and intercedes with the Spirit's own groanings to the Father:

> We know that the whole creation has been groaning in labor pains until now; and not only the creation, but we ourselves, who have the first fruits of the Spirit, groan inwardly while we wait for adoption, the redemption of our bodies. For in hope we were saved. Now hope that is seen is not hope. For who hopes for what is seen? But if we hope for what we do not see, we wait for it with patience. Likewise the Spirit helps us in our weakness; for we do not know how to pray as we ought, but that very Spirit intercedes with sighs [groanings] too deep for words. And God, who searches the heart, knows what is the mind of the Spirit, because the Spirit intercedes for the saints according to the will of God. (Rom 8:22–26)

Thinking theologically about suffering and death helps ministry leaders to enter the suffering of others with a perspective of both realism and hope. Ministry leaders are realistic in that they know that suffering and death are a fact of life in this world. No one escapes it. Yet, suffering and death were not God's original intention. He has been working throughout history to bring suffering and death to an end. In the present moment, we know that God knows and cares what we are going through. God suffers with us. He is present and is ultimately bringing us all to the kingdom where all suffering shall end.

Comforting the Sick

It is not always clear what a ministry leader is supposed to do when hearing of someone in their congregation who is ill or who has died. Ministers have to enter uncomfortable situations where they may feel awkward or even unwelcome in order to see the person who needs their comfort. They may have to drive through unfamiliar neighborhoods and visit different hospitals, and they may have to interact with unfamiliar medical personnel and family members who are not immediately receptive. When all realize, however, who the ministry leader is and why he or she has come, the visit is almost always appreciated. In other words, ministry leaders, especially those serving in new ministry settings, sometimes have to go through a gauntlet of obstacles to make it to the side of one who is hurting, but enduring the ordeal is worth it and important.

The more that ministry leaders can learn about the process of going to be with a person in their home or in the hospital or being present in the time of death, the less intimidating these situations become. With increasing confidence, the ministry leader can provide more effective comfort. In making any visit, there are five basic steps: call, go, enter, listen, and leave.

Call

Congregational leaders waste time and effort when they do not know where they are going or the situation they are walking into. Often, the person is not at home, does not want a visitor at the moment, or has already been released from the hospital. So, calling ahead is always a smart idea. When going to see someone in their home, it is always best to call and set up an appointment, and when going to the hospital it is always best to call the hospital for information. Very few people like drop-in visits in their homes from their ministry leaders, especially when the person is sick. Calling ahead shows sensitivity and consideration. The exceptions to calling ahead are when the situation is an emergency or in the event of a death. When ministry leaders get a call that someone has had some sort of emergency (injury, heart attack, etc.), then they should just go and try to see the person immediately. In the event of a death, ministry leaders should drop everything and go to the home or the hospital. Otherwise, calling ahead is the best procedure. Hospital receptionists can provide the patient's room number (make sure you know the patient's full name) and can give directions to the location in the hospital, the location of elevators, and even the best place to park. The patient information receptionist can also explain any safety protocols for visitors. Some hospitals require visitors to check in and wear a color-coded wrist band. Some hospitals take a photograph and create an adhesive visitor label to be worn on one's shirt. One thing the patient information receptionist cannot tell you is anything about the medical condition of the patient. At most, the receptionist can transfer the call to the nurses' station on the floor of the patient. Someone at the nurses' station usually can tell ministry leaders if there are any visiting restrictions, how to proceed through control doors, and whether there are any isolation protocols like wearing protective masks, gloves, and gowns.

Other than the patient information receptionist or the nurses' station, the best source of information is often the chaplain's office in the hospital. Many hospitals have full-time chaplains, and almost all have part-time or voluntary chaplains. Chaplains can be of great help to ministry leaders. A chaplain is a religious leader who is assigned to work in an institution rather than a congregation. Chaplains serve in the military, in hospitals, with first responders, in businesses, and in many other settings. The work of chaplains includes ministering in crisis situations, leading worship services in institutional chapels, administering sacraments or ordinances, providing spiritual counsel and prayer for both patients and staff personnel, helping with ethical decision-making, conducting funeral services, and coordinating care of patients with community ministry leaders.[2] Chaplains are required to work with people of all religious traditions or of no religious tradition. They are not to push their own faith on others but help patients find comfort in their own forms of spirituality. It is wise for ministry leaders to get to know local chaplains. Most chaplains can help congregational leaders get oriented to surgery waiting rooms and hospital procedures, and can provide identification badges and parking permits to make entering the hospital easier and even to save some money if parking is not free.

Go

An old adage of ministry leaders is "When in doubt, go!" Once one has gathered as much information as possible by calling ahead, then one should just go. No matter what qualms one may be feeling, there are few situations in which one would regret going to be with someone in need.

2. K. Smith, "Chaplain/Chaplaincy."

In fact, the ministry leader and the person in need both benefit from the visit. Nothing is as rewarding in Christian ministry than the knowledge of having helped someone in her or his time of need. Another old adage of ministry is "The hardest door to get through is your own." Some ministry leaders are glued to their desk chairs by the comfort and safety of their offices. Getting up and getting out the door may take all the effort one can muster, but it has to be done. If, for some reason, it is not possible to make a visit in person, then calling the person on the phone or sending someone else can still provide comfort. Remember, however, that the actual presence of ministry leaders in the hour of need is what provides the most comfort for their people and what they remember most.

Enter

When a ministry leader goes to see someone, there comes the moment of actually entering the house or the hospital room. Immediately prior to entering, one should say a brief prayer for the visit and the person, asking God to be present and to guide the conversation. Nothing prepares a ministry leader more effectively than prayers confessing his or her limitations, acknowledging God's presence, and asking for his help. Paul was absolutely correct that with prayer comes "the peace that passes understanding" (Phil 4:7). Along with cleansing the heart through prayer, ministry leaders need to clean their hands. Outside of every hospital room today, there is a hand sanitizing dispenser and it is required to be used prior to entering a room and upon exiting a room. When visiting someone in their home, ministry leaders should have hand sanitizer in the car or in a pocket or purse, and they should be careful to clean hands before entering and upon exiting. Also, prior to entering a hospital room, it is always good to stop at the nurses' station and make sure it is a good time to visit. Nurses may give instructions to wait a few minutes for some reason, or they may provide a protective gown, mask, or gloves if necessary. Usually, however, the nurse says just to go on in.

Upon entering the room, knock on the door, whether it is open or closed, and listen for a response. Many times the patient can't hear the knock. If there is no response, then slowly open the door and voice a greeting, e.g., "Hello, it's Pastor Bill." While entering, quickly look around the room and assess the situation. Is the patient awake or asleep? Is he or she in obvious pain or emotional stress? Are family members in the room? Are doctors or nurses tending to the person? If there is any sense that this is not a good moment, then one should ask, "Is this a good time for a visit? Should I wait outside or come back later?" A doctor or nurse will quickly let you know what they want you to do. A family member or friend may not know what to say, however. So you have to make a judgment about how this visit should go. If there is more than one person visiting with the patient, then your visit should be very short with a promise to come back later. If there is only one person with the patient, particularly a spouse or close relative, then a normal visit may be in order. If the patient is alone and asleep, then it is best to leave a business card with a handwritten note, e.g., "Mary, I came by to see you, but you were asleep (or out of the room for a test, etc.). I'll come again later. You are in my prayers. Pastor Maddie." If doctors or nurses are in the room, stay out of their way. They are in the room to tend to the patient, not to interact with you. The presence of ministry leaders is important, but, when they enter the hospital, they are on the turf of the medical staff, and they dictate how things go in the hospital. Most of the time, hospital staff are very receptive to ministry leaders, because they appreciate the fact that the patient has spiritual as well as physical needs.

Listen

Everything to this point has been leading up to the actual visit with the person. The primary goal of the visit is to *listen*, not to talk. Listening begins with getting in a good position to attend to the person. In a home, sitting in a chair near the person or together at a table are best. In a hospital room, it is best to pull a chair near the bed, if possible. Try to get close to their eye level and establish good eye contact. If one or two others are in the room and no chair is available near the patient, then just make the best of standing within the person's field of vision. Start the conversation with a greeting, but keep comments to a minimum. The purpose of the visit is to let the person speak and to listen to what she has to say. Remember that the primary comfort ministry leaders provide is their presence. It is not the time to give advice, to tell personal stories, or to ask a bunch of invasive questions. It is common for congregational leaders to be uncomfortable with silence, but a visit to a suffering or grieving person is not the time to talk much.

Other important aspects of listening include the length of the visit, the need for empathy, and maintaining confidentiality.[3] The length of the visit tends to follow how much the person wants to talk. Most ill or grieving people have little that they feel like sharing, so this means that visits should be brief. It is not unusual for a hospital visit to be only five minutes. Visits of more than thirty minutes should be avoided, unless the visit is for some sort of an event like surgery or the birth of a baby. In that case, a ministry leader should stay with a family member until the end of the event (e.g., the doctor reports the surgery is over and successful, or the baby has been born and is healthy). If there is an unexpected crisis stemming from a surgery or birth, then one should to stay as long as needed.

Another aspect of listening is the need for empathy. Empathy is the ability to understand or sense another person's feelings. Empathy is produced by observation and imagination. A ministry leader needs to observe carefully what a person says, how she says it, and the look on her face to gain insight into what the person is feeling. Ministry leaders also need to imagine how they themselves would feel in the same situation. Imagination is helped by asking oneself questions: "How would I feel if I just found out I had cancer?" or "How would I feel if it was my mother who just died?" Sometimes empathy can become sympathy, which means not only understanding but also *sharing* the person's feelings. Ministry leaders sometimes are themselves moved emotionally by the suffering of others, and that's okay. When Jesus was about to raise Lazarus from the dead, he still wept upon seeing the grief of his friends:

> When Mary came where Jesus was and saw him, she knelt at his feet and said to him, "Lord, if you had been here, my brother would not have died." When Jesus saw her weeping, and the Jews who came with her also weeping, he was greatly disturbed in spirit and deeply moved. He said, "Where have you laid him?" They said to him, "Lord, come and see." Jesus began to weep. (John 11:32–35)

Ministry leaders must be careful not to let their feelings interfere with the care they are trying to provide for others, but, when others know that their leaders are suffering with them, they may find great comfort in that alone. There is much truth in the old proverb "A sorrow shared is a sorrow halved."

The final aspect of listening is the need to maintain confidentiality. Ministry leaders have a great responsibility to keep personal information private. The Health Insurance Portability and Accountability Act of 1996

---

3. Riecke, *How to Talk*, 52–67.

(HIPAA) protects the rights of patients to keep their medical records private unless a patient gives permission to release those records. Sometimes ministry leaders talk openly about the medical conditions of their people in prayer meetings or other settings. There is absolutely no need to tell others about the specific medical issues of someone. It is the person's news to tell, not the ministry leader's. If there is a need to say something, then ask permission of the patient, e.g., "We are going to be praying for you tonight at church; I will not say anything about your condition, unless you want me to do so. What would you prefer?" The need for privacy applies not only to medical conditions but also to most things a person says to a ministry leader in confidence. All caregivers are obligated to report information about child abuse or sexual assault to proper authorities, but, in general, personal information shared with a ministry leader should be kept in confidence.

Leave

As much as ministry leaders need to go and be present with persons who are suffering or grieving, they also must be ready to leave after an appropriate amount of time. Some ministers can be insensitive to the circumstances of a person who is suffering. Personal interaction for one who is sick or grieving is very tiring, especially when one is trying to be cordial and nice to a ministry leader. Short visits, like short sermons, are almost always well received. An important question is whether to offer to say a prayer upon leaving. It is almost always appropriate to offer to say a prayer; however, some people will indicate that they are not comfortable with a prayer or they just don't want it. Leaders need to respect the patient's wishes and never insist on voicing a prayer for someone who does not want it. When a prayer is welcomed, it should be a brief acknowledgment of God's presence and love, along with a request for comfort, e.g., "Dear Lord, we know that you are here with Mary and that you love her very much. Help her now with your comfort and strength . . ." Following the prayer, it is time to leave. The ministry leader's job is done for the moment, and it is time to leave the person in God's hands.

Comforting the Grieving

Ministry leaders need to be present with their people in all kinds of suffering, and no more so than in the time of death. Death is an overwhelming event of loss. A person's beloved family member or dear friend is gone, and, with the loss of that life, a vital piece of the surviving person's identity and purpose is also lost. Death threatens to swallow all meaning and hope. Ministry leaders bring the hope of Christ and the resurrection into this moment of profound loss. They also bring with them an understanding of the experience of grief. Grief describes the mental and emotional suffering brought on by death. Grief is complex. It is not a single feeling or a momentary event. It is an experience or a process that one passes through. According to Colin Parkes, "grief is a process through which people pass and that, in doing so, most tend to move from a state of relative disorientation and distress to one of growing understanding and acceptance of the loss."[4] There are a number of ways that the stages of grief have been described, most notably the five stages described by Elisabeth Kübler-Ross in her classic book *On Death and Dying*: denial, anger, bargaining, depression, and acceptance. Kübler-Ross's stages apply more to those who are facing their own terminal illness rather than to those who are grieving after the death of a loved one.

A better description of grief experienced by a close relative or friend of a deceased person is Parkes's four-phase description: numbness, pining, disorganization, and acceptance.[5] The news of terminal illness or sudden death may bring on numbness and disbelief, which characterize the first phase of the grieving process. As grief progresses, people may experience pining or painful yearning or longing for the deceased. Pining can then be followed by disorganization and aimlessness. With the death of a loved one, structures of the old life collapse. Wandering through the rubble of this collapse may bring about depression and despair. Only as people develop new routines and begin to focus thoughts and energy on the present and future do they enter the fourth phase of acceptance, in which they reorganize their lives and begin to recover.[6] Although, the description of the phases indicates a sequential progression, in reality the experience of grief is not so linear. Grief can be more chaotic and disordered than the description suggests. The length and severity of grieving process depends on many variables, but most influential are the closeness and depth of the relationship between the bereaved person and the deceased. Ministry leaders play an important role

---

4. Parkes, quoted in Switzer, "Grief and Loss," 472.
5. Switzer, "Grief and Loss," 473.
6. Switzer, "Grief and Loss," 473.

in helping people through the grieving process by the initial care they give at the time of death and the conduct of the funeral service.

The Moment of Death and the Funeral

Upon notification of a death, ministry leaders should go immediately to be with the person closest to the deceased (spouse, parent, or adult child). Gentle greetings, light hugs, and soft words are in order, e.g., "Linda, I am so sorry for you" or "John, I have no words, we are all hurting for you." In this stage, the ministry of presence and quiet listening with little comment are the best comfort ministry leaders can provide. They may also need to assist with calling the police, the funeral home, or both, if the family has not yet made these calls. The hours and days immediately after a death are also the time to help people prepare for the funeral service. The ministry leader can be of valuable assistance in working with the funeral home. A few days after the death, ministry leaders usually schedule a meeting with the family to gain information for the funeral service and funeral sermon. This meeting also can be an important moment of helping the family share fond memories of good things about their loved one's life and personality. It is very appropriate to bring a pad of paper and take careful notes on what the family says. By doing so, family members can be even more motivated to share memories, because they see that the ministry leader is really interested in what they are saying. Ministry leaders should ask questions that pertain to the funeral service, but be careful not to ask questions that are too invasive. Questions like "What are some of your good memories of John?" or "What are some character traits that come to mind when you think about John?" are appropriate. It is also appropriate to ask about favorite Scriptures, hymns, or special desires for the funeral service. One of the most helpful things to request is to see the deceased's Bible. Some people store in their Bibles a wealth of personal reflections on Scripture texts, sermon quotes, or notations about special moments in life.

Funeral services may be conducted within a few days or delayed for several weeks if the situation dictates. They may be conducted in a church building, a funeral home, or at the graveside. Some families may have no service of remembrance at all. Having a funeral service of some kind is important for several reasons. Most importantly, funerals help people move through the process of grief. Funerals bring a sense of reality to what may feel like a dream. The gathering of family and friends in a solemn public ceremony helps to honor the deceased and comfort those who mourn. Funerals also are times to reaffirm faith and hope in the promises of God and the work of Christ, but the purpose is not to evangelize the lost. Certainly, if unbelievers come to faith through the service, it is a welcome outcome, but the primary spiritual purpose is to remind those who are grieving that God is present, that God understands their suffering, and that God will bring the ultimate victory over death. The funeral service itself should be dignified but not elaborate, and it should not be lengthy. Forty-five minutes is plenty of time. Graveside services should be no more than fifteen to twenty minutes. A typical order of service for a funeral might look something like the following:

    Organ or piano prelude

    Greeting

    Scripture reading(s)

    Prayer

    Hymn/solo

    Obituary

    Eulogy

    Hymn

    Solo

    Sermon

    Hymn/solo

    Final viewing

    Procession to the graveside

The service does not have to have all of the elements listed above, but the order of elements is fairly standard.

    Christian funeral services should be bathed in Scripture. As we have seen, the biblical story forms the ultimate context for all of life and ministry, so it also forms the context of the funeral service. Many texts of Scripture speak of the hope of consolation and resurrection. Ministry leaders do well by beginning a funeral service with a greeting and readings of biblical texts, for example:

PART FOUR: THE PRACTICES OF MINISTRY LEADERSHIP

Greeting

On behalf of the family of John Doe, I welcome all of you, his dear friends, to this service of remembrance. Our great help and comfort comes from the word of God.

Scripture Readings

Blessed be the God and Father of our Lord Jesus Christ, the Father of mercies and the God of all consolation, who consoles us in all our affliction. (2 Cor 1:3-4)

[Jesus said] Do not let your hearts be troubled. Believe in God, believe also in me. In my Father's house there are many dwelling places. If it were not so, would I have told you that I go to prepare a place for you? And if I go and prepare a place for you, I will come again and will take you to myself, so that where I am, there you may be also. (John 14:1-3)

What will separate us from the love of Christ? Will hardship, or distress, or persecution, or famine, or nakedness, or peril, or sword? . . . No, in all these things we are more than conquerors through him who loved us. For I am convinced that neither death, nor life, nor angels, nor rulers, nor things present, nor things to come, nor powers, nor height, nor depth, nor anything else in all creation, will be able to separate us from the love of God in Christ Jesus our Lord. (Rom 8:35, 37-39)

For since we believe that Jesus died and rose again, even so, through Jesus, God will bring with him those who have died. For this we declare to you by the word of the Lord, that we who are alive, who are left until the coming of the Lord, will by no means precede those who have died. For the Lord himself, with a cry of command, with the archangel's call and with the sound of God's trumpet, will descend from heaven, and the dead in Christ will rise first. Then we who are alive, who are left, will be caught up in the clouds together with them to meet the Lord in the air; and so we will be with the Lord forever. Therefore encourage one another with these words. (1 Thess 4:14-18)

Other Scripture texts that may be read at the beginning or anytime during the service: Ps 23, 46; Job 19:25-27; Eccl 3:1-4; Isa 4:28-31; Matt 11:28-30; Rev 21:1-7; John 3:16, 11:25-26.

The greeting and Scripture readings are often followed by a prayer of invocation, which includes thanksgiving for God's presence, request for

God's comfort for those in attendance, and thanksgiving for the deceased. In most funerals in churches or chapels, two or three meditative instrumental music pieces, congregational hymns, or inspirational solos are interspersed between the spoken elements of the service.

The reading of an obituary, the giving of a eulogy, or both may come next in the service. An obituary is simply a description of the basic facts of the deceased's life. Dates of birth and death, marriage, employment, achievements, and a list of survivors are the usual components of an obituary. Some ministry leaders use selected verses from Eccl 3:1–8 to guide the obituary, to add dignity and gravitas, and to communicate a sense of divine providence:

> The book of Ecclesiastes says, "For everything there is a season, and a time for every matter under heaven."
>
> The Scripture says there is a time to be born and a time to die.
>
> John Doe was born February 21, 1956, and he died April 22, 2020. He was sixty-four years old.
>
> The Scripture says there is a time to plant.
>
> John Doe planted his life in this community and built houses all over this area.
>
> He retired recently after forty years of hard work.
>
> The Scripture says there is a time to embrace.
>
> John Doe embraced and married Mary Smith Doe on June 15, 1977.
>
> The Scripture says there is a time to mourn.
>
> John Doe is mourned by his wife Mary, daughter Jane, son Bob, three brothers, two sisters, and five grandchildren.

In a eulogy, a close friend or family member shares fond memories of the deceased, tells a brief story, reads a poem, or simply describes the deceased's good qualities. Deep emotions and humor often characterize the eulogy. Not every funeral has a eulogy, so the funeral sermon often combines elements of eulogy along with reflection on the Scripture. The funeral sermon should be very brief compared to sermons in regular worship services. Five to ten minutes is long enough. Funeral sermons of thirty or more minutes are not well received and can be exhausting for family members who are already tired and stressed by the events of the past few days. In the words of a wise pastor, funerals sermons should "be biblical, be personal, and be brief."[7] All of the Scripture texts above can be the basis of a good funeral sermon, along with many other possibilities. Over time, experienced ministry leaders develop a number of standard funeral sermons that they have ready at hand, since deaths are unexpected and there is little time for preparation. Even if the sermon has been preached many times, it can always be renewed and personalized to each new situation. Funeral sermons become personal to the family by associating some quality or characteristic of the deceased with some truth from the Scripture text. In one of my funeral sermons, entitled "The Master Craftsman," I related the wisdom of God as Creator in Prov 8:30 to the deceased who had been a master woodworker and cabinetmaker: "Then I was beside him, like a master worker; and I was daily his delight, rejoicing before him always."

The funeral sermon should conclude with a brief prayer. Then the ministry leader steps to the head of the casket (if present) and leads the casket out of the building with the pallbearers following. It is becoming more common for funerals or memorial services to be conducted after the interment or after the cremation of the body, so there is no casket at the front. If there is a casket, it may have been opened briefly prior to the funeral service for viewing and then closed. In some traditions the casket may be reopened for people to pass by for a final viewing at the conclusion of the service. Ministry leaders should ask the funeral director about the funeral traditions in the community and talk them over with the family.

The final aspect of the funeral service is the interment at the cemetery. Traditionally the funeral service concludes at the graveside, not at the church or funeral chapel. At the graveside the minister goes to the back of the hearse and leads the pallbearers as they carry the casket to the grave. Here the ministry leader reads an additional Scripture or two, prays, and then reads the committal. The committal is a benediction that concludes the service. Many ministry leaders continue to use the traditional committal from the Book of Common Prayer:

> In sure and certain hope of the resurrection to eternal life through our Lord Jesus Christ, we commend to Almighty God our *brother/sister John/Jane Doe.*, and we commit *his/her* body to the ground;
>
> earth to earth, ashes to ashes, dust to dust. The Lord bless *him/her* and keep *him/her*, the Lord make his face to shine upon *him/her*

---

7. Powell, *New Ministers' Manual*, 24–25.

and be gracious to *him/her*, the Lord lift up his countenance upon *him/her* and give *him/her* peace. Amen.[8]

In some traditions, it is still customary to throw a handful of dirt on the casket, but many no longer observe this practice. The final act by the minister is to go to each of the family members sitting in front of the casket and quietly speak a blessing, e.g., "May the Lord bless you and give you his peace."

After the Funeral

The ministry leader's work to provide comfort is not over with the conclusion of the funeral. The process of dealing with grief has just begun. As much as the funeral service helps, when it is over, family members are left to grieve alone. So ministers need to stay in touch with the grieving family members by visiting them a few days after the funeral and multiple times during the first few months. In those visits, the goal is to help the person work through the grieving process and get a handle on what he or she may be feeling. The goal is not to deny or cover over the feelings but to become more aware of them. When the mind can comprehend what is happening in the heart, one can begin to regain some control of life.

There are a number of ways to help the grief-stricken with their emotions. Feelings of anger, guilt, loneliness, fear, and depression are not easily expressed to other people. So privately writing or recording one's thoughts and feelings can help externalize what is hidden deep inside. Some people keep a daily journal in which they describe their feelings and experiences from day to day. Others put their feelings into words by verbally recording their thoughts each day. Another method is setting aside a time each day to mourn. Mourning is the outward expression of grief. When people schedule a timed, thirty-minute session to mourn each day, they give themselves permission to grieve while also gaining some control. At the end of the set time of mourning, it is helpful also to have some productive task or activity scheduled (e.g., take a walk, work in the garden, read a book, go to the grocery store, wash the dishes, pay the bills, etc.). One fear that grieving people have is that they will forget about their deceased loved ones, so they continually rehearse images and experiences in their minds. One way to hold on to these memories while also moving on is by writing down a word, a phrase, or a one-line statement of something that comes to mind about

---

8. Episcopal Church, *Book of Common Prayer*, 501.

person. The statements might be kept in a journal of memories or written on small slips of paper, folded up, and placed in a "remembrance" jar or box. Periodically, then, one can take out the slips of paper and read through each of the memories. The collection can continue indefinitely, but eventually, as the grief eases, the memory jar can become an artifact of a time that has passed. The slips of paper within it can be reread and memories revived whenever the pangs of grief again arise.[9]

The ministry leadership practices of proclamation and care meet the needs of people for hearing the word and receiving the consolation of God. The third sphere of ministry practice supplies one other area of human need—the need to love God and to love neighbor.

---

9. H. Wright, *Complete Guide*, 115–21.

11

Guidance of Worship

IN THIS CHAPTER AND the next, we examine the third sphere of the practice of ministry leadership, the practice of guidance. Like the spheres of proclamation and care, guidance is an extension of the person and work of Christ. Jesus reveals God, restores people, and rules over all. The two great commands of Christ are to love God and to love others. Ministry leaders, under the rule of Christ, guide their people toward obedience to these commands. By guiding worship, ministry leaders help people to express their love for God, and, by guiding the work of ministry, they help people to express their love for others.

Worship is the moment in space and time that the body of Christ jointly and publicly acknowledges the ultimate worth of God. Ministry leaders have the privilege and the responsibility of guiding their people in this endeavor. The word worship comes from the Old English *weorthscipe*, which meant to regard something as worthy of honor or reverence. When we worship, we are acknowledging God as of greater worth than anything else, including ourselves. The Bible speaks of that worthiness as God's *glory*. The word glory (*kabod* in Hebrew, *doxa* in Greek) expresses the great worth, value, or "weight" of God. The biblical words most often used for worship indicate the actions of bowing down or prostrating oneself (*shachah* in Hebrew, *proskuneō* in Greek). Worship is humbling ourselves before God, recognizing that we are in the presence of one who is far greater and deserves our glory, honor, and praise. The book of Revelation displays the kind of worship God deserves from his creation:

> And the four living creatures, each of them with six wings, are full of eyes all around and within, and day and night they never cease to say,

> "Holy, holy, holy, is the Lord God Almighty,
>
> who was and is and is to come!"
>
> And whenever the living creatures give glory and honor and thanks to him who is seated on the throne, who lives forever and ever, the twenty-four elders fall down before him who is seated on the throne and worship him who lives forever and ever. They cast their crowns before the throne, saying,
>
> "Worthy are you, our Lord and God,
>
> to receive glory and honor and power,
>
> for you created all things,
>
> and by your will they existed and were created. (Rev 4:8–11)

The practice of worship by the earliest Christians was rooted in the Jewish tradition from which the church originated. Israel was steeped in worship. The Torah laid out the worship practices that Israel would follow. God led the people of Israel to establish sacred space (the tabernacle with the ark of the covenant) and sacred time (the seventh-day Sabbath and three yearly festivals) in which they could come and worship. God also provided priests to lead the people in worship and to bring their offerings to God. In Judaism, the priests, who were the leaders of worship, were described as rendering a service or ministry for the people. When Zechariah, the father of John the Baptist, concluded his priestly "service" in the temple, the word used was *leitourgia* (Luke 1:23). We get our English word liturgy from this Greek noun, which literally means public service or public ministry. The earliest Christian churches used the Greek verb *leitourgeō* to describe their worship: "While they [the church at Antioch] were worshiping [*leitourgeō*] the Lord and fasting" (Acts 13:2). Hence, we see the understanding of worship shifting in the book of Acts from the service of priestly individuals to the service of the "holy priesthood" of the entire body of Christ (1 Pet 2:5). Worship in the earliest church had come to mean the work of all the people to God.

Elements of Worship

When the church was born on the day of Pentecost, the earliest believers in Christ were still faithful Jews practicing Jewish patterns of worship. They were still observing the Sabbath and going to the temple for prayer.

Yet, their new faith in Christ and guidance by the Holy Spirit would soon change their ways of worship. They would still set aside sacred space and time to gather for worship. They would, however, begin to see sacred space not as a building made with human hands but as the person of Christ himself indwelling the gathered people of God. They would also begin to see sacred time not as the seventh day but as the first day of the week, the day of the resurrection of Jesus. Luke describes their immediate actions as new Christians: "They devoted themselves to the apostles' teaching and fellowship, to the breaking of bread and the prayers. . . . All who believed were together and had all things in common; they would sell their possessions and goods and distribute the proceeds to all, as any had need" (Acts 2:42, 44–45). The worship of the earliest church included five things: gathering (fellowship), hearing the word (apostles' teaching), breaking bread (communal meal with the Lord's Supper), praying, and giving to those in need. Although the earliest Christians appear to be in a continual state of worship rather than holding a singular worship "service," these five elements became the structural basis of worship throughout Christian history down to the present day.

In the decades following the close of the New Testament period, Justin Martyr, around 150 CE, described the same five elements of worship:

> And on the day called Sunday, all who live in cities or in the country gather together to one place, and the memoirs of the apostles or the writings of the prophets are read, as long as time permits; then, when the reader has ceased, the president verbally instructs, and exhorts to the imitation of these good things. Then we all rise together and pray, and, as we before said, when our prayer is ended, bread and wine and water are brought, and the president in like manner offers prayers and thanksgivings, according to his ability, and the people assent, saying Amen; and there is a distribution to each, and a participation of that over which thanks have been given, and to those who are absent a portion is sent by the deacons. And they who are well to do, and willing, give what each thinks fit; and what is collected is deposited with the president, who succor's the orphans and widows and those who, through sickness or any other cause, are in want, and those who are in bonds and the strangers sojourning among us, and in a word takes care of all who are in need.[1]

---

1. Martyr, "First Apology," 287.

With some modification and refinement, the five elements evident on the day of Pentecost had become aspects of structured worship in Justin's description. In whatever circumstances, Christians were gathering together on a Sunday (sacred time). The personal teaching of the apostles had become, a century after Pentecost, the reading of their "memoirs" (the Gospels and Letters) and the Old Testament writings (the prophets), followed by comments and exhortation by the worship leader. Justin then says the people rose to pray together. His description indicates that prayer was at the center of the worship service and may have lasted for some time. Following the time of prayer, bread and wine were distributed. The communal meal in the homes of the believers following Pentecost (the breaking of bread) had become a ritual element (communion or Lord's Supper) within the worship service. The worship service concluded with the collection of funds for those in need. By Justin's day the "offering" had been incorporated as a final element of worship.

These same elements are at the heart of Christian worship today. They take many forms, but all are usually present, with the possible exception of the Lord's Supper, which may be included in every worship service or only occasionally. Table 11.1 depicts the basic elements of worship today alongside common components and various approaches for each area.

Table 11.1 The Elements of Worship

Basic Elements	Typical Service Components	Various Approaches and Styles
Gathering	Greeting	(may be at the beginning or at any point in the service) words of welcome, invitation to greet each other, "passing of the peace"
	Call to Worship	Scripture reading, choral introit, anthem or gathering song, instrumental prelude, procession, lighting of candle, chiming the hour, dramatic/media presentation, opening worship music set list by team or band
	Invocation	prayer, hymn, song

Basic Elements	Typical Service Components	Various Approaches and Styles
Praying	Pastoral Prayer	pastoral prayer, guided prayer, moment of silence
	Congregational Prayers	prayer of adoration, call to confession and assurance of pardon, unison reading, responsive reading, informal time of intercessory prayer with requests from the congregation, kneeling at the front or in place
Hearing	Scripture Reading	lectionary readings of OT, Psalms, Gospels, and Letters—(distributed throughout the service) responsive reading, dramatic or antiphonal reading, reading of a verse prior to a hymn or song, narrating of a text of Scripture, singing of a Scripture text with media projection of Scripture, Scripture readings in between song set list
	Sermon	topical, textual, expository, narrative, dramatic monologue
	Response	call to faith and discipleship, hymn or song, silent reflection, invitation to come forward, invitation to meet pastor/counselor after the service
Lord's Supper		(frequency determined by congregation) passing of the elements, procession to the front, gathering around tables
Baptism	As needed or special occasion (e.g., Easter), beginning, middle, end of a worship service. Performed in a baptistery or outdoors at a specially arranged time and place (pond, pool, river, etc.)	
Giving	Offering	(middle or end of service) passing offering plates, processional to the front, box at the entrances, online portal

Basic Elements	Typical Service Components	Various Approaches and Styles
Sending	Benediction	prayer, individual or unison reading, hymn or song, "go in peace"
	Post-Service Gathering	reception with coffee and snacks, communal meal, "Dinner on the Grounds," meeting with a ministry leader

Whether formal or informal, in a large sanctuary or small home fellowship, worship will usually include most of the basic elements in some form. Each congregation has to determine the style of worship through which it can best serve Christ. Far more important than style, however, is that worship is done *well*. Ministry leaders are the planners and guides who enable the people to worship well; they help the people connect with God and with one another through their words, attitudes, and actions.

The task of those who guide worship is to call the people together and to help them participate in the genuine worship of God. In doing so, ministry leaders must not underestimate the power of their influence. Too often leaders use language haphazardly as if words were of little value, but well-chosen words inform minds, evoke emotions, and direct actions. The attitudes of worship leaders can either inspire or bore people, and the actions of leaders can foster active participation or produce passive observation. Participation by all the people is a primary goal of a worship leader. Unison Scripture readings, prayers, and music enable participation. Music has always been a part of Christian worship, not only because it expresses and stirs the emotions but also because it provides the melodies and rhythms by which people can sing together the words of faith and praise. Although occasionally an individual or group may perform for the people, the emphasis should always be on participation rather than performance. If leaders are not careful, solos, choral anthems, or band set lists can convey that the musicians are there to entertain the people. Ministry leaders must be vigilant to insure that worship does not become a show.

Balancing Worship Approaches

Another aspect of leading worship is the need to balance, or at least bring variety, to the ways ministry leaders appeal to and involve people. Humans have different capacities and preferences for ways that they participate in worship and are affected by worship. Figure 11.1 depicts three ways participation in worship may be directed: action, thought, or emotion.

Figure 11.1 Worship Emphases: Action, Thought, and Emotion

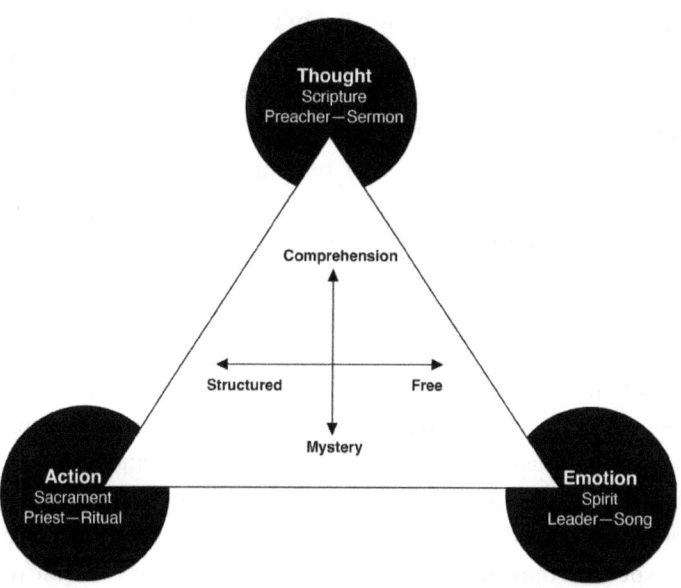

All three ways of participation are involved to a greater or to a lesser degree in any worship service, but over the course of Christian history congregations have tended to focus on one or the other according to cultural factors or the prevailing winds of the Spirit. In the Middle Ages, levels of literacy were low, so worship was more structured and action oriented. Rituals (e.g., kneeling, making hand gestures, verbal responses, etc.) characterized worship. Ritual actions preserved a sense of mystery and divine power in worship. The habitual actions also instructed and strengthened the faith of the people. With the invention of the printing press and the rise of literacy, worship became more thought oriented. The Protestant Reformers saw the emphasis on ritual as prone to pagan magical thinking, so they moved the sermon to the center of worship. The things that mattered most in worship were words, ideas, and comprehension of the Christian message. With the rise of the Pentecostal movement at the beginning of the twentieth century, the focus of worship shifted once again from thought to emotion. For the Pentecostals, the rationalist bent of

Protestant worship obscured the immediacy and free flow of the Holy Spirit. So the change of heart and depth of feeling produced by the power of the Spirit became central to their worship. While worship in various Christian traditions will always follow particular theological views and historical emphases, ministry leaders should try to pull from all of these traditions to increase the participation of their people.

Many people in the more rationalistic traditions long for the mystery of ritual and the flow of the Spirit. These traditions might consider introducing some appropriate ritual actions. Examples of rituals might include adding vocal responses to reading the Scripture like "Thanks be to God," encouraging a vocal "Amen," inviting people periodically to kneel at the front for prayer, increasing the frequency of the Lord's Supper, processing to the front to take the elements, raising hands in song or prayer, lighting an altar candle, or saying a benediction together at the conclusion of the service. Rationalistic traditions can also introduce elements that appeal to the emotions. Examples include less structured moments for free-flowing congregational prayer and incorporating some contemporary music. Traditions that are emotion and Spirit-oriented may benefit by adding more ritual and rationalistic elements, especially Scripture reading. All traditions can benefit by looking at how other traditions speak to the deep needs of people. There is a reason these different emphases emerged throughout the history of Christianity; they reflect the basic nature and needs of all humans.

Following the Christian Year

Some ministry leaders approach each Sunday with a "blank slate" on which they have to draw up all the elements of worship. They may not be aware that there is a wealth of material developed over the centuries of Christian heritage and tradition. Two resources useful for worship planning are the Christian year and the lectionary of Scripture readings. The Christian year is a thematic calendar marking the major events in the life of Christ over a twelve-month cycle. Various Christian denominations have their own versions of the Christian year, but for the most part the versions are similar. Table 11.2 lists the major worship themes of the Christian year. In many congregations each worship theme is identified by a color, which helps the people, especially children, follow the calendar. The use of colors is optional, but when used they are often in the form of a banner on a wall, a drape on the pulpit, or a table covering on the altar.

Table 11.2 The Christian Year

Worship Theme	Length & Date	Color
Advent—waiting for the coming of Jesus	Four weeks, beginning the fourth Sunday of November	Purple
Christmas—the birth of Jesus	Twelve days, beginning with Dec. 25	White
Epiphany—Jesus revealed to the nations	Jan. 6, followed by Ordinary Time until Lent	Green
Lent—reflecting on human mortality and repenting of sin in preparation for the crucifixion and resurrection	Forty days prior to Holy Week	Purple
Holy Week—remembering the events of the journey of Jesus to the cross	Seven days, Palm Sunday through Holy Saturday	Red
Easter—celebrating the resurrection of Christ	Forty-nine days, Easter Sunday until Pentecost Sunday	White
Pentecost—celebrating the coming of the Holy Spirit and the birth of the church	Fiftieth day after Easter	Red
After Pentecost or Ordinary Time—Scriptures and themes on Christian living	about six months	Green

The Christian year begins four weeks before Christmas with the season of Advent (literally, "arrival" or "coming"). Advent looks back at the long years of waiting by the people of Israel for the coming of the Messiah, and it looks forward to the hope of the church for the second coming of Christ. The Christmas season (twelve days, beginning with December 25) celebrates the birth of Christ and the incarnation of God. The day of Epiphany (January 6) reminds the church of the coming of the magi or wise men to worship Jesus. The word Epiphany means "manifestation" and celebrates the revelation of God to the nations of the world. The season of Lent (forty days prior to Palm Sunday) is a period of preparation, reflection, and repentance that parallels Jesus's journey to the cross. In the ancient church, the season of Lent was a time of fasting and prayer, particularly by those who were awaiting baptism on Easter Sunday. Holy Week is the seven days prior to Easter Sunday beginning with Palm Sunday and including Maundy Thursday, Good Friday, and Holy Saturday. The season of Easter begins with Easter Sunday and continues for seven weeks until Pentecost Sunday. The Easter Season celebrates the resurrection of Jesus and the eternal life given to believers. Pentecost Sunday celebrates the coming of the Holy Spirit and the birth of the church. Following the day of Pentecost is the long season of "Ordinary Time" or undesignated Sundays leading once again to the season of Advent.

Using the Lectionary

Following the Christian year is especially helpful when coupled with the Scripture readings in a lectionary. A lectionary is a set of preselected Scripture readings for weekly or daily use. From the early centuries of Christianity until today, churches have developed collections of Scripture readings or lections for use in worship. One version of the lectionary used by many congregations today is the Revised Common Lectionary, which was produced by the North American Consultation on Common Texts.[2] The daily readings can be useful for personal Bible reading or special services, but, for the purposes of planning regular worship, the Sunday readings are most important. Many congregations follow the lectionary continually throughout the year, but others use the lectionary more selectively for particular Sundays or seasons of the year.

The Revised Common Lectionary is a three-year cycle of readings built around three of the four Gospels (table 11.3). Year A follows the Gospel of Matthew, Year B follows the Gospel of Mark, and Year C follows the Gospel of Luke. Readings from the Gospel of John are distributed throughout all three years. Included with readings from the Gospels are readings from the historical or prophetic books of the Old Testament, from the Psalms, and from the rest of the New Testament. The lectionary readings go along with the worship themes of the Christian year, and there are some words or themes in common between the readings for each Sunday. It is not always apparent, however, why certain Scripture texts have been selected alongside others. The lectionary does not cover all of the texts of the Bible, but it

2. Consultation on Common Texts, "Revised Common Lectionary."

covers much more of the Bible in a year than most ministry leaders would select on their own. So an important outcome of using the lectionary is that ministry leaders read and preach texts that challenge their exegetical skills and expose their people to much more of the biblical story. Following the Christian year and using lectionary readings also keeps congregations on a steady diet of the life and teachings of Christ.

Table 11.3 Example of the Revised Common Lectionary[3]

Year A	First Reading	Psalm	Second Reading	Gospel
Advent First Sunday Nov. 27, 2022	Isa 2:1–5	Ps 122	Rom 13:11–14	Matt 24:36–44
Lent First Sunday Feb. 26, 2023	Gen 2:15–17; 3:1–7	Ps 32	Rom 5:12–19	Matt 4:1–11
Season after Pentecost Proper 5 (10) Second Sunday after Pentecost June 11, 2023	Gen 12:1–9 Ps 33:1–12	Hos 5:15–6:6 Ps 50:7–15	Rom 4:13–25	Matt 9:9–13, 18–26

Sacraments or Ordinances

One final issue in the guiding of worship is the distinction between sacraments and ordinances and how these are administered in worship. The word sacrament comes from the Latin *sacramentum*, meaning "to consecrate" or to make something sacred or holy. The word ordinance means "an authoritative decree" and is used by churches that hold non-sacramental views. In the Roman Catholic Church and Eastern Orthodox Church there are seven sacraments: baptism, confirmation, Eucharist, penance, anointing of the sick, marriage, and holy orders (ordination). Among sacramental Protestants groups (e.g., Anglican, Lutheran, Presbyterian, and Methodist) there are only two sacraments: baptism and the Lord's Supper. Baptism, in all of these traditions, can be administered at any age, including infants, and removes the effects of original sin (although interpretations vary as to whether

---

3. Consultation on Common Texts, *Revised Common Lectionary*.

actual guilt is forgiven or only the inclination to sin is removed).[4] Baptism may take many forms in sacramental groups. Most often, especially if the baptism is of an infant, the water is dripped or poured on the head; however, in Eastern Orthodox churches it is common to immerse infants completely three times in the name of the Father, Son, and Holy Spirit. Baptism in sacramental churches is often administered apart from a regular worship service in a special ceremony just for that purpose.

In non-sacramental churches, baptism is included as an occasional aspect of a regular worship service or may be scheduled at a special time and place (e.g., river, pond, or pool) just for that purpose. In non-sacramental churches, baptism is not administered to infants. Baptism is considered a *symbol* of salvation and administered subsequent to a person's profession of faith. So the person must be old enough to understand and respond to the gospel (sometimes called "the age of accountability"). Baptism is seen as an act of obedience to the command of Christ. It is an outward portrait of a person's inward commitment, of dying to one's self, being buried, and then being raised with Jesus. For this reason, baptism usually takes the form of full immersion in water. Not the water, nor the ritual, nor the officiant, however, have power in themselves to effect salvation. Salvation is the result of a personal response of faith to God's personal offer of grace.

The Eucharist or communion is the most prominent and frequently performed ritual in sacramental churches. For Roman Catholics and Eastern Orthodox, the Eucharist is the heart of worship. The bread and wine become the body and blood of Jesus as the priest raises the elements to be consecrated by God.[5] While sacramental Protestant churches have a greater emphasis on the preaching of the word, they still see Christ as in some way truly present in the elements. On the other hand, non-sacramental churches believe the risen Christ is already present within the believer. They view the Lord's Supper as a symbolic reminder of the salvation a Christian has already received through personal faith. This raises the issue, then, of how often to observe the ordinance of the Lord's Supper in worship. Wanting to avoid all appearance of holding a sacramental view, some non-sacramental churches rarely observe the Lord's Supper (some only two or three times a year). The avoidance of taking the Lord's Supper is unfortunate, because, no matter

---

4. See Harwood and Lawson, *Infants and Children*.

5. In Roman Catholic Churches the change of the bread and the wine is called *transubstantiation*. The Eastern Orthodox consider the Eucharist to be the body and blood of Jesus but leave it as a mystery. In many Protestant churches, Christ is considered present in the elements (*consubstantiation*), but the elements themselves are not transformed.

the theological viewpoint, it has been a part of worship since the beginning. Non-sacramental churches that want to balance an overly rationalistic or thought-oriented worship would do well to observe the ordinance of the Lord's Supper regularly (at least once a month). The taking of the Lord's Supper incorporates mystery and tangibility that not only reminds the believer of the past but helps to experience Christ in the present.

12

Guidance of Work

JESUS COMMANDED HIS DISCIPLES not only to love God but also to love others. At the beginning of his earthly ministry, Jesus expressly called his disciples to the work of reaching others: "And Jesus said to them, 'Follow me and I will make you fish for people'" (Mark 1:17). Fishing for people meant to go and make disciples, to baptize, and to teach others to obey Jesus's commands (Matt 28:1–20). This work was not reserved for ministry specialists but for the whole body of Christ. Paul understood that he and other leaders were called to prepare and lead the people in work and not do the work for them. "The gifts he gave were that some would be apostles, some prophets, some evangelists, some pastors and teachers, *to equip the saints for the work of ministry, for building up the body of Christ*" (Eph 4:11–12). Everything ministry leaders do should be with an eye to guiding their followers to love others and build up the body of Christ. The study of Jesus's ministry reveals three basic steps that enable the people of God to serve effectively: setting forth the vision, instructing in the faith, sending out to serve.

Setting Forth the Vision

Jesus could see what his followers could not. He had a clear vision of the kingdom of God, and, as the Good Shepherd, he guided his followers toward it. Ministry leaders are visionaries. More important than what ministry leaders do is what ministry leaders *think* they are doing. "To lead" means to guide toward a goal by going before those who follow. The most important aspect of "going before" is the vision of the goal. What mental pictures do ministry leaders have of where they are guiding the people? Ministry leaders may see themselves doing all kinds of things: helping people, building a church, fulfilling a career, pleasing mom, impressing colleagues, getting famous, or hanging on until retirement. It is only with a vision of Christ and the kingdom, however, that ministry leaders guide their people in the right direction. The vision of Christ and kingdom includes the entire biblical story as laid out in the first chapter above. Ministry leaders must have Jesus and his commands as the focal point of all they do. Their work is to bring people to Christ, help people to understand the teaching of Christ, and engage people in the work of Christ. Ministry leaders must not be driven by their own personal visions for success or visions for the success of their churches. There can be only one driving vision for ministry, and that is Christ and the kingdom of God.

The example of Jesus as ruler is counterintuitive. Jesus did not try to obtain power or exert force over others; instead, resisting the temptations of Satan, Jesus renounced power and refrained from coercion. He emptied himself of the power of his divinity, taking on the role of a servant (Phil 2:5–11). Jesus's servanthood, however, did not limit him from guiding his followers. At every point that guidance was by invitation, not coercion. Jesus's disciples accepted that invitation and committed themselves to follow his guidance, but we never see Jesus forcing any of them to do anything. Jesus guided and motivated others by the power of his love for them. Jesus's methods of guidance included his character, his words, and his deeds. Humility, self-denial, courage, kindness, compassion, righteous anger, honesty, endurance, faithfulness, and integrity guided Jesus's followers to imitate the example of his character. Jesus's words in preaching, teaching, and conversations guided all who would listen to find the kingdom, and Jesus's deeds of touching, listening, dining, feeding, praying, fasting, yielding, and dying guided his followers to be caring, worshipping, and self-sacrificing people. In all of this, Jesus was ruling over salvation history and guiding it toward its culmination with the reign of Christ. He was founding the church, calling and preparing its leaders, admonishing and redirecting them when they failed, and giving them a guiding vision for the future.

Having such a vision does not come quickly or easily. Hearing a sermon, reading a book, or taking a class can birth a vision; but a mature, lasting, and compelling vision comes only through living out the biblical story and following Christ. The human mind is cluttered with many competing visions. Satan's best tool is confusion. Ministry leaders who are confused about what they are doing are living in a fog, and they may be leading their people in circles or even off a cliff. Those who lead others in ministry must be vigilant to keep Christ as their only vision, or they will be derailed by attractive visions from other spheres. The business world offers a vision of making a profit from selling a product or service. Many businesses contribute to the common good of society, and ministry leaders can glean some good ideas from business principles. The idea of making a monetary profit is not a kingdom vision, however. "No one can serve two masters; for a slave will either hate the one and love the other, or be devoted to the one and despise the other. You cannot serve God and wealth" (Matt 6:24). The "profits" of the kingdom of God are transformed people who love God with all of their hearts and love others as they love themselves. Like business, the world of art and entertainment offers an alluring vision to ministry leaders. Art and entertainment bring aesthetic and emotional satisfaction. Ministry leaders can learn much about influencing people through beautiful music, visual art, and dramatic narrative. However, ministry leaders are not putting on a show. They are not in the entertainment business. When ministry leaders have a vision of Christ alone, they might appropriate a few helpful ideas or methods from the world, but they will be ever vigilant that the vision and values of the world do not creep in and obscure or replace the vision of Christ and kingdom.

In recent decades, it has become common for ministry leaders and congregations to tout vision as a *means* to ministry success. One prominent writer describes vision as "a clear mental image of a preferable future imparted by God to His chosen servants to advance His kingdom and is based on an accurate understanding of God, self, and circumstances."[1] This definition sounds impressive, but ideas from spheres other than the Bible have crept in. The vision described is not of the kingdom *itself* but of how *to advance* the kingdom. Vision has become a business plan that God gives "to His chosen servants." Market-driven ideals have replaced the singular vision of Christ; if ministers can discover God's special vision for their situation, they can succeed in their own corners of the church market. The vision of Christ and kingdom, however, has been given to *all* followers of Christ, and God is the one advancing his own kingdom. God's kingdom is not *a* "preferable future," but *the* present and future rule and reign of Christ as King of kings and Lord of lords. A truly biblical vision is not about the success of a minister or the growth of a church but about what God is guiding all Christians in all churches to be and do. In the words of Bonhoeffer, "God hates visionary dreaming; it makes the

---

1. Barna, *Power of Vision*, 18.

dreamer proud and pretentious. The man who fashions a visionary ideal of community demands that it be realized by God, by others, and by himself.... He acts as if he is the creator of the Christian community, as if his dream binds men together."[2] Ministry leaders who guide their followers properly have in their minds the vision of Christ and the kingdom that is for all to see in the biblical story. There is no secret formula or plan for loving God and loving one's neighbor. Again, in the words of Bonhoeffer, "it is in fact more important for us to know what God did to Israel, to His Son Jesus Christ, than to seek what God intends for us today.... I find no salvation in my life history, but only in the history of Jesus Christ."[3] Ministry leaders must have a singular vision—"to seek first the kingdom of God and his righteousness" (Matt 6:33).

To guide others to Christ and the kingdom, therefore, ministry leaders must communicate this vision to their followers. Jesus himself spoke early and often about the kingdom. Communicating this vision takes many forms: telling, listening, discussing, conversing, demonstrating, and praying. Jesus did all of these with his disciples, and they bought into his vision. It took a long time and much heartache, however, before the disciples could see the vision clearly. They had other visions dancing in their heads—visions not of the kingdom of God but of the kingdom of Israel, visions not of loving their neighbors but of destroying the Romans, visions not of serving one another but of sitting in power at the right and left hand of the messiah. The words kingdom and messiah were inflammatory words in first-century Israel. Jesus knew that his followers did not understand these words in the same way that he did, but he had to use these words to get their attention. Ministry leaders today have the same dynamic going on with the people they guide. Congregations are embedded in the values of human society and culture, and they do not comprehend well the vision of Christ and kingdom. So, congregations must be taught the biblical story, not just piecemeal but as a whole. Many Christians do not know the whole story of their faith. They know bits and pieces, but the fabric that holds those pieces together is more likely to be the stories of their surrounding culture rather than the story of the Bible.

Communicating the vision of Christ and kingdom comes with the risk that people will not understand, but the vision must be shared anyway. Jesus took that risk, and at times he felt the pain of the rebuke of his

2. Bonhoeffer, *Life Together*, 27–28.
3. Bonhoeffer, *Life Together*, 54.

disciples. Immediately after Peter declared Jesus to be the Messiah, Peter proceeded to rebuke Jesus:

> He asked them, "But who do you say that I am?" Peter answered him, "You are the Messiah." And he sternly ordered them not to tell anyone about him. Then he began to teach them that the Son of Man must undergo great suffering, and be rejected by the elders, the chief priests, and the scribes, and be killed, and after three days rise again. He said all this quite openly. And Peter took him aside and began to rebuke him. But turning and looking at his disciples, he rebuked Peter and said, "Get behind me, Satan! For you are setting your mind not on divine things but on human things." (Mark 8:29–33)

Jesus rebuked Peter, telling him that he had the wrong vision in his head. Peter understood that Jesus was the anointed one, the Messiah, but he was not yet ready to submit to Jesus and his self-denying vision. Ministry leaders who instruct others in the vision of Christ and kingdom must understand that each person, like Peter, goes through a process of growth and increasing understanding. Although people may believe, they may not fully understand their faith.

Instructing in the Faith

Wayne Oates notably argues that ministry leaders would be wise to build their identity around teaching. It is common for ministry leaders to identify themselves as preachers, but they may be missing a great opportunity to influence the lives of their people.

> Again, your best strategy is to assert and activate your own identity as a teacher . . . if your *pastoral* instruction as a Christian shepherd is activated, you can equip many lay persons to be pastors to one another. . . . Two-way communication in teaching groups creates a healthy dialogue between the person in the pew and the message being preached. . . . The point of the suggestion here, then, is that the identity of yourself as a pastor can be integrated most effectively around your sense of being a teacher.[4]

Ministry leaders typically see themselves as proclaimers of the gospel but not necessarily as instructors or educators. Witness and preaching clearly are aspects of proclamation, but teaching may not seem to fit. Scholars also

---

4. Oates, *Christian Pastor*, 136–37.

are inclined to distinguish preaching (*kērugma*) from teaching (*didachē*). Yet, there is not a clear difference in the content of *kērugma* and *didachē*. Both *kērugma* and *didachē* ultimately communicate the word of God and Jesus Christ in particular. The common content is not surprising when we consider the example of the master Teacher. Jesus himself moved seamlessly between announcing the kingdom of God and teaching about the nature of the kingdom. Throughout the first three Gospels, people often referred to Jesus as "the teacher" (*didaskalos*). In all four Gospels, we see Jesus addressing a large crowd one moment, speaking privately with his disciples in another moment, and having a personal conversation with someone in another moment. So how can preaching and teaching be distinguished? Preaching is typically for the gathered community *as a whole* to hear a word from God, but teaching is for individuals and groups, in settings appropriate to their age and capabilities. The purpose of teaching is for the formation of spiritual character and for the work of serving others through learning of the biblical story and the beliefs and practices of the Christian faith.

Lucien Coleman defines teaching as "helping others to learn," not merely giving people information. According to Coleman, "Bible study is the creation of teachers and learners together. . . . Lessons aren't made just to be presented. They should be struggled with, tugged at, pulled apart and put back together, mulled over, and grasped by learners interacting with teachers as both interact with other resources."[5] The need for interactive teaching and learning lies in the fact that what is being learned is not mere facts but faith. Ministry leaders are tasked not with teaching *about* the Bible but helping others to live the faith of the Bible. According to John Westerhoff, "there is a great difference between learning about the Bible and living as a disciple of Jesus Christ. . . . Faith is expressed, transformed, and made meaningful by persons sharing their faith in an historical, tradition-bearing community of faith. An emphasis on schooling and instruction makes it too easy to forget this truth."[6] Teaching, therefore, must be by people who themselves have been shaped by what they are teaching. Various settings and methods of teaching can be employed, but there is no substitute for teaching that expresses the story that has become the teacher's own story. For faith to be learned, people must come to understand the biblical story as their own story, and they must become participants in that story. The goals of teaching then are ultimately faith and obedience. Proven methods of instruction

---

5. Coleman, *How to Teach Bible*, 15.
6. Westerhoff, *Will Our Children*, 19.

and learning certainly contribute to these goals, but ministry leaders must always be aware that they depend on the winds of the Spirit and not purely on human strategies and formulas for learning. Teachers guide the learning process, but only God speaks to the heart.

Ministry leaders who teach must have a thorough understanding of the biblical story, and they need to know how to interpret and apply the Scripture. So they need the same skills in hermeneutics and exegesis for teaching as those for preaching (see ch. 8). Effective teaching also requires knowledge and employment of sound pedagogical procedures and methods to help others learn well. Five steps are basic to effective teaching:

1. Establish learning goals and outcomes.
2. Plan and prepare teaching methods and learning activities.
3. Create a learning environment.
4. Lead the learning sessions.
5. Evaluate learning.

These five steps are general and basic, so they can be followed with any age group and any setting, whether in a formal classroom or informal small group, or even when mentoring an individual.

Establishing learning goals and outcomes is the essential first phase in the learning process. A learning goal pertains to the broad subject area of study, and a learning outcome to a specific aspect of the larger goal. Learning goals are typically stated in terms what of the teacher wants to accomplish, and learning outcomes are stated in terms of what the student should be able demonstrate after the lesson. Here are some examples of learning goals and learning outcomes:

> **Learning Goal:** Students will develop knowledge of the book of Genesis.
>
> **Learning Outcome:** Students will be able to list the major events in Genesis in chronological order.
>
> **Learning Goal:** Students will develop personal spiritual disciplines.
>
> **Learning Outcome:** Students will complete a personal four-week plan of Bible reading and prayer.
>
> **Learning Goal:** Students will develop skill in personal witness.

GUIDANCE OF WORK

Learning Outcome: Students will explain four basic themes of the gospel to another person.

Learning outcomes should be measureable or observable in some way, so they are usually stated using action verbs that correspond to the levels of learning desired. Bloom's taxonomy has become a standard system of classifying levels of learning. The six levels rise from lower-order to higher-order learning. Figure 12.1 shows the levels with some of the action verbs that might be used in the creation of learning outcomes. Learning outcomes can be written various ways, but a common way of doing so follows this pattern: "Students will be able to *(action verb) + (content)*." A learning outcome at the level of remembering might be "Students will be able *to list* the *first five books of the Bible*." For a learning outcome at the level of understanding, the learning outcome might be "Students will be able *to explain Paul's idea of justification by faith*," and a learning outcome at the level of application might be "Students will be able to apply the idea of context to the meaning of a Bible verse."

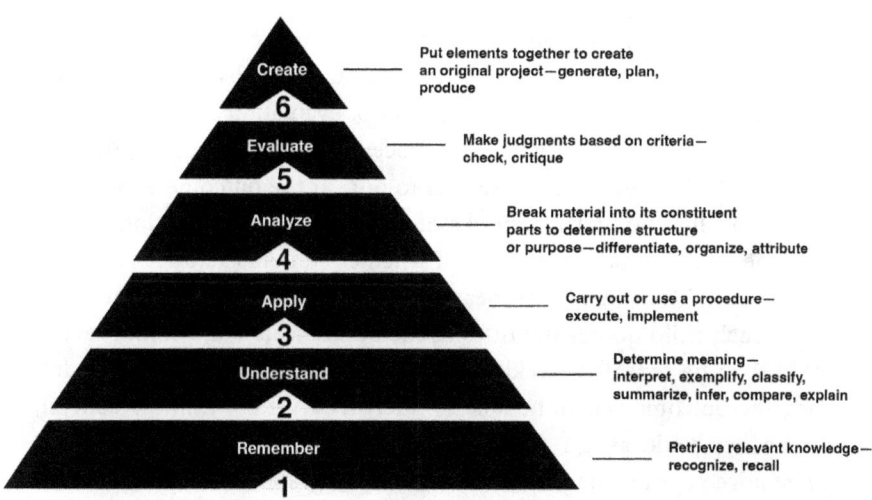

Figure 12.1 Bloom's Taxonomy (Revised)[7]

Based on the learning outcomes, the teacher then plans and prepares teaching methods and learning activities. Common methods of teaching include lecture, question and answer, or breaking into small discussion

---

7. Based on descriptions in Krathwohl, "Revision of Bloom's Taxonomy," 215.

groups. Learning activities might include a drawing or craft, game, role play, case study, written response, project, or practice of a skill. Creating the learning environment for these methods and activities is the next phase. Learning environments must be appropriate to the ages and capacities of the learners and fitted to the learning methods and activities. Formal classrooms with good lighting, acoustics, climate control, desks, writing boards, and projection equipment are ideal for a lecture method with adults. Other learning environments might be quite different if the method is more interactive or activity-based, e.g., a small group gathered in a circle, children sitting on a floor or at craft stations around the room, a home group sitting around a dining table, a group walking around a neighborhood, a mentor and student in a corner of a restaurant, etc.

Goals, outcomes, methods, activities, environments—all come to bear in the moment of leading the learning session. Teachers must have a well-developed plan for how the session will proceed. All learning sessions should have some kind of introduction that gains the learners attention. Following the introduction, the focus shifts to addressing the learning outcome(s) for the day. At the end of the session there should be an assignment to apply the learning (studying a text, memorizing a Bible verse, telling a friend, helping a parent, praying for a co-worker, etc.). The final phase in effective teaching is evaluation. If the learning outcomes have been properly constructed, the basis of evaluation has already been established at the beginning of the process. Evaluation simply asks the question "Did we do what we set out to do?" If the outcome was for the students to list the first five books of the Bible, then evaluation of that outcome would be some measure of whether students actually could list the books. With children, the measure might be a simple verbal review in which each child quotes the titles of the books. This same verbal review could then be repeated weekly to reinforce the learning. If, in an adult class, the outcome was to be able to interpret a verse within its context, the teacher could assign a homework project with a specific verse and the requirement for the learner to write a paragraph or draw a picture of showing how the context in a paragraph, book, and historical background enables clarity. The key to evaluation is that the method actually measures whether the learning outcome has been accomplished. Based upon the evaluation of learning outcomes, then, the teacher can make adjustments to the methods and activities of learning, if necessary.

Sending Out to Serve

The vision of Christ and kingdom comes into full focus when people engage in ministry. Classroom instruction, small group study, or private mentoring can go only so far. In fact, teaching stalls out if there is no follow-through in actual Christian service. The ultimate evaluation of learning is in the doing, in practicing what one has learned. Jesus understood this well. The disciples loved being with Jesus, and they would have been very happy to stop moving about and just enjoy being in his presence. On the Mount of Transfiguration, Peter suggested that staying on the mountain was a really good idea. "And there appeared to them Elijah with Moses, who were talking with Jesus. Then Peter said to Jesus, 'Rabbi, it is good for us to be here; let us make three dwellings, one for you, one for Moses, and one for Elijah.' He did not know what to say, for they were terrified" (Mark 9:4–6). Peter often spoke out of fear and attempted to gain some control over a situation. This time the Father himself responded to Peter's "good" idea: "Then a cloud overshadowed them, and from the cloud there came a voice, 'This is my Son, the Beloved; listen to him!'" (Mark 9:7). Listening to Jesus for Peter and the other disciples would not mean sitting on a remote mountaintop in Galilee but following Jesus to Mount Zion, the city of Jerusalem, and to the cross. So how do ministry leaders guide people to do the work of the ministry? The actual practice of ministry consists of extending the love of Christ to others in some concrete way—to the people of the congregation, to the surrounding community, and to the world beyond. The possibilities are endless, but in general the people of God engage in ministry in four ways: praying, blessing, helping, and witnessing.

The Work of Prayer

Praying for others or "intercessory" prayer is asking God to help another person or group of people. Those of almost any age can engage in prayer. It should be the first ministry practice taught to children and should be encouraged among the oldest adults. Children can pray for family members, members of the church, missionaries, public officials, or people suffering in various parts of the world. Intercessory prayer should be as concrete and specific as possible. It can be prayer during a time of illness, but intercessory prayer also should be for spiritual growth, protection from evil, and for provision for well-being. Jesus himself interceded for his disciples, asking for their protection and unity: "I am asking on their behalf.... And now I am no longer in the world, but they are in the world, and I am coming to you. Holy Father, protect them in your name that you have given me, so that they may be one, as we are one" (John 17:9, 11). Paul is particularly noted for his prayers of intercession for the spiritual growth of churches or individuals:

> And this is my prayer, that your love may overflow more and more with knowledge and full insight to help you to determine what is best, so that in the day of Christ you may be pure and blameless, having produced the harvest of righteousness that comes through Jesus Christ for the glory and praise of God. (Phil 1:9–11)

> For this reason, since the day we heard it, we have not ceased praying for you and asking that you may be filled with the knowledge of God's will in all spiritual wisdom and understanding, so that you may lead lives worthy of the Lord, fully pleasing to him, as you bear fruit in every good work and as you grow in the knowledge of God. May you be made strong with all the strength that comes from his glorious power, and may you be prepared to endure everything with patience, while joyfully giving thanks to the Father, who has enabled you to share in the inheritance of the saints in the light. (Col 1:9–12)

Ministry leaders need to guide their people to establish individual and corporate times of prayer, find prayer partners, and form prayer groups. Leaders can create space in a sanctuary or set aside a classroom for prayer during the week, and they can also put up lists of people, places, events, and needs for prayer. Leaders can also guide the people in prayer walking through the neighborhoods around a church, around a school, or down a city street. Guiding people in the work of prayer benefits everyone involved—those prayed for and those doing the praying.

The Work of Blessing

The ministry of blessing is a good way to learn how to communicate God's grace. Acts of blessing remind the givers that they have received freely God's blessing of mercy and forgiveness, while the givers also communicate God's free grace to the recipients. Blessing is doing something kind for others with no expectation that the act will gain something for the giver in return. Only a failure of the imagination can limit the ways blessing can be bestowed. A group of youth can hand out cold water bottles to passersby on a hot street corner. Children and adults can make cookies to take to a nearby hospital staff working through Christmas Eve. A children's or youth choir can sing Christmas carols at local nursing homes or for the elderly homebound. A college group can have a free car wash (no payment or donations accepted). An adult Bible study class can purchase gift cards for the faculty members of a local grade school. Instead of meeting in the church building, an entire congregation can assemble in a homeless area on Sunday morning, bringing food and hygiene supplies. Most important in the ministry of blessing is that ministry leaders help their people understand that God has called the people of God to bless the world. The kingdom of God is a reversal of selfish actions and self-interested motivations. Unselfish blessing and merciful kindness reveal God to the world.

The Work of Helping

Whereas the goal of the ministry of blessing is to extend God's grace in a general and broad way, the ministry of helping is deliberate and focused on meeting a particular need or performing a particular task. A significant amount of a ministry leader's time and effort goes into guiding the helping work of the people of God. That work may be assisting with the internal operations of a congregation, the instruction or care for the people within the congregation, or care for people beyond the congregation in some way. Ministries within the body of Christ span a wide range: greeters at the doors and welcome centers, nursery workers, Bible study teachers, committee chairs and members, deacons, choir members, worship team members, sound technicians, ushers, and mission team members—all these and many other volunteer roles contribute to the internal processes of life in the body of Christ. Beyond the internal process, helping work extends ministry to the community: serving at a food pantry or homeless shelter, working as a volunteer in a chaplain's office or information desk at a hospital, traveling with a disaster relief ministry, building houses for low-income families, serving at a women's shelter or crisis pregnancy center, developing a job training and networking ministry, tutoring children in an afterschool program, or being a big brother or sister to an underprivileged youth. The list of possibilities goes on and on, but what is key is that ministry leaders understand that a significant part of their work is helping God's people to serve.

PART FOUR: THE PRACTICES OF MINISTRY LEADERSHIP

Church people have become comfortable with ministry leaders doing most of the ministries of the church themselves, but this is not biblical. To be a Christian is to be a minister, and ministry leaders are there to guide their people to find their particular way of serving Christ. Rick Warren describes this process as "turning members into ministers."[8] Ministry leaders guide their people to engage in helping ministries in a number of ways. They teach people why participation in the work of ministry is biblical. They help people discover their spiritual gifts and ways they may be particularly suited to help others. They also provide training, placement, job descriptions, and resources. As they do all of these things, ministry leaders also must be willing to delegate authority and responsibility. Delegation is the greatest challenge for ministry leaders, because the human tendency is to want to control and do things one's own way. Delegation is also challenging because it is hard; it requires thinking through a task, recruiting a person suited to the task, showing that person how to do the task, providing resources for the task, and then backing away and letting the person do her or his work. Although delegation is hard, the rewards far outweigh the difficulties. When God's people engage in the work of the ministry, they find fulfillment in their faith and help far more people than ministry leaders can by themselves.

In guiding people in the work of helping, ministry leaders also need to make sure that genuine helping is the result of their work. Steve Corbett and Brian Fikkert have done ministry leaders a great service by showing how ministries, especially ministries for the poor, do not always provide real help. Helping "hurts" when ministers focus only on *relief* rather than *development*.[9] Relief is immediate help for people who have just suffered some sort of catastrophe like a fire, natural disaster, job loss, etc. Giving help *to* people in this situation is appropriate. Providing food, shelter, clothing, and other basic staples of life is necessary for those in the throes of disaster. Most people, however, are not in immediate danger or distress. So giving things to them may not help them get out of poverty and may actually keep them in poverty. What is needed is for helpers to focus on *development*, which means doing things *with* the people who need help. The best helpers focus on helping others *to help themselves*. In fact, according to Corbett and Fikkert, everyone is impoverished in some way, including the helpers. Helpers sometimes are trying to meet their own needs to feel good

---

8. Warren, *Purpose Driven Church*, 365.
9. Corbett and Fikkert, *When Helping Hurts*, 99–105.

about themselves. When they help others, they feel superior and enjoy the fact that other people depend on them. Helping that actually helps, however, comes from those who, in the words of Paul, "do nothing from selfish ambition or conceit, but in humility regard others as better than yourselves. Let each of you look not to your own interests, but to the interests of others" (Phil 2:3–4). When we consider what is in the best interest of others, we move from giving people a fish to teaching them how to fish—and maybe even how to buy the whole pond.

The Work of Witness

Finally, ministry leaders need to guide their people in the work of witness. As discussed in chapter 7, an important part of being able to lead in ministry is knowing the gospel and being able to share it effectively. Yet, ministry leadership involves not only being a witness but also guiding the people to be witnesses. The elements and process of evangelism are the same as those described above for ministry leaders: cultivating relationships, developing one's testimony, knowing the main points of the gospel with Scripture texts, and engaging in a witnessing conversation. Guiding people in witness requires more than verbal instruction, however. Ministry leaders must model witness with those they instruct. Role play can be effective, but not as effective as being with a ministry leader when talking with a non-Christian about Christ.

It is appropriate that the ministry of witness concludes this book. The ultimate purpose of ministry leaders is to lead people to Christ. The three spheres of ministry leadership—proclamation, care, and guidance—are formed by Christ and come together in Christ. Ministry leaders who know their context, understand their calling, and demonstrate good character are those who proclaim Christ, extend the care of Christ, and guide God's people to obey Christ. Christian ministry leadership has no greater purpose than Christ and his kingdom.

Bibliography

Anderson, Ray S. *The Shape of Practical Theology: Empowering Ministry with Theological Praxis*. Downers Grove, IL: InterVarsity, 2001.

Augustin[e]. *On the Holy Trinity, Doctrinal Treatises, Moral Treatises*. Edited by Philip Schaff. Vol. 3 of *Nicene and Post-Nicene Fathers of the Christian Church*. Grand Rapids: Eerdmans, 1988.

Barna, George. *The Power of Vision: Discover and Apply God's Plan for Your Life and Ministry*. Rev. ed. Grand Rapids: Baker, 2018.

Barth, Karl. *The Word of God and the Word of Man*. Translated by Douglas Horton. New York: Harper Torchbook, 1957.

Blackwood, Andrew W. *Preaching from the Bible*. New York: Abingdon, 1951.

Bonhoeffer, Dietrich. *Letters & Papers from Prison*. Edited by Eberhard Bethge, incorporating translations by Reginald Fuller et al. Enlarged ed. New York: Touchstone, 1971.

———. *Life Together: The Classic Exploration of Christian Community*. Translated by John W. Doberstein. New York: Harper & Row, 1954.

Bosch, David J. *Transforming Mission: Paradigm Shifts in Theology of Mission*. 20th anniversary ed. Maryknoll, NY: Orbis, 2011.

Broadus, John A. *On the Preparation and Delivery of Sermons*. 4th ed. Revised by Vernon L. Stanfield. New York: HarperCollins, 1979.

Browning, Dan S. *A Fundamental Practical Theology: Descriptive and Strategic Proposals*. Minneapolis: Fortress, 1991.

Buechner, Frederick. *Wishful Thinking: A Theological ABC*. New York: Harper & Row, 1973.

Calvin, John. *Institutes of the Christian Religion*. Edited by John T. McNeill. Translated by Ford Lewis Battles. Library of Christian Classics 20–21. Philadelphia: Westminster, 1960.

Carkhuff, Robert R. *The Art of Helping*. 9th ed. Amherst, MA: HRD, 2009.

Catechism of the Catholic Church. With modifications fr. Editio Typica. New York: Doubleday, 1995.

Childs, James M., Jr. *Ethics in Business, Faith at Work*. Minneapolis: Fortress, 1995.

———. *Faith, Formation, and Decision: Ethics in the Community of Promise*. Minneapolis: Fortress, 1992.

BIBLIOGRAPHY

Choung, James. *True Story: A Christianity Worth Believing In.* Downers Grove, IL: InterVarsity, 2008.

Coleman, Lucien E., Jr. *How to Teach the Bible.* Nashville: Broadman, 1979.

Consultation on Common Texts. *The Revised Common Lectionary.* Vanderbilt Divinity Library, 1992. From print ed., Nashville: Abingdon, 1992. https://lectionary.library.vanderbilt.edu/.

———. "The Revised Common Lectionary." Consultation on Common Texts, 2015. http://www.commontexts.org/rcl/.

Conyers, A. J. "The Meaning of Vocation." *Christian Reflection* (2004) 11–19. https://www.baylor.edu/ifl/christianreflection/VocationarticleConyers.pdf.

Corbett, Steve, and Brian Fikkert. *When Helping Hurts: How to Alleviate Poverty without Hurting the Poor . . . and Yourself.* Chicago: Moody, 2012.

Dentan, R. C. "Heart." In *The Interpreter's Dictionary of the Bible*, edited by George Arthur Buttrick, 2:549–50. Nashville: Abingdon, 1962.

Episcopal Church. *The Book of Common Prayer: And Administration of the Sacraments and Other Rites and Ceremonies of the Church.* New York: Oxford University Press, 2006.

Estep, William R. *The Anabaptist Story: An Introduction to Sixteenth-Century Anabaptism.* 3rd ed. Grand Rapids: Eerdmans, 1996.

Fee, Gordon D., and Mark L. Strauss. *How to Choose a Translation for All It's Worth: A Guide to Understanding and Using Bible Versions.* Grand Rapids: Zondervan, 2007.

Friend, W. H. C. *The Rise of Christianity.* Philadelphia: Fortress, 1984.

Gallagher, Timothy M. *The Discernment of Spirits: An Ignatian Guide to Everyday Living.* New York: Crossroad, 2005.

Gerkin, Charles V. *Crisis Experience in Modern Life: Theory and Theology for Pastoral Care.* Nashville: Parthenon, 1979.

Grenz, Stanley J. *Theology for the Community of God.* Nashville: Broadman & Holman, 1994.

Guinness, Os. *The Call: Finding and Fulfilling the Central Purpose of Your Life.* Nashville: Word, 1998.

Harwood, Adam, and Kevin E. Lawson, eds. *Infants and Children in the Church: Five Views on Theology and Ministry.* Nashville: B&H, 2017.

Hinson, E. Glenn. "1–2 Timothy and Titus." In *Corinthians—Philemon*, Broadman Bible Commentary 11, 299–308. Nashville: Broadman, 1992.

Humphreys, W. Lee. "Hermeneutics." In *Mercer Dictionary of the Bible*, edited by Watson E. Mills, 372–75. Macon, GA: Mercer University Press, 1991.

Ignatian Spirituality. "How Can I Pray?" Ignatian Spirituality, n.d. https://www.ignatianspirituality.com/ignatian-prayer/the-examen/how-can-i-pray/.

Ignatius of Loyola. *The Spiritual Exercises of St. Ignatius of Loyola or Manresa.* Gastonia, NC: Tan Classics, 2010.

Kicklighter, R. W. "Origin of the Church." In *What Is the Church? A Symposium of Baptist Thought*, edited by Duke K. McCall, 28–45. Nashville: Broadman, 1958.

Kohler, Kaufmann. "Binding and Loosing." In *Jewish Encyclopedia*, 1906. From 3:215 in print ed. http://jewishencyclopedia.com/articles/3307-binding-and-loosing.

Koskela, Doug. *Calling and Clarity: Discovering What God Wants for Your Life.* Grand Rapids: Eerdmans, 2015.

Krathwohl, David R. "A Revision of Bloom's Taxonomy: An Overview." *Theory into Practice* 41 (2002) 212–18.

BIBLIOGRAPHY

Kübler-Ross, Elisabeth. *On Death and Dying.* New York: Macmillan, 1969.

Lea, Thomas D., and Hayne P. Griffin Jr. *1, 2 Timothy, Titus.* New American Commentary 24. Nashville: Broadman, 1992.

Luther, Martin. *Christians Can Be Soldiers: From Martin Luther's "Whether Soldiers Too Can Be in a Holy Estate."* Edited by Paul Strawn. Translated by Holger Sonntag. Minneapolis: Lutheran, 2010. http://www.lutheranpress.com/docs/CCBS-fulltext.pdf.

———. *Commentaries on 1 Corinthians 7, 1 Corinthians 15, Lectures on Timothy.* Edited by Hilton C. Oswald. Vol. 28 of *Luther's Works.* St. Louis: Concordia, 1973.

Marshall, I. Howard. *1 Peter.* IVP New Testament Commentary 17. Downers Grove, IL: InterVarsity, 1995.

Martyr, Justin. "The First Apology of Justin Martyr." Edited and translated by Edward Rochie Hardy. In *Early Christian Fathers*, edited and translated by Cyril C. Richardson, vol. 1 of *The Library of Christian Classics*, 225–89. Philadelphia: Westminster, 1953.

Maxfield, John A. "Luther and the Lutheran Confessions on Vocation." *Logia* 24 (2015) 29–36.

McAdams, Dan P. *The Redemptive Self: Stories Americans Life By.* New York: Oxford University Press, 2006.

———, and Kate C. McLean. "Narrative Identity." *Current Directions in Psychological Science* 22 (2013) 233–38.

McGrath, Alistair E. *A Life of John Calvin.* Oxford, UK: Blackwell. 1993.

Meilaender, Gilbert C., ed. *Working: Its Meaning and Its Limits.* Notre Dame, IN: University of Notre Dame Press, 2000.

Moody, Dale. *The Word of Truth: A Summary of Christian Doctrine Based on Biblical Revelation.* Grand Rapids: Eerdmans, 1981.

Moser, Drew, and Jess Frankhauser. *Ready or Not: Leaning into Life in Our Twenties.* Colorado Springs, CO: NavPress, 2018.

Myers & Briggs Foundation. "MBTI® Basics." Myers & Briggs Foundation, n.d. https://www.myersbriggs.org/my-mbti-personality-type/mbti-basics/.

Newman, Randy. *Questioning Evangelism: Engaging People's Hearts the Way Jesus Did.* Grand Rapids: Kregel, 2004.

Niebuhr, H. Richard. *The Purpose of the Church and Its Ministry: Reflections on the Aims of Theological Education.* New York: Harper, 1956.

Nouwen, Henri J. M. "Moving from Solitude to Community to Ministry: Jesus Established the True Order for Spiritual Work." *Leadership* 16 (1995) 81–87.

Oates, Wayne E. *The Christian Pastor.* 3rd rev. ed. Philadelphia: Westminster, 1982.

———. "Settling on Your Personal Ethical Code." In *A Practical Handbook for Ministry: From the Writings of Wayne E. Oates*, edited by Thomas W. Chapman, 141–50. Louisville, KY: Westminster/John Knox, 1992.

Oden, Thomas C. *Pastoral Theology: Essentials of Ministry.* San Francisco: HarperSanFrancisco, 1983.

Placher, William C., ed. *Callings: Twenty Centuries of Christian Wisdom on Vocation.* Grand Rapids: Eerdmans, 2005.

Pennington, M. Basil. *Lectio Divina: Renewing the Ancient Practice of Praying the Scriptures.* New York: Crossroad, 1998.

Powell, Paul W. *The New Ministers' Manual.* Waco, TX: Truett Theological Seminary Press, 1994.

Ramm, Bernard. *Protestant Biblical Interpretation: A Textbook of Hermeneutics.* 3rd ed. Grand Rapids: Baker, 1970.

BIBLIOGRAPHY

Riecke, Patrick Shawn. *How to Talk with Sick, Dying, and Grieving People: When There Are No Magic Words to Say*. Fort Wayne, IN: Emerald, 2018.

Riso, Don Richard, and Russ Hudson. *Understanding the Enneagram: The Practical Guide to Personality Types*. Rev. ed. Boston: Houghton Mifflin, 2000.

Robinson, Haddon W. *Biblical Preaching: The Development and Delivery of Expository Messages*, 3rd ed. Grand Rapids: BakerAcademic, 2014.

Schnitker, Sarah A., et al. "9 to 5." *Christianity Today* 65 (2021) 70–76.

Sittser, Jerry. *The Will of God as a Way of Life: How to Make Every Decision with Peace and Confidence*. Grand Rapids: Zondervan, 2004.

Smith, C. Christopher, and John Pattison. *Slow Church*. Downers Grove, IL: InterVarsity, 2014.

Smith, K. W. "Chaplain/Chaplaincy." In *Dictionary of Pastoral Care and Counseling*, edited by Rodney J. Hunter, 136. Nashville: Abingdon, 1990.

Stassen, Glen H., and David P. Gushee. *Kingdom Ethics: Following Jesus in Contemporary Context*. Downers Grove, IL: InterVarsity, 2003.

Stevens, R. Paul. *The Other Six Days: Vocation, Work, and Ministry in Biblical Perspective*. Grand Rapids: Eerdmans, 2000.

Stone, Howard W. *Brief Pastoral Counseling: Short-Term Approaches and Strategies*. Minneapolis: Augsburg Fortress, 1994.

———, and James O. Duke. *How to Think Theologically*. 3rd ed. Minneapolis: Fortress, 2013.

Switzer, D. K. "Grief and Loss." In *Dictionary of Pastoral Care and Counseling*, edited by Rodney J. Hunter, 472–73. Nashville: Abingdon, 1990.

Thompson, W. Oscar, Jr., with Carolyn Thompson. *Concentric Circles of Concern: From Self to Others through Life-Style Evangelism*. Nashville: Broadman, 1981.

Vanhoozer, Kevin J. "Exegesis and Hermeneutics." In *New Dictionary of Biblical Theology*, edited by T. Desmond Alexander and Brian S. Rosner, 52–64. Leicester, UK: InterVarsity, 2000.

Veith, Gene Edward, Jr. *God at Work: Your Christian Vocation in All of Life*. Wheaton, IL: Crossway, 2002.

Warren, Rick. *The Purpose Driven Church: Growing without Compromising Your Message & Mission*. Grand Rapids: Zondervan, 1995.

Weber, Max. *The Protestant Ethic and the Spirit of Capitalism: And Other Writings*. Edited and translated by Peter Baehr and Gordon C. Wells. New York: Penguin, 2002.

Westerhoff, John H., III. *Will Our Children Have Faith?* 3rd rev. ed. Harrisburg, PA: Morehouse, 2012.

Willard, Dallas. *The Spirit of the Disciplines: Understanding How God Changes Lives*. New York: HarperOne, 1988.

Willimon, William H. *Pastor: The Theology and Practice of Ordained Ministry*. Rev. ed. Nashville: Abingdon, 2016.

Wingren, Gustaf. *Luther on Vocation*. Translated by Carl C. Rasumssen. Eugene, OR: Wipf & Stock, 1957.

Wright, H. Norman. *The Complete Guide to Crisis & Trauma Counseling: What to Do and Say When It Matters Most*. Bloomington, MN: Bethany, 2011.

Wright, N. T. *Simply Christian: Why Christianity Makes Sense*. New York: HarperCollins, 2006.

Yoder, Perry B. *Toward Understanding the Bible*. Newton, KS: Faith and Life, 1978.

www.ingramcontent.com/pod-product-compliance
Lightning Source LLC
Chambersburg PA
CBHW071441150426
43191CB00008B/1200